The Denham Massacre

19th Century Britain's
Most Shocking
House of Horror
Murders

Neil Watson

Mango Books

First edition published 2018

The right of Neil Watson to be identified as the author
of this work has been asserted in accordance with
the Copyright, Designs & Patents Act 1988.

ISBN: 978-1-911273-34-9 (hardcover)
ISBN: 978-1-911273-35-6 (ebook)

Published by Mango Books
www.mangobooks.co.uk

18 Soho Square
London W1D 3QL

The Denham Massacre

For my family
Gillian, Samantha & Thomas

and

In memory of my father,
Andrew Nicholson Watson

The Denham Massacre:
List of Contents

Introduction

The Denham Murders of 1870 have somewhat taken over my life since 7th May 2013, when I first stumbled over this case completely by accident. I inadvertently came across the Denham Murders when I was rummaging in a box of old photos at John Peters' home in Pinner, Middlesex. We were discussing John's grandfather, PC Thomas Piner who had served at Pinner Police Station at the turn of the 20th Century. I had also served at Pinner Police Station myself at the end of my police career.

As I searched the box I came across a black-edged memorial card. I had seen many of these cards before, but this one was different. The card listed the names of Emmanuel Marshall and six other members of his family, covering three generations.

John could not tell me anything about the card or indeed the story of the deaths. The card mentioned that the family had all been cruelly murdered in 1870. Surely a crime of this scale must have been big news? Why had John and I never heard of it?

The hunt was then on for me to find out as much as I could about the crime. Who were the victims? What was the motive? And who had committed the murders? My research took me to a number of record offices, ranging from the National Archives to the Uxbridge Local Studies Archive.

I have had a lot of luck during my research. I was lucky to have met John and seen the memorial card, but I was also lucky to have placed

In Memory

OF

EMMANUEL MARSHALL, AGED 35 YEARS;

CHARLOTTE, (HIS WIFE,) 34;

MARY MARSHALL, (HIS MOTHER,) 77;

MARY ANN MARSHALL, (HIS SISTER,) 32;

MARY, 8; THIRZA, 6; AND GERTRUDE, 4,

(HIS CHILDREN;)

Who were all cruelly Murdered on Sunday May 22, 1870,

And Interred in Denham Church-yard, May 27th, 1870.

Memorial card
Courtesy John Peters

a call to the Thames Valley Police Museum. The curator immediately returned my call and invited me to visit. This was a very profitable meeting with Colin Boyes, which led the museum to produce a new glass display cabinet with items from the murders. I had never been responsible for anything in a glass case in a museum before! Huge thanks to Colin for all his help and encouragement.

The Thames Valley Police Open Day in 2015 proved to be a useful coincidence. Luckily for me, a descendant of Superintendent Thomas Dunham, who solved the crime, visited the Open Day and met with Colin Boyes, and was completely unaware that myself and the Museum were collaborating on the history of the Denham Murders. Trevor Ford has been assisting me with information on Dunham and other police descendants.

The search for information revealed a huge amount of material just waiting to be harvested. The crime was one of awful violence and brutality where three generations of one family were axed to death by a cold blooded murderer, John Jones. The house must truly have resembled a house of horror. Can you imagine breaking into the house to discover seven badly mutilated corpses?

These heinous 1870 murders were eighteen years before the emergence of the world-famous Jack the Ripper mystery. The question for me was why had a single mass killing of six females and one male been forgotten, when the Ripper, who had probably killed only five women, was still making the headlines and exciting interest all around the world?

I could only imagine that the Whitechapel Murders had the London fog, the letter to the newspapers from the Ripper in red ink, and the many colourful theories about the culprit being a high-ranking Freemason, a member of the Royal family, or a renowned writer or painter, etc, to keep the pot boiling. When we think of Victorian crime in London, many people think of Jack the Ripper.

The Denham Murders had no fog and no famous suspects, but it does have a lot to offer the crime addict. This is an important crime. It produced a successful police investigation lead by the notable Superintendent Dunham, the hero of the story. The press did not make jokes at the expense of the police as they did during the Ripper investigations later.

This account is not for the faint hearted. The finding of the bodies and the subsequent inquest make for painful reading. Was anyone safe in their bed? If seven people could be murdered in their home, was anyone safe from Victorian villainy?

I have found this whole case completely fascinating. I hope you will too.

Neil Watson
January 2018

Neil Watson was a Metropolitan Policeman for 30 years during the turbulent times of the mid 1970s, ending his career in 2005. He served at Cannon Row, Wembley, Harrow and Pinner Police Stations. Neil has recently retired for a second time from his job as an anti-social behaviour officer in north west London. He has written several articles about police history including the History of Pinner Police Station, as well as a chapter of the book "Discovering More Behind the Blue Lamp, policing central, north and south west London" by Peter Kennison, David Swinden and Alan Moss. The chapter covers the history of all five Harrow police stations. Neil has a passion for all things history. He has also been researching his and friends family history for 25 years.

Acknowledgements

Ancestry.com
Genealogical information regarding the characters mentioned in this book has been obtained using the Ancestry website. www.ancestry.co.uk

British Newspaper Archive
Authority to reproduce images from the BNA with the kind permission of The British Newspaper Archive. www.britishnewspaperarchive.co.uk

Bronwyn BIDWELL
Freelance journalist (Pinner News) and editor who introduced me to John Peters.

Centre for Buckinghamshire Studies
County Hall, Walton Street, Aylesbury, HP20 1UU

Colin BOYES
Curator, Thames Valley Police Museum, Sulhamstead House, Sulhamstead, Reading, Berks RG7 4DU. www.thamesvalley.police.uk/aboutus-museum

Ann COLLINS
Whose parents and grandparents lived in the Marshall house.

Carolynne COTTON
Local Studies, Archives and Museum Manager, Uxbridge Library, 14-15 High Street, Uxbridge, Middlesex. www.hillingdon.gov.uk/26066

Nigel EAGLING
Retired Thames Valley Police Officer and police historian.

Trevor FORD
Direct descendant of Superintendent Thomas Dunham.

David GREEN
Huge thanks to my genius editor, David for spotting my many mistakes in the text and for making so many brilliant suggestions about how to improve this book. He is the most meticulous and eagle-eyed of editors. I ended up changing quite a bit in the book but I am very happy with the finished product. I can't thank him enough.

Samantha HERLIHY
My favourite daughter, who gave me lots of critical advice and grammatical guidance.

Pam HICKS
Editor, The Byword, Village magazine for Byfield, Northamptonshire.

National Archives
Kew, Richmond, Surrey, TW9 4DU. www.nationalarchives.gov.uk

Susan PARRY
History writer, for encouragement and publishing advice.

John PETERS
Owner of the Memorial card to the Marshalls' funeral, which started this book off.

Pamela REED
Denham Local History Society.

Michael SHAW
Retired police officer who runs Buckinghamshire Constabulary website. www.mkheritage.co.uk/bch/index.html

Jean SMITH
Church Warden, St Mary's Church, Slough.

Gillian WATSON (My Wife)
Who allowed me time off for good behaviour in order to complete the mammoth job of researching the history of the Denham Murders.

Thomas A. WATSON
My son who gave me lots of technical advice regarding putting the book together on my computer.

Adam WOOD
My excellent publisher from Mango Books for all his helpful advice and his superb graphics on the cover of this book.

Jane WOOD
Owner of the cottage in Maids Moreton in which Supt Dunham lived from 1859 to 1861.

Len WOODLEY
Retired Thames Valley police constable and criminal history writer.

Dedication

This book is dedicated to the men and women of the British Police Service who give so much of themselves to keep the citizens of this country safe. It's a thankless task sweeping up after the worst acts of murder, terrorism and depravity, not to mention the casual violence used on the streets of Britain by alcohol-fuelled louts.

The hard-pressed British Bobby has always, with some notable exceptions, done his or her best to keep the Queen's Peace and uphold the laws of the day. Some citizens don't always like laws made by Parliament. The police don't make the laws but are paid to enforce them. Protesters usually take out their anger against the police, who have been at the sharp end of public protests for almost 200 years.

There is no hiding place when you are a police officer. No looking the other way, or flinching from making the difficult decision. No avoiding of going in where it hurts to make the arrest. It's a tough job, both mentally and physically.

Police officers put their safety on the line every day of the year, in all weathers, at all times of the day and night and in all situations. It's often scary. And it's impossible to get every decision right all of the time. The police live in constant danger of being assaulted. The danger of high-speed vehicle use is also a threat to officers' safety.

By and large we get the police service that we deserve, and the police service represents its citizens. The officers that patrol our streets, both now and back in Victorian days, are doing their best in very difficult circumstances. We want our police officers to be perfect. This would be to ask them not to be human, people who sometimes make mistakes.

I worked with police officers in the Metropolitan area 'family' for thirty years. During that time I worked alongside hundreds of officers, the vast majority of whom were 'good people', who believed in the law and doing the right thing. I saw lots of brave acts being carried out during my time and I take my hat off to all honest, hardworking officers who go out every day, not knowing what they are going to be faced with.

I believe the office of constable is a noble profession, but it takes leadership, integrity, bravery, common sense and hard work. We are lucky to have such a professional police service. We should applaud all our officers and thank them for what they do.

At the time of writing, the police service is having to cope with massive budget cuts imposed by the Government. The service is being so badly damaged by these cuts that it may never recover. During my time in the Met, the officers of Scotland Yard were widely regarded as the best in the world. At present, police buildings are being sold off at an alarming rate. Even the world-famous Scotland Yard has recently been sold. The Thin Blue Line is getting very much thinner. I hope it won't break.

I also dedicate this book to my father Andrew Nicholson Watson. After service in the RAF Regiment during WWII he joined the Metropolitan Police in 1946. He was a fine man who was blessed with honesty, dedication, integrity and a wonderful sense of humour. It was in his footsteps that I followed to the Metropolitan Police in 1975.

Our combined family service to our country stretched from 1942 until 2005. Of this, I am immensely proud. It was my father who set me on the career path that I chose. A lot of the officers mentioned in this book followed in their fathers' footsteps into the police as well. Indeed the Dunham family, of whom you will hear a lot later, produced a number of fine officers.

My final dedication is to police families. My wife and children supported me through thick and thin for thirty years, which included the long and unsociable hours. Police spouses have the added worry of whether their partner will return unscathed after a tour of duty. Being a member of the police family is not for the faint hearted.

Three cheers for Mrs Watson and all the others.

CHAPTER 1

Peace and Tranquillity

In May 1870, Emmanuel Marshall was the head of his own small family business in the rural idyll that was Denham, Buckinghamshire. He was surrounded by his wife Charlotte and their young children, together with his elderly widowed mother. He earned his living as one of the village blacksmiths, having his own forge attached to the house in Cheapside Lane. Marshalls had lived in the house for forty years – Emmanuel's father had lived in the property before him and had planted an orchard there. The family was comfortably off and they were about to celebrate the forthcoming marriage of Emmanuel's sister. Though many people in Victorian England had hard and difficult lives, Emmanuel had attained a comfortable living. What could possibly go wrong?

One newspaper described the house thus:

> The house is in a very pretty spot ... The cottage itself stands at a point where the high road from London to Oxford parts by way to Denham on the one side, and Slough & Windsor on the other. The house parted the bye lane while his orchard planted by his father forty years ago stretches behind it to the Oxford Road. Away beyond the cottage towards Denham stretched two magnificent rows of ancient elm trees forming a long shaded avenue.

> The place is by no means lonely. From the cottage to Denham at an interval of one hundred yards are other cottages, all tenanted by apparently well-to-do agricultural labourers.

The Marshall house in Cheapside Lane, Denham,
showing the forge on the left.

> Within the cottage there is evidence the family lived in comfort.
> Rooms were tastefully furnished. There was a well-filled larder.[1]

In the front room and in each of the bedrooms there was a little carpeting. This was perhaps what we today would call 'Middle England'. A hard-working family of God-fearing people. A family with roots in the village and a craftsman plying his trade.

Another newspaper recorded details of the pantry and what would have been the family's Sunday meal:

> In the pantry was evidence of comfortable preparations for Sunday dinner. A leg of mutton, some pounds of beef steak, butter, bread, eggs, rhubarb and a small cask of ale.[2]

The same paper added a sad note about a present that had been given to the firstborn child, Mary. It wrote:

> On the front room table was a religious book called 'Heaven our Home', which bore on its flyleaf in a neat woman's handwriting an

inscription telling it as a birthday present a year or two ago from Mother to the eldest child.[3]

In 1870, people got the news by reading newspapers. Any new scandal or bloodthirsty crime was devoured by eager readers. There were many local and national newspapers at the time, and the reporters of the day often covered stories in greater detail than is typically seen in the press today.

The Illustrated Police News was a weekly illustrated newspaper which was one of the earliest British tabloids. It featured sensational and melodramatic illustrations of murders, hangings and other crimes, and was a direct descendant of the execution broadsheets of the 18th century.

It was one of the few newspapers in circulation in the mid-nineteenth century that contained pictures on the front page. It first appeared in 1864 and ran till its demise in 1938. The front covers always contained sensational images of the important crimes of the day, typically murders, serious accidents, as well as executions. The pictures were melodramatic in style. A typical front page of the *Illustrated Police News* in 1870 around the time of the Denham Murders might contain up to nine separate drawings, though in later years one main drawing was more common.

What was about to happen to the Marshall family would have the *Illustrated Police News* reporters and artists scurrying to Denham. The goings-on in the sleepy little village were about to become international news and the front page story on two consecutive weeks.[4]

---

1   *Freeman's Journal*, 26 May 1870.

2   *Bucks Advertiser*, 28 May 1870.

3   Ibid.

4   *Illustrated Police News*, 4 June 1870 and 11 June 1870. Their front page of 18 June covered the recent death of Charles Dickens.

CHAPTER 2

Denham Then and Now

Census records show that Denham had a population of 1,234 souls in 1871.[1] Had the Denham Tragedy not occurred, that figure would have increased by seven. The murder of seven people in one act of cruelty is still one of the most horrific crimes of its type. If you look at lists of British serial killers famous names such as Dr Harold Shipman, John George Haigh, Dennis Nilsen, Peter Sutcliffe and John Reginald Christie appear in the 'premier league' of murderers. The Denham Murderer cannot compete with Dr Shipman's estimated 300 victims, or even those of Peter Sutcliffe or Fred and Rose West.

That said, what is special about the Denham Outrage is that all the murders were committed in a single incident and without the use of a firearm. Most serial killers at the top of the list killed people over time rather than in a single violent act.

In 1870, Denham was a sleepy village on the outskirts of London but just within the county of Buckinghamshire. It marginally fell outside of the catchment area of the Old Bailey. The main London to Oxford road lay to the south of the village. The village is dissected by the pretty Misbourne River as well as the River Colne and the Grand Union Canal to the east. The nearest town was Uxbridge in Middlesex (now in the London borough of Hillingdon), which was policed by the Metropolitan Police; the Buckinghamshire town of Slough, now part of the Thames Valley Police area, was seven miles

The main Village Road, Denham, looking west, c.1910.
The Swan is shown on the right with its large sign.
Neil Watson collection

away and policed by the Bucks Constabulary.

The parish of Denham covers 3,939 acres and was mentioned in the Domesday Book in 1086. The old English name for Denham, 'Deneham', means 'homestead in a valley'. Denham is a typical English village, with a parish church, main street and pubs. St Mary's Parish Church is a Grade I listed building with a flint Norman tower. There are many fine old houses in the main street of the village, and a Grade II listed manor house, Denham Court. (The village currently has eighty-six buildings within the parish, and parts of the village now form a conservation area.)

There were several pubs in the village, including the Green Man, which acted as the village hostelry and coaching inn, and the Swan, the Plough, the Falcon, the Dog & Duck, the Gravel Diggers Arms, the Hare & Hounds and the Lambert Arms. The village also had two schools and a Methodist Church.

The village had a resident policeman at the time of the murders in the shape of 28-year-old PC Charles William Trevener.

Our story starts not far from the centre of the village in Cheapside Lane, a quiet road both then and now.[2] It was here that the Marshall family resided in a two-storey cottage set in an acre of land. Adjoining it was a small wooden building containing a forge and a lathe.

The highly-respected *Illustrated London News* published its own artist's impression of the Marshall abode, and they described the property as follows:

> Two miles and a half from the Uxbridge railway station, and about 100 yards down a shady lane off the old Oxford road, is a six-roomed cottage,[3] with a small workshop or smithy on its western side, a prettily laid-out flower-garden in front, and on the eastern side a fruit and vegetable garden 70 or 80 yards in length. The whole is enclosed by low wooden palings, and the calling or trade of the tenant is indicated alike by a signboard over the smithy, bearing the words 'Emmanuel Marshall, wheelwright and engineer', and by several wheels and parts of agricultural implements in the open space leading up to the workshop.
>
> The cottage is not situated in an isolated position, the nearest house to it being at the end of the garden on the eastern side. This house is not, however, sufficiently near for its inmates to have heard any cries for help that might have been raised by the unfortunate victims at the time of the attack.[4]

---

1   1871 Census.

2   At the time of the murders, Cheapside Lane contained only twenty-two households. The 1871 Census lists the following families residing there: Alsford, Baiste, Bowler, Briant, Calder, Cannon, Flitney, Halsey, Harris, Hearst, Jacobs, Mason, Meade, Pendry, Perkins, Pevesell, Pike, Rolf and West.

3   Some newspaper reports describe the house as an eight-room cottage. A plan of the house shows there were definitely four rooms on the ground floor.

4   *Illustrated London News*, 4 June 1870.

CHAPTER 3

The Marshall Family ~ The Victims

The unfortunate victims of the Denham Outrage were seven members of the Marshall family.

The head of the household was a 35 year old blacksmith, Emmanuel Marshall.[1] Emmanuel had married Charlotte Sparke in 1860,[2] and by 1870 they had raised a family of four. The children were daughters Mary aged 8, Thirza aged 6, and Gertrude aged 4, and son Francis aged 19 months.[3]

Emmanuel's parents, William and Mary, had lived in the house for many years until William's death in 1857. Mary had become a widow at 64 but stayed on in the house with Emmanuel and soon after his new wife, Charlotte.

He had started out in his career working for John Smith at the Albert Iron Works in Falcon Yard, Uxbridge. Here he would have learned the trade of making agricultural tools out of iron.[4] It's likely that Emmanuel left the Albert Iron Works in the mid 1860s to become a blacksmith in Denham, working from the smithy attached to his cottage.[5]

As the local blacksmith, Emmanuel would have been a working-class man, but a man who was a cut above the average unskilled labourer, such as a farm labourer or a factory worker. He would have been viewed as a skilled local artisan. He was also independent of a master over him and he would have been regarded as an

7

important member of the community. He would have needed to have possessed intellect, numeracy and business skills to become a successful blacksmith.

1870 was still the age of the horse, and as such his work would have been plentiful. We tend to have a picture of an old-fashioned blacksmith simply making horseshoes, but they did much more than that. Cars had not yet arrived and so fitting iron rims to wooden wheels of carts and wagons would have kept him busy. Drawings of the Marshall house show sets of wheels in the garden as well as a sharpening wheel.

Agricultural tools and machines would also have been a major source of work for the local blacksmith. In addition he may have been involved in the manufacture of metal hoops for barrels, ploughs, nails, fireplaces and cooking tools.

With agricultural methods improving all the time, Emmanuel would probably have had busy periods and would have had to occasionally take on temporary labour to help him fulfil his orders. The significance of this will become apparent later in this story.

Inventions were being made all the time developing machines to help the farmers save on labour. It was a time of huge progress in this field. Indeed, Emmanuel's former employer John Smith in Uxbridge, apart from manufacturing agricultural machines, had also invented them too.[6]

Blacksmiths were an important part of the workforce. Records from 1867 recorded that there were 130,000 blacksmiths in England and Wales.[7] The records also showed that blacksmiths were paid more than ordinary manual workers. Soldiers earned 12 shillings a week, farm labourers 14 shillings; miners and postmen 21-23 shillings. Blacksmiths, seamen and lace makers earned 25 shillings. Further up the scale came the likes of bakers, butchers and cabinet makers on 28-30 shillings. Watch makers, jewellery makers and perhaps surprisingly engine drivers made 35 shillings a week.

Emmanuel would not have been on a wage himself but would have made a reasonable living from his efforts. It was clear that he was a hard-working man and that he would have spent much of his life in

Emmanuel and Charlotte Marshall
Illustrated Police News

the wooden smithy which was attached to the house. This building, which was painted black, would have contained a forge with bellows, an anvil, lathe, and other tools and appliances, which significantly would include a sledgehammer and an axe. There was no lock on the smithy door, so anyone tramping the roads could easily have found a way in for a night's shelter. *The Windsor & Eton Express* described Marshall's attitude to intruders:

> Marshall appears to have been annoyed by trespassers of this kind: and according to one witness at the inquest had threatened to give such visitors an unpleasant reception. The smithy is accessible from the roadway, but anyone could, without himself being seen, have easily watched him through the patched and broken window at the side, as he stood there at work in the ruddy glow of the fire.[8]

Although no photographs of Emmanuel exist, a drawing of him from the *Illustrated Police News* shows him to be a fine looking man of early middle age, well dressed in his waistcoat, jacket, high collar and tie. He sports a thin beard, though with no moustache and a slightly high forehead. Although old portraits don't tend to show the subject smiling, he does look a serious man.

The Bucks Advertiser described Emmanuel's character thus:

> Emmanuel Marshall is described as a good workman, generally a sober man, and very industrious and hard working. He was a well conducted man but was somewhat excitable, and his temper was not the best. He was a very kind husband and father.[9]

Emmanuel's wife of ten years was a country girl from Suffolk, 31 year old Charlotte Sparke. She was the daughter of her grandly named father, Loyal Sparke. He was a wheelwright who came to live in Uxbridge.

We don't know a lot about Charlotte Marshall but the *Bucks Advertiser* spoke well of her:

> Said by her neighbours to be an excellent housewife, as well as the most respectable woman in all her habits and conduct, a very superior woman. Some intelligent persons described her children as models of neatness and the best behaved in the parish.[10]

Two drawings exist of Charlotte. One is from the *Illustrated Police News*,[11] and the other from the poster in the possession of Thames Valley Police Archives.[12] Both pictures portray her as a neatly dressed, dark-haired, unremarkable looking woman.

Emmanuel's mother Mary was described in favourable terms by the local newspaper:

> Mary Marshall, the mother, aged 77 was described as a very worthy and respectable woman, to whom her son was exceedingly kind.[13]

Another drawing from the ever-helpful *Illustrated Police News* depicts Mary, describing her simply as 'The old lady'. She appears from this drawing as a respectable and upright old lady with a good head of grey hair.

As we have heard already, the children of Emmanuel and Charlotte were described as being neat and well-behaved. But unfortunately we know little of them as individuals, and no portraits of the children are known to exist. They would have attended the village school in Cheapside Lane, just down the road from where they lived.[14]

Also resident with the Marshall family was Emmanuel's sister, Mary Ann. This would have been a happy time for the family. As

Mary Marshall
Illustrated Police News

the end of May 1870 approached, the family had a wedding to look forward to. Mary Ann, was engaged to be married. The ceremony was due to take place on Tuesday, 24th May in Denham Parish Church. The banns were read on 8th, 15th and 22nd May. Sadly, we have no pictures of Mary Ann, but there is this brief mention of her in the *Bucks Advertiser*:

> She was a housekeeper in the family of Robert Crook Walford Esq of Uxbridge, by whom she is highly spoken. She was about to be married to a respectable young man to whom she has been engaged for four years. He is a gardener from Sawbridgeworth.[15]

On 21 May 1870 the Marshall family were doing well by comparison to a large part of the British population. They lived in 'relative' comfort, had enough to eat and had employment which would keep them in money for the foreseeable future.

---

1   The 1861 Census for Denham gives Emmanuel Marshall's birthplace as Hillingdon, Middlesex and the year of birth as circa 1835 (reference RG9/850 page 8, entry 41).

2   Marriage no 353 in 1860 at Stowmarket, Suffolk.

3   Mary Charlotte Sophia (baptised 10 August 1862), Denham Parish Church, Baptism Register (page 27, entry 213); Thirza Agnes (baptised 17 April 1864), Denham Parish Church, Baptism Register (page 35, entry 274); Gertrude Maud (baptised 11 November 1866), Denham Parish Church, Baptism Register (page 44, entry 346); Francis William (baptised 21 November 1868), Denham Parish Church, Baptism Register (page 51, entry 406).

4   The Works were a successful enterprise, and indeed, John Smith was honoured to have been one of the exhibitors at the 1851 Great Exhibition in Hyde Park (page 59, *Great Exhibition Catalogue*). The Works were advertised for sale by auction in 1864 (*Windsor & Eton Express*, 24 September 1864).

5   By 1866 the baptism register for Emmanuel's children stated that he was a smith & engineer, rather than an engineer in 1862.

6   In 1850 John Smith applied for a patent for a chaff-cutter, cylindrical iron sifter, thrashing-machine, barley hummeller (a machine or tool which removes the awns or beards of barley), oat and bean mill, iron skim plough, winnowing machine and turnip-cutter. Design number 2588. National Archive, Ref BT45/13/2588.

7   Geoffrey Best, *Mid Victorian Britain – 1851-1875*.

8   *Windsor & Eton Express*, 28 May 1870.

9   *Bucks Advertiser*, 28 May 1870.

10 Ibid.

11 *Illustrated Police News*, 11 June 1870.

12 Thames Valley Police Archives. Glass case in the museum on the Denham Murders.

13 *Bucks Advertiser*, 28 May 1870.

14 Denham Village School, Cheapside Lane, still exists and operates from the same early Victorian structure. It was built in 1832 and is a listed building.

15 *Bucks Advertiser*, 28 May 1870.

CHAPTER 4

The Owen Family

John Jones is possibly the most common name that anyone in Victorian England could choose. It is the 'name' of the villain of the piece. But who was he? Much more will be revealed as our story progresses, but the 'John Jones' I will refer to throughout this book was an alias taken by a common criminal called John Owen.

In the Victorian period the police kept records of criminals, but fingerprinting and DNA were many years away, so there was often no absolute way of positively identifying people. It was a common thing in those days for lawbreakers to use false identities to try and hide their criminal past, as harsher sentences could be handed out to prisoners who were habitual criminals. Our John Jones was indeed a small time thief of no great note until he committed a crime which was right off the scale of seriousness in comparison to what he had done before.

John may have used four different surnames during his life, but he only ever went by the Christian name of 'John'.

He was born as John Owen on 8 June 1832 in Byfield, Northamptonshire, a small farming community south of Daventry and north of Banbury. His parents were John Owen, a tailor, and Elizabeth Bush. They had married in Byfield on 30 April 1818.[1] The first child was delivered five months after the wedding. They had a total of eight children, and John was the sixth born.

Thomas   (baptised 21 September 1818)[2]
Mary   (born 15 November 1820, baptised 14 January 1821)[3]
Caroline   (born 14 November 1823, baptised 21 March 1824)[4]
George   (born 20 June 1826, baptised 16 July 1826)[5]
Emma   (born 13 September 1828, baptised 5 October 1828)[6]
John   (born 8 June 1832, baptised 22 July 1832)[7]
Elizabeth   (born c.1840)[8]
Fanny   (born c.1843)[9]

The marriage between John Owen and Elizabeth Bush and the baptisms of their first few children would have taken place at the Byfield Parish Church (Holy Cross). In 1827 an Independent Protestant Chapel was built in Byfield, and John Owen was baptised there in 1832 rather than the parish church.[10]

In those days, fathers often passed their professions down to their sons. John's father was a tailor. John's brother George did learn the trade from his father, and indeed was still a tailor residing in Byfield at 'The Green' at the time of the 1891 census.[11]

John apparently decided that he did not wish to become a tailor, and so was apprenticed out to Thomas Mason, a master blacksmith who lived in the village. By the time of the 1851 census John was 18-years-old and living with Mr and Mrs Mason, along with their three children. Mr Mason's only son, also called Thomas, was twelve years old and serving as an apprentice blacksmith.[12] Learning such a trade could have set John up for life, but he would follow a very different path.

---

1   Byfield marriage register (Ref OPR 56P/7, page 8, number 24).

2   Byfield baptism Bishops transcripts (page 19, entry 153).

3   Byfield baptism Bishops transcripts (page 27, entry 215).

4   Byfield baptism Bishops transcripts (page 37, entry 302).

5   Byfield baptism Bishops transcripts (page 45, entry 357).

6   Byfield baptism Bishops transcripts (page 57, entry 412).

7   Byfield Independent Chapel baptism (Ref RG4/2860, page 5).

8   1851 Census (Ref HO107/1741; page 23, schedule 75).

9   1851 Census (Ref HO107/1741; page 23, schedule 75).

10 The chapel is now a private house on The Green, Byfield.

11 1891 Census (Ref RG12/1205; page 6, schedule 51).

12 1851 Census (Ref HO107/1741; page 25, schedule 275).

CHAPTER 5

Jack the Cat Killer

John Owen came from a respectable family but went off the rails and started getting himself into trouble with the law. The question is, why did this happen to him? What turned him into a killer? Although this subject is discussed further in Chapter 37, it is important to set the scene about his offending. He was what would have been described as a 'habitual' criminal, regularly in and out of prisons in Worcestershire, Oxfordshire, Berkshire and then London.

Owen left his home town of Byfield, Northamptonshire and eventually settled twenty miles away in the small market town of Shipston-on-Stour, where he married a widow named Hannah Russell (née Alexander) on 6th February 1853.[1] The wedding took place in the Roman Catholic Chapel in Brailes to the east of Shipston. He gave his real name of John Owen, and his occupation as blacksmith. His bride was a 44-year-old widow, who was described as a 'confectioner' and whose father was William Alexander. Her confectionery shop was situated in Stratford Road, Shipston.

The marriage certificate gave John Owen's age as thirty, but the truth of the matter was that he was only twenty. A 24-year age difference may have been something that the couple wanted to reduce on paper.

We can only speculate, but the marriage may have suited them both. Hannah may have needed a man to help with her business,

Wedding certificate of John Owen and Hannah Russell

and the opportunity was probably a good one for Owen as well. According to the *Berkshire Chronicle*, Hannah claimed her husband always treated her with kindness.[2]

John had not long been married when he had his first brush with the law. In April 1853 he was prosecuted for selling tobacco on a Sunday. He told the court that he had been unaware of the new law and that his wife had neglected to tell him of the new regulations. He was fined 5 shillings and ordered to pay costs.

This matter would have brought him to the attention of the local police. Later that year, it emerged that while Owen had been working for local blacksmith Robert Lovett he had stolen a pistol from a trunk in the workshop. The *Worcestershire Chronicle*[3] reported that the pistol had not been missed for seven months, but when its loss was finally discovered, local policeman Henry Churchley found the firearm in Owen's possession.

He was taken into custody by Superintendent Thompson of the Warwickshire Constabulary and committed for trial. On 2 January 1854, at the Worcester Epiphany Sessions, he was found guilty and sentenced to six weeks in Worcester Gaol. This would be his first period of incareration, but would not be the last. He was to hear the clank of the prison gates behind him on a further six occasions.

While Owen had given no explanation to the court regarding the pistol, it was said locally that he had been shooting cats with the weapon. It was further suggested in newspapers that he was possibly using the cats' flesh in the pies his wife was selling in the confectionery shop. The locals had given him the unfortunate title of 'Jack the Cat Killer'. The *Luton Times & Advertiser* described Mrs Owen's shop as being

> famed for sausage meat and pork pies, but when it became known that Owen killed his neighbours' cats by shooting them with a pistol, his trade was spoilt.[4]

While he was away in prison his wife lost the confectioner's business, and instead took on the Roebuck beerhouse. But having a conviction for a firearms-related offence was bad news for Owen. When he was released from custody, the police objected to the licence and the beerhouse was lost too.

The *Manchester Evening News* published a letter from Superintendent Thompson of the Warwickshire Constabulary explaining the background to this decision:

> In October, 1855, a man called John Owen was resident in Shipston-On-Stour as a journeyman blacksmith. He was married to a widow named Russell, but they did not live together long. While here he was convicted of a felony, which of course rendered his licence to sell beer null and void. In consequence of which I laid an information against him for selling beer without a licence. He left the neighbourhood, and I have lost sight of him since that time.[5]

Hannah's marriage to Owen was fast becoming something of a disaster. She had lost a confectionery shop and now a beershop as a direct consequence of her husband's behaviour.

One can only imagine what may have passed between John and Hannah, but it seems likely that it must have soured their relationship. Owen must have known that Shipston was not a place where he was ever going to prosper in the forseeable future; his reputation preceeded him.

In 1870 the *Bucks Herald* recounted another of Owen's ventures which ended in failure:

> John and Hannah left Shipston for a time. On his return, he went into the sweetmeat business, set up a goat and cart, and travelled the country round; but his old name [Jack the Cat Killer] stuck to him, and the boys shouted after him, which made it too hot for him.[6]

At this point he must have decided on a life on the road, but without Hannah. He took the dramatic decision to leave her and the town, and to go on the road to seek his fortune. He was a blacksmith by trade so had that skill to fall back on in order to earn money for his food and lodgings. According to the *Berkshire Chronicle*, Hannah returned to live in Brailes with her friends.[7]

Jones had violence on his record as well as theft offences. In 1870, *Aris's Birmingham Gazette* reported that in November 1859, while living in Wolverhampton, he assaulted a policeman in a fight of extreme violence. This incident shows a dark side of Jones which would surface again in 1870. Was he simply drunk or was he suffering from mental illness? Whatever the cause, this was a man that would use violence to get his own way. The *Gazette*'s report ran as follows:

> We learn from Wolverhampton that John Jenkins, alias Jones, alias Owen, is believed to be a man who some years ago lived in that town where he was known as of a violent and ferocious disposition, and who got into difficulties there as a consequence.
>
> The description given of the accused man at Uxbridge is exactly that which would describe the man of the same name (John Jenkins), who was known in the Staffordshire town named. He did not reside a great while in Wolverhampton but whilst there worked at one of the neighbouring iron works near to which (Shrubbery Street) he lived.
>
> In November 1859 his violent conduct got him into durance. At about ten at night he was passing through one of the leading thoroughfares assaulting the passersby indiscriminately, and like a madman or a wild beast who delighted in cruelty.
>
> Directly a policeman came up he struck at him with both fists, and marked him on each eye to an extent even now visible. The officer, a powerful man named Nightingale, grappled with him and a severe struggle ensued in which Jenkins got in turn overpowered. Owing to the beating he received from the officer in self defence, the fellow got off with a fine of 10 shillings plus costs. Since that time he has not been heard of.[8]

Touring the country and finding constant work must have been difficult. One also wonders about the quality of his workmanship. This was to be a key factor later in his relationship with Emmanuel

Marshall. Here was a man who appears to have turned his back on his family in Byfield, as well as his wife in Shipston.

John must have had a hard life during this period, given the uncertainty of where he might be sleeping on any given night or whether he had enough food to keep him sustained. There could not have been any love or affection in his life, and his prospects for the future looked dim. His self-esteem could not have been very high, but a sense of injustice may have pervaded his thoughts: Why has this happened to me?

Petty crime was a problem in Victorian England. The authorities had for a period solved prison overcrowding by giving felons a one-way ticket to Australia. Transportation only ended in 1868, after Her Majesty's Government had rid the country of 165,000 prisoners.

Sentencing in Victorian courts was harsh even for the most minor offences, and prisoners would often be forced to do hard labour whilst in custody. It's perhaps not surprising that John Jones ended up in the criminal justice system given his personal circumstances. One other factor that we may speculate about is his mental health. Jones made lots of bad choices during his life. Why did he not learn tailoring with his father and continue the family business? What caused him to assault passersby and fight with the police? Why did he shoot cats?

What is known is that John took to theft to supplement his income, and he would often get caught. A history of offending and disregard of authority was developing within him, and there did not seem to be much prospect of a happy ending.

A criminal record sheet given below shows a record of his 'known' offending. It also records the offences, as well as the name which he gave to the police on arrest, which varied from Owen to Jenkins to Reynolds to Jones. Incredibly, considering the minor nature of most of his crimes, all but one of them made it into the columns of the local papers.

Research into his criminal record indicated that he was an unsophisticated but opportunistic thief. Typically, his offending indicates a man who would steal anything that was unattended which he could carry away with him. Although he was prosecuted ten times, this may well have been the tip of an offending iceberg. Without a regular income, criminality was probably his only chance of keeping himself afloat financially.

The next conviction that Jones received, ended up with him being sent to Reading Gaol for a month with hard labour. The *Reading Mercury* as well as the *Windsor & Eton Express* gave details of the case.[9] On 24 April 1866, calling himself John Reynolds, he was described as a tramp, who with another tramp called Henry Withington appeared before the bench at Maidenhead Petty Sessions charged with stealing a pair of leather driving reins valued at two shillings and sixpence.

The men had entered the tap room of the Coach & Horses pub at White Waltham where Jones had spotted the unattended reins hanging up, which belonged to a Mr Mason. After drinking half a pint of cider, Jones 'acquired' the reins, then tried to sell them to a Mr James Hudson at a shop in Maidenhead. Unluckily for Jones, Mr Hudson had himself repaired the reins for the owner and had recognised them. Jones pleaded guilty to the crime, while his companion Henry Withington was discharged due to lack of evidence.

Jones' arrest for this theft was a double whammy for him as when he was apprehended, the police found him to be in possession of a wheelbarrow, a spade and two baskets. The *Berks Chronicle*[10] reported that the items were later reported missing by market gardener, Mr J. Pounsett, from his garden shed in South Street, Reading. Jones tried to say that he was a market gardener and had bought the items in Birmingham. No sooner was he 'released' from his sentence for the reins theft than he was being sentenced on 21 May 1866 at Reading Petty Sessions after pleading guilty for the theft of the wheelbarrow etc. The outcome was another month in Reading Gaol.

The *Oxford Times*[11] reported another court appearance. It stated that on 29 February 1868, Jones was again up before 'the beak', this time at the Oxford Lent Assizes on a charge of theft of two fowls valued at four shillings and six pence, the property of Alfred Speck from Ambrose Farm, Nuffield, Oxfordshire. Jones said that he was a blacksmith from Southampton. The birds cost Jones six weeks in Oxford Gaol with hard labour.

On the same day while being sentenced for the bird theft, the *Reading Mercury, Oxford Gazette & Newbury Herald*[12] reported that Jones was also appearing in the same courtroom on an unrelated charge. This one involved the theft of a basket, needles, thread, tape and other articles, which were the property of a licensed hawker called Joel James. The items had allegedly been stolen from a truck outside the Feathers Public House, Henley-on-Thames. The case was not proceeded with for some reason at the Assize.

The *Oxford Chronicle & Reading Gazette*[13] newspaper report from the initial court appearance at the Henley Petty Sessions was quite revealing about the character of John Jones. The article described him as a wretched looking tramp. The victim had left his truck unattended outside the pub at 6.00 am when he went inside for breakfast. When he emerged from the premises his basket and contents had gone. The basket as well as the two fowls in the other case, which were still alive, were found in a lodging house in Watlingford. Tellingly, the newspaper described how Jones stole anything that came his way.

Without wishing to cast more doubt onto the character of Jones, theft of unattended items was his modus operandi, and its seems unlikely that he was not guilty of stealing the hawkers basket as well as all the other items.

The *Oxford Times*[14] reported that on 7 May 1868, Jones was again appearing before the magistrates on another theft charge, this time at Neithrop Petty Sessions, Oxfordshire. The crime involved the appropriation of a whip belonging to a Mr D.T. Gardener of Adderbury, Oxfordshire. Jones had been seen by a Robert Wyatt on side of the road with no whip. Fifteen minutes later Wyatt saw him again in possession of a whip. Jones then told William Burchill that he had found the whip on the road. Burchill bought it from Jones for six pence. After being arrested by Sgt Daniel Hayward, Jones told him that he had bought the whip for three pence from some chap.

Jones stated that he had committed the offence in order to get some breakfast as he had travelled a long way without food. He gave his name as Jones and stated that he came from Southampton and was travelling to find work as a smith. After he was locked up, he admitted to the police that he came from Byfield. He did not need to worry about obtaining food for a while as he was sentenced to a month's imprisonment in Oxford Gaol with hard labour. Jones was not very adept at making a clean getaway during his offending. On the other hand, we have no way of knowing how many other crimes he may have got away with. Offending was a way of life for Jones.

A few weeks later, Jones was back in court on 8 July 1868. The *Reading Mercury, Oxford Gazette and Newbury Herald* reported that he was appearing at the Berks Midsummer Assizes,[15] where he was being tried on a more serious charge than before. He and a woman called Elizabeth Keble had been charged with the theft of a ewe and a lamb belonging to famer, Edward Franklin, of Cumnor. After the animals had been discovered to be missing, Jones was seen driving the animals down the Botley Road towards Oxford very hastily.

Jones had killed the ewe, and had taken the head, liver and heart to Mrs Keble's shop. Jones pleaded guilty and was sentenced to eighteen month imprisonment with hard labour at Reading Gaol. Keble was charged with handling stolen goods. Perhaps not surprisingly, she was acquitted by the jury. Jones had only ever been sentenced to six weeks imprisonment previously. Eighteen months was a different matter altogether. It was a sentence that he did not want to repeat.

John Jones's Criminal Record

Date
9 April 1853
Court
Shipston-on-Stour Petty Sessions

Plea
Pleaded guilty (pleaded ignorance of the new law).
The case was the first of its kind in the district

Court record
Court record not yet found

Charged in the name of
John Owen

Offence / Method used
Selling tobacco on a Sunday.
Prosecutor; Sgt Phillips.
Wife had notice of the new police regulations but she had
neglected to inform her husband, John Owen of them.

Sentence
Pay 5 shillings costs

Prison to which sent
N/A

Source
Worcestershire Chronicle, 13 April 1853;
Manchester Evening News, 21 June 1870

Date
2 January 1854

Court
The Shirehall Worcester, Epiphany Sessions

Plea
Found guilty after trial

Court record
Criminal Record Sheet, page 460, entry no 5, HO27/107

Charged in the name of
John Owen

Offence / Method used
Larceny (Theft) of a Pistol, from Mr Robert Lovett's workshop, Shipston-
on-Stour, on 25 November 1853, the property of Robert Francis Insull.

Sentence
6 weeks Imprisonment

Prison to which sent
Worcester Gaol

Source
Worcestershire Chronicle, 4 January 1854;
Worcester Journal, 7 January 1854

Date
November 1859

Court
Wolverhampton Petty Sessions

Plea
Unknown

Court record
Court record not yet found

Charged in the name of
John Jenkins

Offence / Method used
Assault on Police. Whilst intoxicated, at the corner of
St James Square in Horsely Fields, Wolverhampton, assaulted
PC Nightingale by punching him in the face and fighting with him.

Sentence
Fined 10 Shillings & costs

Prison to which sent
N/A

Source
Case reported in 1870 newspapers;
The Daily Courier, 28 May 1870;
Aris's Birmingham Gazette, Saturday 28 May 1870

Date
24 April 1866

Court
Maidenhead Petty Sessions

Plea
Pleaded guilty.
(Co-defendant Henry Withington was discharged)

Court record
Court record not yet found

Charged in the name of
John Reynolds

Offence / Method used
Larceny (Theft), of a pair of leather driving reins, value 2 shillings and
6 pence, on 21 April 1866 The Coach & Horses public house, White
Waltham, near Maidenhead, the property of Mr Charles Mason

Sentence
1 month imprisonment with hard labour

Prison to which sent
Reading Gaol

Source
Reading Mercury, 28 April 1866, page 6, col 6;
Windsor & Eton Express, 28 April 1866, page 6, col 2.

Date
21 May 1866

Court
Reading Petty Sessions
Before Mayor E. Blackwell

Plea
Pleaded guilty

Court record
Court record not yet found

Charged in the name of
John Reynolds

Offence / Method used
Larceny (Theft) of a wheelbarrow, a spade and two baskets, on 20 April
1866, from a garden shed in South Street, Reading.
The property of Mr J. Pounsett, market gardener of London
Street, Reading. PC Foster Berks Constabulary, Supt McGrath

Sentence
1 month imprisonment

Prison to which sent
Reading Gaol

Source
Berks Chronicle, 26 May 1866, page 3, col 1.

Date
29 February 1868

Court
Oxford Lent Assizes

Plea
Pleaded guilty

Court record
Criminal Record Sheet, page 410,eEntry no 6. HO27/150

Charged in the name of
John Jones

Offence / Method used
Larceny, (Theft) of two fowls, value 4 shillings and 6
pence at Ambrose Farm, Parish of Nuffield, Oxfordshire,
on 25 January 1868, the property of Alfred Speck.

Sentence
6 weeks imprisonment with hard labour

Prison to which sent
Oxford Gaol

Source
Oxford Times, 1 February 1868, page 6;
Banbury Advertiser, 5 March 1868, page 4

Date
29 February 1868

Court
Oxford Lent Assize

Plea
Indictment not gone into

Charged in the name of
John Jones

Offence / Method used
Larceny (Theft) of a basket, needles, thread, tape and other articles,
the property of Joel James, licensed hawker from an unattended
truck outside the Feathers public house, Henley-on-Thames.

Sentence
Committed for trial on 27 Jan 1868.
Case was not proceeded with.

Source
Oxford Chronicle & Reading Gazette, 1 February 1868
(re appearance on 27 January);
Reading Mercury, Oxford Gazette & Newbury Herald, 7 March 1868.

Date
7 May 1868

Court
Neithrop Petty Sessions, Oxfordshire

Plea
Pleaded guilty

Court record
Court record not yet found

Charged in the name of
John Jones

Offence / Method used
Larceny (Theft), of a whip on 4 May 1868, the property
of Mr D.T Gardener of Adderbury, Oxfordshire.

Sentence
1 month imprisonment with hard labour

Prison to which sent
Oxford Gaol

Source
Oxford Times, 16 May 1868, page 7 col 6;
Northampton Mercury, 23 July 1870, page 3.

Date
8 July 1868

Court
Berks Midsummer Assize at Abingdon

Plea
Pleaded guilty.
Co-defendant, Elizabeth Keble was acquitted.

Court record
Criminal Record Sheet, Page 31, entry no2. HO27/149

Charged in the name of
John Jones

Offence / Method used
Larceny (Theft), of lamb & ewe, the property of
Mr Edward Franklin, farmer of Cumnor.

Sentence
18 months' imprisonment with hard labour

Prison to which sent
Reading Gaol.
Released 8 January 1870

Source
Reading Mercury, Oxford Gazette and Newbury Herald,
11 July 1868, page 4, col 1.

Date
28 March 1870

Court
Uxbridge Petty Sessions

Record of Jones stealing a sheep at Abingdon Assize

Plea
Pleaded guilty

Court record
Court record not yet found

Charged in the name of
John Jenkins

Offence / Method used
Larceny (Theft) of 2 pairs of worsted stockings at Rockingham Road, Uxbridge, belonging to Joseph Hickman.

Sentence
2 months' imprisonment

Prison to which sent
Coldbath Fields Prison.
Released Saturday 21 May 1870.

Source
Bucks Advertiser, 26 March; 2 April; 28 May 1870.

No set of 'official' previous convictions for John Jones exists. There was no centralised Criminal Record Office in mid-Victorian times as there is today - individual forces kept their own local paper records. The above summary of previous convictions is what I believe to be the best guess of his convictions. It is hard to be sure about his complete record, as it is likely that a number of convictions may not be known about. He 'came to notice' ten times that we are currently aware of.

The *Bucks Advertiser* gave a considerable insight into Jones's situation in Spring 1870. The article was entitled 'LARCENY – A miserable looking creature who gave his name as John Jenkins.'[16]

The last offence for which Jones was imprisoned prior to the murders taking place tells us a lot about him and also social welfare of the times. Jones found paid employment hard to find. He would tell the court that he 'had been long out of employment'. Where would he have got money for food and shelter from? Perhaps begging or stealing? It's likely that he had a poor diet. One also wonders how often he had a warm bed in which to sleep?

The items stolen were a thick pair of socks. Perhaps cold and wet weather, combined with a poor diet, had contributed to the skin condition that afflicted him? The *Advertiser*'s comment regarding the skin problem 'which caused no pleasant sensation to those who happened to be near him' hints that it may have made him smell.

He did not attempt to deny the offence in court. It is more than possible that he may have been happy to go to prison; at least in gaol he would be guaranteed a dry bed, regular food and possible treatment for his skin condition. It's interesting to note that the *Advertiser*'s reporter noticed a marked improvement in his appearance, reporting that 'He looked all the better for his 4-5 days lodgement in the House of Detention'. On his initial court appearance they described him as 'miserable looking'.

One also wonders about the mental health of Jones. Was this a man in his right mind? Had his lifestyle affected him mentally as well as physically?

The victim of Jones's offence was 60-year-old furniture broker, Joseph Hickman. It's interesting to note that by the time of the 1881 census Mr Hickman was now described as the 'town crier'.[17]

The *Glasgow Daily Herald* gave further valuable information about the sock case and Jones's foot problem:

> *The Standard* says the following statement by a furniture dealer named Hickmans [sic], carrying on his business in Buckingham Lane, Uxbridge: Early on the morning of 23 March, I was awoke out of my sleep by a cry of 'Thieves'. Upon getting out of bed I discovered a man had been found stealing some stockings from the back garden. A neighbour living opposite to me was the person who gave the alarm.

He and I succeeded with some difficulty in arresting him.

When he was secured he was taken before the Magistrates, and upon being asked why he attempted to steal the stockings, he said, - 'I had an itch, and I felt it necessary to change my stockings in order that I might be cured.' The Magistrates then sentenced him to six weeks imprisonment, and he was allowed out, after the expiration of his sentence on last Friday morning.

I know the man well, for I watched him carefully while he was before the Magistrates, and he corresponded in every particular to the man who is charged with the murder of the Marshall family. He had long black hair, his nose was straight, he wore a black moustache and he was about 5 feet 8 inches in height. When he was searched by the police a complete set of burglars instruments were found upon him. A screw driver, a chisel and a bunch of skeleton keys were found upon him.[18]

The same Glasgow newspaper article also had information from a local ironmonger who knew the suspect 'Jenkins'. The article gave details of the ironmonger's opinion:

Mr Tapnidge (FASSNIDGE),[19] a manufacturing ironmonger, carrying on business in Uxbridge, states that the deceased man Marshall was apprenticed to him, and that he had known him for the last 20 years. He states that he frequently saw the accused murderer Jenkins, and that that man often came into his shop to ask for work.

He is of the opinion that Jenkins never premeditated the murder of the whole Marshall family, and in support of that opinion he states that it is well known that Jenkins was frequently convicted of petty robberies. He thinks he went to the bottom of Marshall's forge or smithy for the purpose of committing a theft.[20]

Another significant piece of information about Jones and his battle with authority was reported in the *Morning Post*. This information has not been corroborated in any way and may be a fanciful boast, but equally, given his history, does have the ring of truth. The newspaper reported:

A woman who was in the company of Jenkins on the Sunday evening in the Bell Tavern, Uxbridge makes the following statement: He said to me – 'I have been abroad. When I was quite a young man I enlisted in the army. While in it I was flogged. I was tied up to a cross bar while they flogged me.

> 'When they were done flogging me they untied me. I then turned round to them and said, 'Thank you for that'. They then let me go.' The landlord of the Bell Tavern states that Jenkins frequently told him that he had been abroad, and he boasted that he could tell the accent of any person, no matter what country they came from.[21]

The mention of recognising accents is interesting. When Jones was initially arrested he gave the name of MacKenzie and was said to have spoken with a Scottish accent. Perhaps his travels had given him the ability to mimic other dialects?

The information about the army has the ring of truth. It was a period in history where Britain was involved in a number of military campaigns abroad. Flogging in the military was not abolished until 1881, so this sort of punishment could have been inflicted on Jones. It's probable from what we know of him that he would have been a likely candidate for military punishment.

The other aspect which suggests that Jones undertook a period of military service is the absence of any convictions between the period 1859 to 1866. Could a prolific thief like Jones have stayed out of trouble for seven years? It seems unlikely. A period of service abroad in HM Forces may also have taught him how to kill people. It's an interesting thought.

---

1   John Jones' wife Hannah Alexander was born c.1808 in Brailes to parents William Alexander and Agnes Dorcas Waddup. She married John Russell on 25 December 1841 at Shipston-on-Stour. Russell died in 1850. The census of the following year reported a woman called 'Ann' Russell as a 41-year-old widow, occupation 'confectioner', born in Brailes and living at Stratford Road, Shipston-on-Stour. The age, place of birth and unusual occupation fit with her being Hannah. She married John Owen on 6 February 1853 in Brailes Catholic Chapel. Hannah was illiterate and made her mark on the wedding certificate, but John was able to sign his name. We know that they did not live together long. Owen was still in Shipston in 1855, but by 1858 he was in Wolverhampton. The 1861 Census for Brailes makes interesting reading. By this stage, Hannah had moved back to the village. The Census read as follows: Dorcas Alexander, 78 years, head of family, widow, pauper, born Little Tew, Oxfordshire: Hannah Owen, 53 years, daughter, married, laundress, born in Brailes: Sarah Alexander, age 52, daughter, unmarried, laundress, born Brailes. Sarah was a witness at the marriage of Hannah to John Owen. Hannah Owen died in 1871 aged 63, less

than a year after Owen's execution. Information from census returns, birth, death and marriage certificates

2   *Berkshire Chronicle*, 13 August 1870.

3   *Worcestershire Chronicle*, 4 January 1854. See also *Worcester Journal*, 7 January 1854. Criminal Record Sheet, page 460, entry no 5, HO27/107.

4   *Luton Times & Advertiser*, 16 July 1870.

5   *Manchester Evening News*, 21 June 1870.

6   *Bucks Herald*, 2 July 1870.

7   *Berkshire Chronicle*, 13 August 1870.

8   *Aris's Birmingham Gazette*, 28 May 1870.

9   *Reading Mercury*, 28 April 1866; *Windsor & Eton Express*, 28 April 1866, page 6, col 2.

10 *Berks Chronicle*, 26 May 1866, Page 3 Col 1

11 *Oxford Times*, 1 February 1868, page 6; *Banbury Advertiser*, 5 March 1868, page 4. Criminal Record Sheet, page 410, entry no 6, HO27/150.

12 *Reading Mercury, Oxford Gazette & Newbury Herald*, 7 March 1868.

13 *Oxford Chronicle & Reading Gazette*, 1 February 1868 (re-appearance on 27 January).

14 *Oxford Times*, 16 May 1868, page 7 col 6; *Northampton Mercury*, 23 July 1870, page 3.

15 *Reading Mercury, Oxford Gazette and Newbury Herald*, Saturday 11 July 1868, page 4, col 1. Criminal Record Sheet, page 31, entry no2, HO27/149.

16 This conviction was allegedly mentioned by a witness named Charles Coombes who sometimes lodged with Jones. This was reported in the *Bucks Herald* of 4 June 1870. A detailed report on the actual offence was published in the *Bucks Advertiser* on 28 May 1870.

17 1881 Census record lists Joseph Hickman as living at 8 The Lynch, Uxbridge. He was aged 71 and employed as the Town Crier.

18 *Glasgow Daily Herald*, 27 May 1870.

19 Tapnidge was a typographical error in the original newspaper report; his name was Fassnidge. *Kelly's Directory for Middlesex* in 1873 shows Fassnidge Brothers, furnishing Ironmakers, as being at 156 High Street, Uxbridge. There were a number of Fassnidge businesses in Uxbridge. James Fassnidge was shown in the 1871 Census at 43 St Andrews, Uxbridge, as being a builder and contractor employing 130 hands. William Fassnidge, Builder was shown at 66 High Street, Uxbridge. Some years later in 1898, Fassnidge & Son started working on the building of Pinner Police Station, where I served almost 100 years later. The company was a mayor employer in the town and operated for 50 years.

20 Ibid.

21 *Morning Post*, 30 May 1870.

CHAPTER 6

Collision Course ~
Marshall and Jones

Emmanuel Marshall appeared to be a normal man without enemies in a quiet rural spot. He had a young family and a devoted wife. He had stability, a home, money and the respect of his neighbours. His sister's wedding was about to bring joy to the Marshall family. How was this situation going to change with such disastrous results?

As it turned out, Marshall was not loved by everyone. When the crime was investigated, several theories were publicised.

The first was reported in the papers in late May, and involved Marshall reporting an assault against him:

> Shortly after Christmas, an incendiary fire took place at Ivy House Farm, near Denham. Marshall was at the fire and on returning home he was stopped on the road and ill-used by four men. Two of them were suitably identified and were sent to prison for two months. Their term of imprisonment has just expired and suspicion rightly or wrongly connected them to the murder. The more so being as on conviction they threatened revenge on Marshall.[1]

Another newspaper reported that Marshall's relation, Job Sparke, told the inquest the following:

> I have never heard of any ill will to Mr Marshall, except that last Christmas, two men assaulted him. He prosecuted one and he was imprisoned for two months.[2]

The Coroner asked Inspector Sutton[3] about this assault incident and the man concerned. The newspaper reported the answer as follows:

The man who was committed, sir, is in the Royal Elthorne Militia. He is now at Aldershot.[4]

The *Herts Advertiser & St Albans Times* also referred to the question of the assault on Emmanuel Marshall.

> The witness [Job Sparke] said that last Christmas two men met Marshall who had been over to his sister's at Iver, and that as he was returning to Denham, he, (the witness) believed they had knocked him about a good deal. He was hurt on the forehead. He sued them and they were committed for 2 months.
>
> Inspector Sutton said the statement of the witness was incorrect. He received the charge. The occurrence took place on Boxing Day. There had been a fire at Iver, and Marshall went to it. On his way he was waylaid and he accused the two men of robbing and assaulting him. They were tried at Slough. The charge of robbery fell through. One of the men was discharged, and the other was sent to two months imprisonment.
>
> The Coroner asked if the man seen by the constable resembled the prisoner Coleshill who was committed at Slough. Inspector Sutton: - Not at all. These men are now at Aldershot with the Elthorne Militia.[5]

The Royal Elthorne Light Infantry was raised in Uxbridge in 1853. The barracks were near the Greenway in Enfield Place, which may take its name from the rifles used.[6]

The second, more crucial theory as to a motive for murder was that Marshall knew Jones. Many murders are committed by people that know the victim, which was the case in this instance. Alfred Hailstone, who compiled a history of Slough, wrote that he had been given this information by Superintendent Dunham's son, James Alfred Dunham:

> Mr. Dunham found, on enquiry, that Marshall, who was the local blacksmith, had employed a travelling wheelwright, a week previously, but the man, Jones, had done the work so badly that the wheel was completely spoiled. As this rendered the blacksmith himself liable for the cost of the wheel - about £2 - he naturally told the man to clear out and not return, refusing to pay him. Jones was

heard to mutter threats of revenge.[7]

Another version of the dispute over work was given in an Australian newspaper, the *Sydney Empire*:

> It has been ascertained that three years ago he worked for Marshall, and while repairing the wheels of a neighbouring farmer's cart, so burnt them that the owner refused to have them, and sent them back. On account of this, Marshall stopped the prisoner's money, and Owen becoming exasperated, struck Marshall in the eye, and a fearful fight between the two ensued.

> For this work, Owen was never able to obtain the money and this fact now throws light on a statement since ascertained to have been made to several persons, 'There is a man near Uxbridge who owes me some money, and if I don't get it off him next time I go, I'll murder him.' This he repeated several times on the two days preceding the murder.[8]

The *Manchester Evening News* also published information that Jones had been seen in the area:

> Several who have seen the prisoner's photo aver that he had been seen in Denham and believed that he occasionally worked for Marshall.[9]

The most telling piece of evidence regarding Jones's relationship with Marshall came from a prison officer who knew Jones at Reading Gaol.[10] This was to later form a key piece of evidence against John Jones, and gave him a motive for murder. This evidence was given at the inquest into the murders and was reported in the press. Daniel Love, a warder at Reading Gaol, said he knew 'Jenkins' as alias Reynolds, Owen and Jones. He identified the jacket found in Marshall's room as one given to Jenkins on leaving gaol in January last, when his imprisonment for 18 months had expired.

The *Windsor & Eton Express* recorded details of a meeting between Daniel Love and Jones following his capture. They reported the following:

> The other day, Daniel Love, the warder of Reading Gaol, told him that he was sorry to see him in for such a crime, to which he replied, 'Why should you be sorry; I ain't sorry; they can't but swing me', jumping

from a chair, and indicating the fall of the drop.[11]

Jones had served time for stealing a ewe and a lamb from Abingdon. When he was discharged, he asked the way to Uxbridge. Love believed his name was Owen, as one day he had cut the name J. Owen in a piece of soap and when it was found he remarked that that was his proper name. Daniel Love continued:

> He asked me how far it was to Uxbridge. I told him I did not know. He said 'I know a man who has got some money, and I will have it rather than have 18 months again, I will murder him.' I think I said I would not do such a thing as that or words to that effect. He did not say the man lived in Uxbridge.[12]

It would appear that some sort of dispute has arisen between Marshall and Jones over the quality of his workmanship and the former had refused to pay. This refusal could have had serious implications for Jones, who may well have been living from hand to

John Jones on discharge from Reading Gaol

mouth at this point. Jones was a man who now held a grudge, and he meant to get the money he was owed. He did not want to spend any more time in prison and had alluded to extreme violence to get what he wanted.

Warder Daniel Love had probably heard it all before from prisoners making idle threats whilst incarcerated. Threats to kill must have been commonplace in prison. Not taking him seriously, he simply told Jones not to say such things. The threat had been made, and was now known by the authorities should anything happen.

The collision course had now been set. Denham was about to be hit by a tidal wave.

———————————

1   *York Herald*, 28 May 1870.

2   *Illustrated Police News*, 28 May 1870.

3   Inspector George Sutton was from the Bucks Constabulary and later rose to the rank of Superintendent.

4   *London Evening Standard*, 25 May 1870.

5   *Herts Advertiser & St Albans Times*, 28 May 1870.

6   The headquarters moved to Hounslow in 1879. The Royal Elthorne Light Infantry Militia became a battalion of the Duke of Cambridge's Own Middlesex Regiment, which was formed in 1881.

7   Slough History Online. This account of the police is taken from chapter 12 of Alfred G. Hailstone's 'Buckinghamshire Constabulary Centenary 1857-1957', an illustrated booklet issued to commemorate the Bucks Constabulary Centenary, available at www.sloughhistoryonline.org.uk/asset_arena/text/pdf/sl/sl/sl-sl- max_chapter12-d-02-000.pdf

8   The *Sydney Empire*, 4 October 1870.

9   *Manchester Evening News*, 21 June 1870.

10 HM Prison Reading was built in 1844 as the Berkshire County Gaol. Designed by George Gilbert Scott, it was based on London's New Model Prison at Pentonville (built in 1842), and is a good example of early Victorian prison architecture. From 1916 it was used to hold Irish prisoners involved in the Easter Rising. Oscar Wilde was the prison's most famous inmate from 1895. The prison closed in 2013.

11 *Windsor & Eton Express*, 4 June 1870.

12 *Bucks Herald*, 4 June 1870.

CHAPTER 7

'I'm a stranger about these parts'

The weekend of 21-22 May should have been a normal one in the village with the family getting ready for the forthcoming wedding of Mary Ann Marshall. She was soon to be moving away to Hertfordshire, to her new life with her new husband. Last minute preparations and the wedding dress needed sorting. The house was being decorated for the wedding. The banns were to be read for the final time on the Sunday morning before the ceremony at Denham Parish Church on the Tuesday.

Due to Mary Ann staying with her brother Emmanuel for the wedding, it had been decided that the youngest child, Francis, who was not yet two years old, should move out to relatives for a few days to make more room. This temporary removal of Francis from his parent's home was to save his life.

It was reported that the village policeman had seen the Marshalls on the Saturday:[1]

> PC Trevener saw Marshall and two murdered children on Saturday morning. He had been to the house on one or two occasions. He believed that the children go to school.

A *Bucks Herald* report of the trial also reported that Mrs Elizabeth Simpson, who lived 100 yards from the Marshalls in Cheapside, saw 'Marshall and the little girl on Saturday night'.[2]

We can be sure, therefore, that the family were alive and well on the Saturday evening, 21 May. Emmanuel Marshall was known to work early on Sunday mornings while the rest of the household still slept, but never on Saturday night:

> At this time of year he was a very early riser and he used to get up at 3 and 4am to let his horse out to graze.[3]

Sunday being the Sabbath, a religious family like the Marshalls would have attended church in the morning, especially as the final reading of Mary Ann's banns were due to take place.

The family had prepared to look their best when they went to bed on the Saturday. The *Belfast Newsletter* remarked:

> Little clean things belonging to the children were all untouched, and their little shoes left cleaned for Sunday remained as they had been placed on Saturday night.[4]

Another significant occurrence that weekend was reported in the local newspaper. It mentioned that one of the main witnesses in the case, Charles Coombes, had news of Jones's release from prison on his theft charge:

> Coombes states that the man that has been captured came out of Coldbath Prison on Friday or Saturday last.[5]

The most crucial incident of the weekend involved local police officer PC Charles Trevener. He would describe his patrol in the early hours of the Sunday morning at the trial:

> I met the prisoner on Sunday morning at about 3 o'clock. I could see the prisoner's features well. My notion of him when I saw him was that he was out after game [poaching]. It was suspicious that he was out at that time of night. I next saw him 9 days later when I recognised the prisoner when he was being examined by the magistrates.[6]

A different newspaper report gave a very interesting account of PC Trevener's 3.00 am meeting with Jones:

> Charles Trevener, No 27 Bucks Constabulary, stationed at Denham, said, 'On Sunday morning the 22nd May at a few minutes before 3 o'clock I was on duty at Denham and met the prisoner, coming from the direction of the canal, in the Uxbridge Road (that is going towards

the murdered man's house). He came up to me and said, 'I wish I had met you before policeman.' I said, 'What's the matter now?' He replied, 'I was coming along the cut (canal) just now, and a man and a woman were quarrelling. The man said he would throw the woman into the cut, and if he had thrown her in, I would have thrown him in.' I said, 'Do you know the party?'

He said, 'No I'm a stranger about these parts.' I said, 'How came you that way if you are but a stranger?' for I knew that there was only a footpath leading from the canal into the road. He said that another man had directed him the way. I asked him what he did that way, and he said he was on his way to Oxford, mentioning some other places.

I let him pass on a distance, but I went after him offering to show the way to the Oxford Road, but really to look at him. I then took particular notice of him and of his dress and as the under coat which he wore under a fustian jacket made him appear very bulky, I purposed to search him, but seeing that the bulk was only the extra coat, I did not search him. I left him after directing him about a third of a mile from the Marshall's house. He would not have to pass Marshall's house the way I directed him but leave it to the left by about a mile.[7]

This meeting in the early hours of Sunday morning was very significant. It placed Jones almost at the Marshall's house at the material time. PC Trevener suspected Jones may have been out poaching, but had no evidence to support this so could not detain him. Clearly this was a man up to no good, but the significance of the meeting would not be known for another twenty-four hours.

Sunday passed without incident. Denham was about to experience a murderous Monday.

---

1   *Staffordshire Sentinel*, 28 May 1870.

2   *Bucks Herald*, 24 July 1870. Mrs Simpson isn't listed among the residents of Cheapside in the 1871 Census, so presumably she left the area shortly after the murders.

3   *Belfast Newsletter*, 26 May 1870.

4   Ibid.

5   *Bucks Herald*, 26 May 1870.

6   *Morning Post*, 23 July 1870.

7   *Bucks Herald*, 4 June 1870, page 7, col 1.

CHAPTER 8

'For God's Sake Mrs Simms, Come Here'

The officers of Bucks County Constabulary probably came on duty on Monday, 23 May 1870 like any other Monday, hoping for a quiet day and not too much aggravation. PC Charles Trevener, the village bobby, had been up late the night before, still patrolling at 3.00 am. He was probably tired already. Officers mostly operated on foot in those days and would have walked many miles each day.

Back at HQ in Slough, Superintendent Thomas Dunham was in the hot seat of authority. Anything important that came in that day would be his responsibility. Dunham had been born in Somerset and worked his way up the ranks in Buckinghamshire. He had had a varied and interesting career, and was never averse to getting stuck in where it hurt on the sharp end of policing.

Little did he know that 23 May 1870 was going to be the defining moment of his career. This and subsequent days were going to be the making or breaking of Thomas Dunham. A major incident was about to blow up in front of him. How would he deal with it, and how would the newspapers react? It will be remembered that the police officers in the Jack the Ripper case were derided and made fun of by the papers due to their inability to catch the culprit.

What also needs to be remembered about this case was that it occurred in 1870 when forensic detection was still in its infancy. The Fingerprint Branch at Scotland Yard would not be established until 1901, some thirty-one years away. Any crime would have had to be solved by old-fashioned police work. The Detective Department at Scotland Yard had been created in 1842, twenty-eight years earlier, and detectives were still relatively new.

No one had seen the Marshalls on Sunday 22 May. The house was closed up, but no one had thought anything was amiss. Come the Monday, however, it was finally noticed that no one was answering at the house.

Lizzie Bampton, the 11-year-old daughter of the innkeeper at the Swan pub, went to the house later in the day. The *Illustrated Police News* reported her visit, as told at the inquest, as follows:

> I went on Monday evening to Mr Marshall's house to take a dress to Mrs Marshall to make. It was after tea. There was no answer to my knocking. Mrs Marshall's sister came when I was there. I then left.[1]

The same newspaper reported the evidence of Mary Ann Sparke, the sister of Emmanuel Marshall's wife Charlotte:

> I saw Charlotte on Friday night. I promised to take tea with her on Monday. I got no answer. Neighbours had not seen anyone. The doors were locked. I saw two men coming along. I asked one of them to get a ladder and he looked in the bedroom window, and he saw bed clothes in a heap. He then looked in the back windows on the ground floor. I heard him shout, 'For God's sake come here.'[2]

Suspicious circumstances led to breaking the door down. A different newspaper described events:

> In consequence of Miss Sparkes's (sic) inability to account for the silence in the cottage and the bolted doors, suspicion arose for the first time and a young labourer from Denham who happened to be passing and was spoken to on the subject burst the door open, when he was horror stricken by the discovery of some of the murdered bodies.

He rushed at once to the police station at Uxbridge and related what he had seen. Superintendent Dunham, Inspector Sutton, Sergeant Bowden and several constables, repaired at once to the

MARSHALL'S COTTAGE AND SMITHY – SCENE OF THE MURDERS

scene of the tragedy.[3]

Another newspaper reported Mary Ann Sparke's testimony:

> I am Mary Ann Sparks [sic]. I reside at 63 Waterloo Road, Uxbridge. I am a single woman. I found the house locked and padlocked. I went to call people at The Plough just down the road and asked if they had seen anything of our people. They said no. I went back to the house but still could not get in. I saw two men, asked if they worked for Mr King and if they knew where my brother was.
>
> A woman called Simms came up. I then saw a ladder behind the house and I asked the man who had stayed if he would get the ladder and look in the window at the back of the house. At first he said he was afraid to do so, but I gave him permission to do it. I said he may break the door open. Mrs Simms had gone to the front of the house and pulled out the bolt from the front window. The man got the bolt out. He cried out 'For God's sake Mrs Simms, come here, Oh it's the old woman'.[4]

The *Bucks Advertiser* gave details of what happened next:

> The man gave a cry of shocked dismay. Stretched out before him was a spectacle seldom seen but among the ghastly realities of the battlefield. Fortunately, Mr Nicholls of Uxbridge Park, butcher, who knew the family well, happened to drive by at the time, being informed of the dreadful truth, he immediately returned home with Miss Sparkes [sic] and gave the first intelligence in the town of Uxbridge of the terrible events that had occurred.

Mr MacNamara and Dr Ferris instantly drove out to Denham to render medical assistance, if occasion should permit. The police were on the alert. Telegraphs were dispatched to London and the Supt of the Bucks Constabulary at Slough to whose division, Denham belongs.[5]

A desperately sad note concluded the report in the *Bucks Advertiser*:

Miss Marshall and her sister in law called last week on the neighbour Mr Dimmock to order a bride cake to be ready on Monday. The order of course was never executed, and the cake in vain waited the call which was to have fetched it.[6]

A truly awful discovery had been made at the Marshalls' house. The police were called for and PC Charles Trevener then attended the scene.

---

1   *Illustrated Police News*, 28 May 1870. Her father, Lewis Bampton, would later sit on the inquest jury. Although the 1871 Census gives his occupation as a butcher, he worked for many years as a beer retailer and licensed victualler at the Swan Inn in Denham. Lizzie was born in 1859 in Fulham. By 1871 she was living away from her parents in Acton and working as a housemaid. She later became a nurse.

2   Ibid.

3   *Maidstone Telegraph & West Kent Messenger*, 28 May 1870. Sergeant Elijah Bowden was from Bucks constabulary. He was on the 1871 census for Upton-cum-Chalvey living at the police station with Thomas Dunham. He ended up as an inspector in Brill, Buckinghamshire, prior to his retirement.

4   *Sheffield Daily Telegraph*, 26 May 1870.

5   *Bucks Advertiser*, 28 May 1870.

6   Ibid.

CHAPTER 9

PC Trevener Attends the Scene

Policemen across the country are used to getting calls from the public to enter premises where it is suspected that persons have passed away. These 'sudden deaths' are a matter of routine and are commonplace, particularly in houses which are occupied by elderly people living alone. Every now and again, the routine non-suspicious death is replaced by a murder. Police officers always have foul play in the back of their minds when they enter premises in order to find dead bodies. Normally, suspicious incidents are quite obvious. While most police officers with a reasonable amount of experience will have been involved in a murder at some point in time, nothing quite prepares them for the sight they are about to encounter.

A single-victim murder can be awful to witness and have an effect on the officer afterwards. What PC Charles Trevener was about to discover would probably have stayed with him all his life. No one, not even the most experienced police officer, would have been prepared for the scene inside the Marshalls' house. It was an orgy of blood and gore combined with the fact that some of the victims were children, and also the fact that he knew the family.

PC Trevener was summoned to the Marshall home just after 7.00 pm. He went there immediately and was the first police officer at the scene. The front door of the house was open.

Newspapers reports of PC Trevener's account of proceedings at

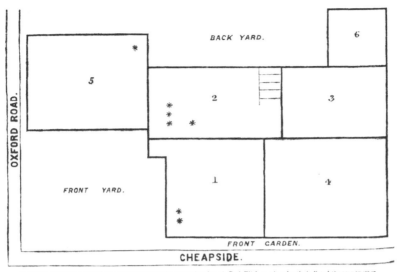

1. Kitchen, where the bodies of Mrs. Marshall and her sister were found.—2. Back Kitchen, where lay the bodies of the grandmother and three children.—3. Pantry.—4. Parlour.—5. Smithy, where Marshall's body was concealed.—6. Outbuildings.
* Position of the Dead Bodies.

PLAN OF MARSHALL'S COTTAGE.

Plan of Marshall's Cottage showing where the bodies were found.

the inquest hearing make harrowing reading:

> I am a member of Bucks Police stationed at Denham for the past 12 months. I have known the deceased during that period.

> A young man residing in the village reported the information. I went to the house and found the doors open. The bodies of the wife and sister were lying immediately inside the door. I found a sledge hammer covered with blood. In the washhouse I found bodies of the three children who lay together. I found the axe which was covered in blood.

> All the deceased persons with the exception of the wife had night clothes on, the wife had her dress partially over her nightdress. Extensive wounds on the hands and bodies, a great deal of blood on the floor. There were pools of blood in some of the rooms.

> I went into the forge. The door was closed. I found there the body of Emmanuel Marshall lying on his face with his arms stretched out. He had apparently been dragged. His body was covered with a sack, an apron and an old coat. A pool of blood and a poker were a few yards from the body.

> The two pieces of a poker corresponded with the shovel and tongs in the parlour.

Some clothes were found in a room of the house on Wednesday morning. I went upstairs, three beds had been used. There was no evidence of a struggle.

The staircase goes down to the back kitchen where four bodies were found.

Some drawers were pulled out. There was blood on the clothes. There was a pair of boots, trousers, coat, cord jacket, a cord vest, a slop, deerstalker hat, red and white common plaid neck cloth.

The deceased man had on his ordinary working clothes. He had clean cord trousers on, was in his shirt sleeves but had no boots on, nor could I find any boots. I examined the bottom of the stockings and found them quite dry and free of grit. He could not have got in that position which I found him without something on his feet. Blood on his trousers was fresh. There was no appearance of a struggle having taken place in the front room. There was blood on the wall, where I should think one of the bodies fell.[1]

The *Windsor & Eton Express* supplied some additional macabre details not gleaned by the other papers. They described the finding of Emmanuel Marshall's body. It was face down, and covered in grit, dust and blood.

The police and his neighbours were utterly unable to recognise him. There was a large hole in his forehead, evidently inflicted by a poker, which was found broken in two, near the body. His head had been beaten to a jelly, and his arms presented several terrible cuts and bruises as though he had struggled with his assailant.[2]

PC Trevener was asked by the Coroner whether anyone had any ill will against the family:

I have never heard of any dispute between the deceased and any other persons. The deceased was a rather excitable man. I heard him threaten to use violence on anyone he caught on his premises. He has asked me several times whether he would be justified in shooting anyone he might find on his premises. I have always told him no.[3]

PC Trevener found a scene of devastation at the house. The murderer appeared to have left behind old clothes and to have searched the house for property. Emmanuel Marshall's boots were missing. He could not have walked across the floor of the forge in his stockinged feet without getting them covered in grit and the like. But

PC Trevener and Supt Dunham discover the body of Emmanuel Marshall in the forge. The body is shown lying on its back, whereas all the reports state that he was lying face down.
Illustrated Police News

his feet were perfectly clean. It would appear that the murderer stole the boots from the feet of the deceased.

Charles Trevener drew the short straw on that day, when he had to go and find the bodies in Cheapside Lane. It's hard to imagine a worse scenario. He only had given three years' service in the force when the crime occurred. It could have been enough to put anyone off for life.

As news of the Denham Murders spread, some newspapers expressed their outrage at the enormity of the crime, while others mourned the death of the young children and the rest of the family. The *Illustrated London News*, which was one on the most important newspapers of its time, printed a sad editorial comment about the tragedy. It accompanied the piece with a drawing of the Marshalls' house. It was a powerful piece, entitled 'The Murdered Family near Uxbridge':

> The horrid slaughter of Emanuel Marshall, his wife and three little girls, his aged mother, and his sister, on the eve of her marriage, in their own dwelling at the hamlet of Denham, near Uxbridge, on the night of Saturday week, has been mentioned in this Journal.
>
> An Engraving shows the house in which this hideous deed of wanton cruelty was done, and where the whole of this innocent family - the strong man, good husband and father, good son and brother, good workman in his skilful and useful industry - the three women, one of them already near the natural end of her life, but revered and cherished, as becomes the grey hairs of a parent, by the filial affection

of others - and the children, of from four to eight years, when their tender lives, passing from babyhood to sprightly girlhood, were daily growing to new sweetness and grace of nature - fell beneath the butcherly axe of a savage with the spirit of a fiend. In this place, a quiet village of Buckinghamshire, an hour before dawn of a peaceful Sunday in the glad month of May, was done by one man, without any provocation or temptation, such a massacre of his kind as would scarcely be effected by a furious horde of Red Indians, or Maories of New Zealand, in their bestial rage of war, swooping with fell purpose of vengeance upon the settler's unguarded home in the wilds.

Civilisation and humanity in England are supposed to prevail above the brutish and the devilish motives of action; it is so with our people in general, as in every other land of Christendom; but the frequent exceptions among us are far worse than the vilest and direst outrages or abuses of nature where law and gospel are unknown.

There is no need here to describe the sickening incidents of this atrocious heap of crimes. The subject of our Engraving requires but a few words of notice.

The cottage is not situated in an isolated position, the nearest house to it being at the end of the garden on the eastern side. This house is not, however, sufficiently near for its inmates to have heard any cries for help that might have been raised by the unfortunate victims at the time of the attack.[4]

---

1   *Maidstone Telegraph & West Kent Messenger*, 28 May 1870.

2   *Windsor & Eton Express*, 28 May 1870.

3   Ibid.

4   *Illustrated London News*, 4 June 1870.

CHAPTER 10

Call for Superintendent Dunham!

Modern day policing demands that squads of officers can be scrambled at a moment's notice whenever a new murder is reported. Highly trained, experienced police officers and forensic support staff flood the scene and start to gather all the evidence.

The police call the start of an investigation the 'Golden Hour'. This is the critical time where evidence is still fresh and witnesses are still available. Mistakes made at this vital part of any homicide investigation can be very costly. Officers and resources are thrown at new murders.

Some murder squads can go on for many months, while others can last literally for years before they are wound up, either due to a conviction or that the possible lines of enquiry are exhausted. The police have a very good clear up rate for murders in the modern era. DNA, the widespread use of CCTV, mobile phone records, taped interviews and fingerprinting have all made the detective's job easier over the years.

Back in 1870, squads of officers waiting to swoop onto a murder scene was a thing of the distant future. Scotland Yard was just developing the detective class around this period and Buckinghamshire Constabulary did not possess any 'detectives' at all. It was still a provincial force with limited resources. Therefore, a crime as serious as the Denham Murders was going to be huge job.

SUPᵀ DUNHAM

The man who was given that task was the 37-year-old hero of our story, Supt Thomas Dunham.

A story as big as this was going to be read by the whole country. The eyes of the world were upon Bucks Constabulary. Would they be up to the job?

As news of the crime emerged on that fateful Monday, officers from Uxbridge (Metropolitan Police) were mobilised and Supt Dunham was informed at the police station at Upton-cum-Chalvey (now a suburb of Slough).

Thomas Dunham must have received quite a shock to be told about seven murders, and during his journey to Denham from Slough his head will have been spinning with concerns about what awaited him and how he was going to solve the crime. The murderer had a head start and had escaped the scene. There were no witnesses to the actual murders, so what clues would emerge? Could he catch the culprit?

The crime scene clearly had an effect on Thomas. The scene of such carnage is hard to imagine, especially as it involved not just adults but young children, as well as an old lady. The house would have been covered in blood.

This book will contain a lot of information about Thomas Dunham and the way he handled the case. It is important to know some background on his police career and personal life.

Thomas Dunham was born in East Coker, near Yeovil, in 1833, and baptised the same year. His father, William, was an agricultural labourer who would never leave the tiny Somerset village of his birth. Thomas was the third boy in a family of four sons and two daughters.[1]

When he was seventeen, Thomas left home and went to work in Yeovil as a grocer's porter.[2] His older brother Robert, aged 20, left home at much the same time, but he travelled to Reading to join the Borough police. Thomas must have heard good reports from his brother about life in the police because a year later, in 1852, he too made his way to Reading and joined up. The younger brother, William, would follow suit three years later. In total, Thomas would spend five years and two months on the Watch Committee at Reading, living with others officers at the police station.

In March 1857, he transferred to the Buckinghamshire Constabulary, joining as a sergeant with no collar number. He met all the Constabulary entry requirements: he was twenty-five years of age, stood 5ft 8in tall without shoes, had a stout build with brown hair and hazel eyes, and was able to read and write. At this time, he was still single.

He rose steadily through the ranks, becoming an inspector in 1859 and a superintendent eight years later. During the first ten years of his service he saw postings in Eton, Maids Moreton, Iver and Chesham, before moving to Slough in Berkshire in 1866. At Maids Moreton, Thomas took lodgings in The Old House on the picturesque village main street, a tiny two-up two-down abode annexed to a seventeenth century detached thatched cottage next door – a far cry from the cramped officer accommodation at Reading.[3]

While stationed in Iver, he began courting Martha Wiggins, a coachman's daughter born and bred in Slough. They were married at St Peter's Church, Eaton Square in Pimlico, London, on 27 January 1864. The newly-weds set up house in St Leonard's Street in Iver.[4]

Nine months later, the couple's first child, Thomas Augustine, was born. By 1871 Thomas and Martha and their five children had relocated to Upton-cum-Chalvey, a village close to Slough, where they resided in the police station on the High Street.[5]

The Thames Valley Police Archives give details of Thomas Dunham's service record up to this point:

Career of Supt Thomas Dunham

14 March 1857	Sergeant on appointment
16 June 1859	Promoted 2nd Class Inspector
27 May 1861	Promoted 1st Class Inspector
19 November 1866	Promoted Acting Superintendent
14 January 1867	Promoted Superintendent
20 November 1876	Credited with £5 per annum
12 November 1881	Pay raised £5 per annum
7 May 1857	South Eastern Division (Eton)
16 June 1859	South Western Division (Maids Morton)
23 April 1861	South Eastern Division (Iver)
25 October 1864	South Western Division (Chesham)
25 November 1866	South Eastern Division (Slough)

At the time of the Denham Murders, Thomas Dunham was 37-years-old and had seventeen years of police service behind him. Most officers in those days retired after 25 years' service, so he was no rookie. Many of his early cases were reported in the local newspapers, and we'll take a look at some of them later on. His dedication and attention to detail was about to be tested at Denham very severely, but he was soon to emerge with an early arrest.

---

1 His siblings were Alfred, Sarah, Robert, William and Mary (1841 Census for East Coker, Somerset).

2 1851 Census for Yeovil.

3   1861 Census for Maids Moreton. In 2016 I had the good fortune of meeting Jane Wood. She is an active local historian who happens to live in the cottage that Dunham lived in between 1859 and 1861. She had managed to work out from the 1861 and other census records that Dunham had lived in the two-up-two-down tiny abode which was an annexe of the main cottage next door. The thatched building, called The Old House Cottage, sits next door to The Old House, and is in the 'picture postcard' Main Street.

4   Marriage certificate. Details of Martha's father's occupation from the 1851 Census for Upton-cum-Chalvey, Slough.

5   1871 Census for Upton-cum-Chalvey, Slough. Over the next eighteen years, the family would grow to ten children: Thomas Augustine (Iver, September 1864), Martha Ann (Chesham, April 1866), Elizabeth Jane (Upton-cum-Chalvey, 6 May 1868), Alice Lucy (Upton-cum-Chalvey, 3 April 1870), Robert William (Upton-cum-Chalvey, 1 September 1872), Sarah Kate (Upton-cum-Chalvey, 13 September 1874), Lotty Louisa (Slough, January 1876), George Albert (Slough, 1877), James Alfred (Slough, October 1879) and Frederick John (Slough, July 1882). See 1881 Census for Upton-cum-Chalvey, Slough and 1891 Census for Slough.

CHAPTER 11

The Murders

There were two crime scenes at the Marshalls' property. One was the house, and the other was the forge. Emmanuel Marshall was discovered face down in the forge with serious head injuries. His wife, sister, mother and three daughters were all also discovered with serious head injuries, but in the house on the ground floor. An early theory was that Emmanuel had murdered his own family and then committed suicide, but this was quickly ruled out by the doctors involved in the case.

Other theories involved the suspect being the 'military man' (Coleshill) from the Royal Elthorne Militia who had assaulted Marshall on Boxing Day (see Chapter 6), or that a brother who had gone to Australia had returned to kill the family.[1]

Another possible motive was plunder. George Armor asserted that his wife-to-be had just withdrawn £26 of her own money from the bank so that she could put it in again in her husband's name after the marriage. Therefore, a large amount of money was in the house. However, as the *Herts Advertiser & St Albans Times* noted, 'No one scarcely attributed the murder to plunder'.[2]

We should look at the facts. A man thought to be John Jones was seen by the village policeman at about 3.00 am on the Sunday morning. Emmanuel Marshall was a man who often used to get up very early in the morning during the summer months to let his

"House of the family murdered at Denham, near Uxbridge".
Illustrated London News, 4 June 1870 (Neil Watson Collection).

horse out to graze and to do some work in the forge. When he was discovered, he was wearing his ordinary working clothes and short sleeves.

All the other inhabitants of the house were discovered in their nightclothes, except for his wife Charlotte, who had a dress partially over her nightdress. This leads to the possibility that Emmanuel had risen in his own time in order to visit the forge to work. He surely got fully dressed to start his working day.

If someone had called at the door in the middle of the night, would he have got fully dressed or would he simply have gone down in his nightshirt?

No one else was dressed, although Charlotte may have possibly been more awake than the others due to her husband recently getting out of bed.

It seems likely that Emmanuel went to the forge himself and had started to work when the murderer approached the house. It may have still been dark, or just starting to get light, when the incident began. The suspect may have seen light coming from the forge or heard the sounds of metalwork being carried out.

Whatever the cause, the suspect must have seized his chance to ambush Marshall. There was no apparent sign of a struggle in the forge. It's possible that the suspect used stealth to enter the forge and strike a blow on Marshall's skull before he knew that an intruder was there. Marshall hated trespassers and would surely have put up a severe struggle had he been aware of his assailant.

It's my view that Emmanuel was the first victim. I consider that the assault on him would have produced a large amount of blood, which would have splattered the suspect's clothing. He would now need some clean clothes to wear, otherwise he would easily be discovered.

At this moment, whatever noise had been made in the forge during Emmanuel's murder may have awakened Charlotte, and possibly the others. She knew that her husband was in the forge and some terrible noises may have alerted her to some awful occurrence. If she had shouted out to him, no answer would be forthcoming. At this stage she may have decided to throw a dress over her nightdress in a considerable hurry. She would then head downstairs.

While she was doing this, the murderer had to think quickly and decide what he was going to do next. We shall probably never know what his intention was that night. Was he going to ask Marshall for the money and hope for the best? Or was he there on a mission of pure vengeance and murder? If he was going to try and negotiate some money, why go there at 3.00 or 4.00 am?

Given Jones's criminal history, simple theft may have been another motive. Was he going to steal Marshall's horse?

It seems likely that the suspect then decided that, having killed Marshall, a capital offence for which he could be hanged, he had to eliminate any potential witnesses. He also needed clean clothing, which was in the house. A supply of money or small items which could be pawned would also be useful to help with an escape away from the area.

PC Charles Trevener and Supt Thomas Dunham examine the murder scene. The 77-year-old grandmother was found holding one of the children.
Illustrated Police News

Having already cold-bloodedly bludgeoned Emmanuel Marshall to death, the suspect's adrenaline must have been running high. He may well then have heard cries from Charlotte within the cottage. There was no turning back.

One can imagine the terror that Charlotte must have experienced at that moment when, not knowing what had become of her husband, the suspect entered the house armed with an axe and a sledgehammer. The killer will have seen Charlotte and Mary Ann cowering in the parlour, and being in a state of extreme excitement he would have despatched both women with terrible blows to the head. Charlotte and Mary Ann were most likely to have been victims number two and three. Following the entry to the cottage the noise would have woken the other occupants of the house.

The *Windsor & Eton Express* paints an awful picture of the panic that must been aroused in the grandmother and the children as they heard Marshall and the two adult women being murdered. Old Mrs Marshall may have taken the children into the back kitchen with the hope of hiding or escaping, but neither was possible. Their final moments must have been terrifying:

> At the back of the house was another door leading into a stone paved kitchen, with an ancient fireplace, or rather hearth for burning wood. This door was found locked. The grandmother and the little ones

> apparently sought shelter in the paved kitchen, where the outer door,
> being barred and locked, they probably hoped to conceal themselves,
> but were easily discovered by the murderer, and were there slain
> without much chance of their cries being heard.[3]

Sister Mary Ann, grandmother Mary, and the three children, all had their skulls smashed by the suspect one by one. The wait in line to be killed must have been like something from a horror film. The suspect managed to break the skulls of all the poor victims before they could escape from the house.

Having killed all the occupants of the cottage, the killer then climbed the stairs in order to search the bedrooms. One interesting action was the smashing of a glass photograph of Marshall that had been in the bedroom. If the suspect had been an ordinary passing burglar, would he have bothered to smash the photo? This question was addressed in the *Manchester Evening News*:

> Suspicion was that the murder was committed in revenge. The last
> photo of Marshall which was taken on glass and which lay on the
> chest of drawers upstairs, was discovered the other day shattered to
> pieces and an indentation on the drawers as if the likeness had also
> received a blow from a sledge hammer.[4]

While in the house, the suspect changed out of his bloodied clothing and helped himself to a suit of nice clothes belonging to Emmanuel. He left his old outfit at the scene, as he could not risk carrying them with him. He also needed some footwear. His shoes would have also been covered with blood and would be another giveaway piece of evidence for his involvement in the crime. His solution was to remove the boots from Emmanuel's feet and put them on before the victim was even cold.

In the bedroom, the suspect helped himself to some items that were later to add to the welter of evidence against him. He was also to steal a watch, a knife, a pistol and a carpet bag. The items of clothing stolen included a coat, waistcoat, trousers, shirt, braces, collar, boots, straw hat and necktie.

1   On 10 May 1855, Emmanuel's brother William Francis Marshall and his wife
    Sarah sailed to Australia on the ship *John Davis* (see Australian Government
    Online Archives at www.archives.qld.gov.au/Researchers/Indexes/Immigration
    /Pages/Immigration1848.aspx, page 98). They had married in Hackney, east
    London, on 10 July 1853. William died on 23 January 1865 aged 42 years, and
    was buried in Toowoomba, Queensland. This meant that the theory that
    Emmanuel's brother had returned to England to commit the murders was
    impossible, as he had been dead for five years by then. Sarah died on 25 August
    1889, aged 57. Emmanuel's younger brother Philip Marshall also sailed to
    Australia aboard the *John Davis* on 10 May 1855. Records show him to be a
    17 year old labourer from Buckinghamshire. There is no evidence whatsoever
    to suggest that Philip ever returned to England.

2   *Herts Advertiser & St Albans Times*, 28 May 1870.

3   *Windsor & Eton Express*, 28 May 1870.

4   *Manchester Evening News*, 21 June 1870.

CHAPTER 12

Call for Scotland Yard!

In 1870, a crime of this magnitude would have attracted the interest of Scotland Yard. Indeed, had a serious crime been committed in another part of the country away from London, a request for a detective to be dispatched from Scotland Yard may have been made. And so it was in the case of the Denham Murders. In all likelihood, a telegraph was sent to Scotland Yard, and Scotland Yard then offered to assist as they were the 'senior' force in the country and had detectives. Inspector William Palmer and Detective Sergeant Robert Walker were promptly despatched to Uxbridge.

Some memos in the National Archives at Kew throw light on the case. Detective Sergeant Robert Walker wrote a report to his superiors dated 24 May 1870 regarding the brief facts of the case.

His report reads as follows:

> I beg to report that a most diabolical murder has been committed in Denham, Bucks, a small village two miles from Uxbridge [Out of the Metropolitan Police District.] A man named Emmanuel Marshall, a smith and esquire, his wife, mother, sister and three female children, aged respectively, 4, 7 and 9 years, were found with their heads almost beaten to pieces, the man Marshall partly dressed in the smithy, the remainder in their night clothes in the bottom part of the cottage. There is no doubt they were cut down with a large axe and their heads afterwards beaten with a large hammer, both these implements were found covered in blood.

The crime is supposed to have been committed on Saturday night last, as the whole of Sunday and Monday till 6pm when a young woman from Uxbridge went to the cottage with a new dress for the sister of the murdered man who was to have been married on the 24th inst. [Tuesday written in pencil.] The motive for the murder is not apparent as nothing is missing except the man's boots. He is supposed to have been murdered in the cottage then dragged into the workshop where he was found.

PS 13X Cooper [Metropolitan Police 'X' Division - Uxbridge] on hearing of the discovery, proceeded to the spot, there being only one constable stationed in the village and tendered all the assistance he could until the arrival of Supt Dunham from Slough and Insp Sutton of the Bucks Constabulary. At present there is no clue to the perpetrators of this horrible crime. Uxbridge and Denham are is a state of great excitement.[1]

This report was signed by a superintendent, but the signature is hard to read. In the margin on page 2 it says 'submitted Robert Walker DS'. On page 1 in the margin is written, 'Had we better send a detective inspector to assist in the enquiry' and is signed by Commissioner Edmund Henderson.

The following day, 25 May, Inspector Palmer sent a telegram to Scotland Yard advising that a man had been detained. He followed this up with a report on the 26th outlining the circumstances of the case. Countersigned by Superintendent Adolphus Williamson, the report made happy reading for Scotland Yard as it made it clear that the case had been solved. The report was written as follows:

I beg to report with reference to the murders at Denham, Bucks, alluded to in the attached report, that as directed, I proceeded to Uxbridge on the 24th and arrived there at 8 ½ pm and in conjunction with Insp Sutton, Bucks Constabulary, and Insp Holloway 'X', made various enquiries at Uxbridge and at 11pm I heard that the murderer had been arrested in Reading.

Yesterday I went to Slough and saw Capt Drake, Chief Constable, and handed him Col Henderson's memo and that gentleman expressed his thanks for the offer of my assistance and stated that the man being apprehended and the case against him being so clear, he thought there was no necessity to my staying any longer. He further requested me to make enquiries at the House of Correction, Clerkenwell with the view to ascertaining if any warden could identify the clothes worn

WILLIAM PALMER

by the prisoner when discharged from that prison on Saturday last.

This I have done this morning and find that warden Thomas PAULTON[2] can speak to the hat and clothing found in the cottage at Denham which has been left behind by the murderer. These particulars I have communicated with Supt Denson, Deputy Chief Constable Bucks.

It would appear that following a breakthrough in the case, Bucks Constabulary kindly declined the continued services of Scotland Yard in helping to solve the crime, other than checking with the prison. Buckinghamshire Chief Constable Captain Drake must have had more than a little satisfaction in informing the Scotland Yard detective inspector that his force were not looking for anyone else, and were happy that they had their man. Supt Dunham was on the case and was doing a good job.

The *Cambridge Independent Press* summarised the intense police activity following the murders and the interest of Scotland Yard:

It should be stated that in the interval which elapsed between the discovery of the murders and the apprehension of the prisoner, every alehouse, lodging house and house of public resort in Brentford, Uxbridge and surrounding neighbourhoods were closely searched for the prisoner and the police were certainly untiring in their efforts. Colonel Henderson sent down an inspector and assistant of the detective police of Scotland Yard, to assist in the search, but the capture was made when they arrived.[3]

1   National Archives: MEPO 3/98. X Division covered west London from Kilburn to Uxbridge which was the last Met outpost before the Buckinghamshire Constabulary area.

2   Thomas Paulton lived a long life, having mostly worked in the field of 'crime and punishment'. He was born in Greenford on 22 September 1833. His first job, according to the 1851 Census, was as a 17-year-old 'pot boy' at the Bessborough Arms in Pimlico. This job had given him a good grounding on how to look after himself. In 1861 he was working at Coldbath Fields Prison as a prison officer, and ten years later as a Gate Warder, a position he held for at least a decade. In the 1891 Census he was recorded as being 57-years-old and employed as an usher. By 1901 he was working at the County Sessions (Court House), where he still was in 1911. He died in September 1922 at the age of 89.

3   *Cambridge Independent Press*, 28 May 1870.

CHAPTER 13

The Press

News of the slaughter of the Marshall family would result in a frenzy of sightseers and reporters descending on Denham. The *Morning Post* of 26 May reported that between 3,000 and 4,000 people had arrived in the village and made entreaties to be allowed to see the corpses. (Only people with the express permission of the Coroner were allowed to enter the cottage and forge.) The murders at Denham would keep the newspapers busy for weeks, and probably increase sales at the same time. The fact that the *Illustrated Police News* ran it as a front page story on two consecutive weeks shows how big this story was. Denham was a picture perfect, quintessential English village, where nothing much ever happened.

A 'Denham circus' had begun. Interest in the newspapers was huge. This story was going to run and run.

The newspapers were outraged that such cold-hearted malice could have been committed by an Englishman. *The Spectator* published an article where you can almost sense the editor banging his desk in outrage at the terrible nature of this dastardly crime.

The newspapers used various headlines to describe the murders: 'Shocking Tragedy', 'Horrible tragedy near Uxbridge', 'The Denham Massacre', 'Fiendish Murder', and so on. The crime was just so shocking that middle England found it hard to contemplate over their breakfast tables.

The mood of the country was typified by the 25 May edition of *The Spectator*. Some of the words used in the article underlined how serious a crime this was. One small article contained these words to describe the event: 'Slaughterhouse', 'massacre', 'outrage', 'savagery', 'ruthless', 'butchery', 'harrowing', 'horrifying', 'barbarous', 'depraved' and 'carnage'.

The article concluded with the following paragraph, showing how embarrassing this atrocity was for the country as a whole:

> In cold blooded brutality, in desperate recklessness and in fiendish atrocity, the deeds of English murderers stand alone, unequalled and unapproachable.[1]

An article by the same newspaper on 28 May gave a further account:

> The special horror of this Denham tragedy, the feature which distinguishes it from vulgar murders, and raises it into the rank of an event in the history of crime, is not the number of the victims, though that no doubt helps to heat the popular imagination, but the illustration it offers of the true blood thirst, that passion in human nature whose explosions are so rare and so terrible that many philosophers have questioned its very existence.

> It was at first supposed that the murderer, believed to be a Staffordshire tramp and thief, named John Jenkins or John Owen, was actuated by some feeling of revenge; that he had sworn some kind of vendetta against his victim Marshall, an engineer living in Denham, Bucks, and it is still uncertain whether he had not some previous grudge or family feud against him.

> He had been repeatedly imprisoned for petty thefts, and on his last release told the warder that he would not be imprisoned again; that a blacksmith of Uxbridge owed him money, and that if he did not get it he would have the villain's blood. Whatever his motive, revenge, or desire for money, or a mere idea of petty robbery, it would seem that on the night of Saturday last he slipped away from a room in Uxbridge in which he had lodged in company with a workman named Coombs, went to Denham, and early in the morning entered Marshall's smithy, probably for plunder, as had he intended to ask for money he would have gone to the house, but possibly to obtain a murderous weapon.

> Marshall, either roused from sleep by a noise, or, as the police think, just getting up to do a spell of work before Sunday began, went down, went out of doors, the smithy being detached, entered the smithy

door, and was felled by a blow from a sledge-hammer, which killed him instantly.

The side of the head was beaten in, and he probably only screamed once, and did not struggle at all. The murderer, whoever he was, then left the smithy, entered the house by the front door,[2] and met in the doorway Marshall's wife, Charlotte, who had evidently been roused by some alarm, for her dress was just thrown over her night-things, and killed her, probably with a chopper taken out of the smithy for the purpose and subsequently found.

Her sister, who under the same alarm had followed her in her night-dress, was next despatched, and then the murderer followed the remainder of the household, Marshall's mother, an old woman of seventy-seven, and three children of eight, six, and four, who, conscious in some way of the horrible tragedy proceeding, were trying in wild alarm to escape by the back kitchen.

By this time the horrible thirst for blood as blood, the delirium of slaughter of which soldiers have been known to speak, must have possessed the murderer, for he not only slaughtered the grandmother, always with blows on the head, but all the children, even a little one four years old, whom he could have secured or frightened with ease, a crime almost as superfluous as that of Williams,[3] a crime suggesting that its perpetrator was no longer sane, but delirious with the delirium of wickedness.[4]

From the modern research point of view, the local and national newspapers of the period are a goldmine of information. Tiny details are recorded. On occasions writers could be annoyingly unhelpful by failing to provide the full name of a person or some other important detail, but on the whole the standard of reporting is good. Liberties were sometimes had when dealing with fact or supposition. Some editors had decided that Jones was guilty a day after the crime had been discovered, and appeared not to need await the verdict of any subsequent jury.

Reports were also written in a wonderfully colourful and exuberant style, almost as if they had been written by Leonard Sachs, the compère of the BBC's *The Good Old Days*. He was famous for using long and outlandishly descriptive words of acts on the show.

The phrase 'Don't believe everything you read in the papers' is certainly correct in the case of Victorian reporting. While researching for this book I found numerous inaccuracies. When one considers

SHOCKING MURDER
OF SEVEN PERSONS
At DENHAM, near Uxbridge.

Last Monday evening, May the 23rd, a dreadful murder was committed at the village of Denham, near Uxbridge. A family of the name of Marshall had retired to rest on Saturday night the 21st, and were not seen by anyone in the neighbourhood. The family consisted of Mr. and Mrs Marshall, the husband s m ther and sister, and three children ; the sister was about to be married, and a friend called on the Monday to see and finding the doors were locked, and receiving no answer, became alarmed ; the police were communicated with, who broke the door, and discovered the dreadful crime. Just inside the door was found the wife and sister, stretched on the floor with their brains knocked out ; a further search was made, and in the kitchen were found the bodies of the grandmother and three children, and in his own workshop, the man Marshall, a wheelwright by trade, was found murdered by the same weapon, which was afterwards found covered with hair and blood in a cupboard. Suspicions are strong against several parties, and the greatest excitement prevails.

Kind Christian friends, pray give attention,
  And listen to a dreadful tale,
Near Uxbridge town what consternation,
  A dreadful murder we must bewail ;
At Denham village, on Sunday morning,
  The shocking tragedy was done,
A family before the dawning,
  Was cruel slaughtered every one.

A Wheelwright by the name of Marshall,
  His aged mother, and loving wife,
His sister and three darling children,
  Seven poor souls deprived of life.
Poor Marshall s sister was to be married,
  A female friend came her to see,
The doors were lock'd and no one answer'd,
  Well might she wonder what could be.

She told the neighbour's her sad suspicions
  And when at last they broke the door,
To see, oh God! six fellow creatures,
  Crushed and mangled on the floor.
Some vile wretches, cruel however,
  His victims in cold blood did slay,
And in each others arms all bleeding,
  The wife and sister together lay.

'Twas in the kitchen the darling children,
  Two little sisters they were found,
And round poor Granny's neck the baby,
  Its little arms had clung around.
The cruel monsters they had no feeling,
  And they slaughtered young and old,
Their brains by dreadful blows were batter'd
  Oh God! it makes the blood run cold.

Oh, where is Marshall, cried the neighbours
  Some thought that he had done the crime
But in his workshop then they found him,
  Fouly murdered in his prime.
He was a sober man and steady,
  Who did his duty without fear,
For which he was ill-used last Christmas,
  By wicked persons so we hear.

They had been caught and sent to prison,
  And both came out the other day,
And swore that they would do for Marshall
  And be revenged, so people say.
May providence reveal the villains,
  The murderers who e'er they be,
And oh God, do thou in heaven,
  Bless the Marshall family.

S. FORTEY, Printer, Monmouth Ct., London, W.C

Handbill with description of the crimes as well as a poem about the murders. The should be compared with a later ballad printed when John Jones was on death row at Aylesbury Gaol. The poem wrongly blames guilt on the man who had assaulted Emmuanuel Mashall the previous year following a fire.

the lack of modern communications such as email, computers and recording machines, the Victorian hack had to do his best to get the story right in double-quick time in order to get it ready for the print deadline. Failing the above, the reporter would try and get the story as nearly right as possible. All things considered, the newspapers did a reasonable job.

Photography was well established by 1870, but the newspapers at the time were still mainly using drawings to give visuals to their reports. As has been mentioned in Chapter 1, the *Illustrated Police News* was big on pictures. Each edition contained an eye-catching drawing, or more often drawings, though only on the front page. Editions would normally have anything between one and twenty or so drawings on the front page.

In the Victorian era, people who bought local newspapers would not simply get stories from their own locale. Most small papers carried local, national and international news. The Denham Massacre was therefore not confined to being reported in the local papers such as the *Bucks Herald* or the *Bucks Advertiser*, but also appeared in provincial newspapers as far away as Scotland and Ireland. The larger national newspapers also carried the story. As it was such huge news internationally, reports of the crime even reached as far away as Australia.

As the original police file for the Denham Murders no longer appears to exist, newspaper coverage at the time has helped enormously at filling in the blanks regarding this case.

---

1 *The Spectator*, 25 May 1870.

2 However, the *Windsor & Eton Express* of 28 May stated, 'There is no door to the front of the house. The principal entrance is on the left side of the cottage. The entrance leads directly into the parlour'.

3 A reference to John Williams, the notorious Ratcliff Highway Murderer. In December 1811, over a period of twelve days, he murdered seven people, including a baby, from two separate families near Wapping in the East End of London. He was never convicted of these crimes because he hanged himself in his prison cell before facing trial.

4 *The Spectator*, 28 May 1870.

CHAPTER 14

Here Comes the Bride?

The enormity of this crime is hard to contemplate when you consider other members of the extended family and how they must have felt on hearing the news.

The family had lost the matriarch of the family, the 77-year-old widow Mary Marshall. Though her time was getting short, her loss would be heartfelt. An old lady did not deserve to die in this way. She would now be joining her late husband William Marshall, who had passed away thirteen years previously in 1857 and who was laid to rest in the churchyard of Denham Parish Church. She would soon be joining him in the same grave.

The loss of both parents, Emmanuel and Charlotte, was cruel as they were still relatively young, being in their thirties.

The three children, Mary, Thirza and Gertrude, were all under ten and had their whole lives ahead of them. Their slaughter was crushing for the relatives, and also very hard to bear for the people of the village.

If the loss of the above was not bad enough, the murder of Mary Ann Marshall robbed her fiancé, George Armor, from Sawbridgeworth, Hertfordshire, of his intended bride.

Tuesday 24 May was supposed to have been the most exciting day of their lives. A wedding dress was due to arrive, the house had

The Denham Parish Church marriage register showing the reading of the Banns between George Armor and Mary Ann Marshall on 8th, 15th and 22nd May 1870.

been decorated and the banns had been read. Mary Ann had a good sum of money to take with her, as after the wedding she intended to journey to Hertfordshire to start her new life as Mrs Armor.

George had been told by his intended to arrive on the Tuesday morning at the station in time for the wedding. He must have been feeling nervous but happy at the prospect of taking his new bride home with him.

He arrived at Uxbridge station not having heard any news of the murders. When he was told what had happened, he was quite overcome.

His evidence to the coroner was later reported in the newspapers:

> I live in Sawbridgeworth and have known the Marshall family for four years. I was engaged to be married to Mary and came here today to marry her. I last saw her a month ago. She always wore a locket with her father's hair in it. I got a letter from her on Friday morning, arranging for me to come this morning. She was going to return home with me after our marriage.[1]

We can only imagine the effect of the harrowing news on George Armor. His life could never have been the same afterwards. Local records revealed that George returned home as a 29 year old bachelor. A year after the murder, he is shown on the 1871 census living with his sister Mary as an unmarried gardener.[2] His address was shown as Hyde Hall gardener's cottage at Sheering, Essex.[3] Each following census up until 1911 gave his marital status as single and his occupation as a gardener.[4] There is no record of a marriage for him. In 1891, he had moved in with his 85 year old mother Elizabeth to a house in Harlow Common, Harlow, Essex, where he was to remain until his death in 1917. He saw out the remainder of his life with his sister Fanny who died in 1916.[5] George passed away in 1917, aged 76.[6] His probate record shows that he left his estate to his brother, livestock dealer, Charles Armor. It is sad to note that his estate only amounted to £3 and 10 shillings.[7]

---

1 The *Illustrated Police News*, 28 May 1870.

2 1871 Census (reference RG10/1641, page 20, schedule 10).

3 Hyde Hall was the local manor house. The magnificent property still exists, but is now divided into apartments.

4 1891 Census (reference RG12/1364, page 1, schedule 6); 1901 Census (reference RG13/1642, page 13, schedule 108) and 1911 Census (reference RG10/1641, page 20, schedule 10).

5 Probate Records London 1916. Fanny Armor, of 'Crumps', Harlow Common, spinster, died 2 August 1916. Probate London 23 September 1916, to Rev James Dudley Elwell, effects £233. One wonders why she did not leave her estate to George?

6 Probate Records, London, 1920, page 60. George Armor of Harlow Common, died 17 August 1917, effects £3. 10s.

7 Biographical note. George was born at Latton, Essex at the start of 1841, being 4 months old at the time of the 1841 Census (reference HO107/330/5, page 10, schedule 8). His parents were James Armor and Elizabeth Harvey. His siblings were Elizabeth, Frances, Mary, Charles and Fanny. In 1841, his father was shown as a gardener, though later he became a farmer (1851 Census, reference HO107/1770, page 5, schedule 13). On James's death on 7 February 1889, he left £12 to George (Probate, London, 12 January 1892). The newspapers and the Denham Parish marriage banns records described George as being from the small town of Sawbridgeworth, Hertfordshire. This was probably given as a place that people may have heard of rather than the unknown village of Sheering. His 1871 census record for Sheering is actually in Essex. The county border runs between Sheering and Sawbridgeworth.

CHAPTER 15

The Chase Was On

Supt Thomas Dunham must have arrived at the Marshall's house around 10.00 pm[1] on the evening of Monday 23 May. He found a scene with bodies everywhere and signs of great violence. There was the smashed glass photograph of Emmanuel Marshall. Items had been stolen including clothing and a pistol. The corpses were no longer warm. They had probably lain in the house for a day and a half.

The suspect had a long head start on him. This was a case that surely had to be solved. But where to start? It must have taken a while to record the crime scene itself. There was a lot to organise; obtaining reinforcements, informing the Chief Constable, arranging the inquest.

Finding out who had committed this crime was going to be just one of a number of jobs for Dunham. He would not be home for dinner that night.

Dunham's head must have been in a spin. He had entered a house full of horrors which included the murder of three young children. He had to think straight and start the investigation immediately in the face of this appalling nightmarish scene. The urge to find the killer must have been deeply held within him, having witnessed such a scene of utter brutality. He also needed luck, and a sloppy suspect. He was about to find both of these, together with some very good policing.

With crime investigations, what always helps the detective is how careful the suspect has been in covering his tracks. Did he take chances, and leave clues behind? Would he be found with incriminating evidence, or say something incriminating? Clever criminals make it hard for the police to catch them and to get a conviction. Other criminals are sloppy and make it easy for the police to find them.

John Jones clearly was not one of the clever variety. The fact that he had a string of convictions indicated that he was not very good at getting away with the crimes he committed. Humans are creatures of habit, and his careless behaviour during this case was probably the same as the way he tried to get away with other crimes. This was a man who had served several prison terms and appears to have been living the life of a criminal tramp. He was ultimately going to make so many mistakes that the police would have their man, but on the evening on Monday, 23 May, no suspect was in sight.

What we should also remember is that Jones was also a man who may not have gone to the house with a careful plan. The fact that all seven members of the family had been killed may not have been his intention. On meeting Emmanuel Marshall, he may have panicked. Whatever the reason for the murders, killing that many people was going to cause a lot of blood to be splattered about and he probably could not think clearly as to the consequences of what he had done. Bad decisions were ultimately going to cost him his life.

Although there was no clue at the scene which pointed to one suspect being responsible on the Monday evening, Tuesday was to be a day of drama and huge developments in the hunt for the killer. It's not recorded when Supt Dunham got to sleep that night. Even if he had gone home to Slough late that night, he could have not got much sleep, if any. His mind would have been full of the victims and the daunting task ahead.

The *Bucks Advertiser* gave details of Supt Dunham's early involvement in the case:

With commendable promptitude, Supt Dunham was on the spot about 10pm the same night, and assisted by other officers made a full examination of the house. Early next morning Mr Dunham was again on the spot, and taking the clothes with him, proceeded to Uxbridge to prosecute enquires.

Meanwhile on Tuesday morning, crowds repaired to the fatal spot. A posse of police guarded the house and prevented entrance, except to some of the reporters of whom, besides those from Uxbridge, there were many from the Metropolis. A brief report of the tragedy been conveyed overnight, partly by telegraph and partly by messenger to the London papers.[2]

A modern police homicide detective would not have been impressed with Victorian forensic methods. Lots of policemen walking over the evidence would not have helped. The fact that Dunham arrived at 10.00 pm in the dark was also a hindrance. Rudimentary lamps and candlelight would not have helped the investigating officers. It's also strange to a modern audience that the police would have allowed some of the gentlemen of the press to enter the crime scene.

---

1   *London Daily News*, 23 July 1870.
2   *Bucks Advertiser*, 28 May 1870.

CHAPTER 16

The Inquest
(First Day)

On Tuesday 24 May the inquest into the deaths of the Marshall family opened at the Swan Inn in Denham before Mr Frederick Charsley, the coroner for South Buckinghamshire.

Situated on the north side of the main road through the village, the Swan was the usual venue for inquest hearings. A strong body of police officers under Captain Drake maintained order within and around the building, holding back the large crowds and ensuring that only those with a valid reason should be admitted.

The *Bucks Advertiser* reported that the coroner took no time in arranging the first hearing:

> Having been appraised at an early hour of the event, Frederick Charsley Esq[1] fixed the inquest for the same day at 12 o'clock noon. Chief Constable Drake arrived and was present at the inquest.

The coroner said it would be necessary for someone to view the bodies who would be able to identify them. The police said the father of Marshall's wife, Mr Sparke of Uxbridge, would be the best person for the purpose.[2]

The jury members were listed as follows:[3]

Rev Charles JOYCE, Curate of Denham parish Church, age 36

Robert RANSHAWE, Agent of farm steward, 69

The Swan at Denham, where the inquest hearings took place.

Thomas HAMERTON, Miller, 44

Edwin WIGGINS, Master tailor, 34

Lewis BAMPTON, Butcher, 47

Charles BROWN, Baker, 31

William HARMAN, Market gardener, 46

William STEVENS, occupation and age unknown

John THOMPSON, Retired baker, 50

Joseph ROSE, Blacksmith, 52

Richard WHEELER, Groom, 73

William BROWN, Groom, 31

Henry PARHAM, Carpenter, 41

George CONNOR, occupation and age unknown

William ARNOLD, Carpenter, 60

The Jury Foreman was the Rev Charles Joyce.

The inquest would be long and painful for everyone who sat in the Swan Inn to hear the evidence. The hearing would be minutely recorded by the newspapers, who reproduced in detail not only evidence against Jones, but also included the findings of the doctors who carried out the post mortems. The details of the injuries sustained by the victims were difficult to comprehend, especially when the ages of some of the deceased were considered.

The jury members did not merely have to listen to the graphic evidence being given by the witnesses. They were also required to visit the Marshall house and view the bodies. This must have been an even more severe test of their emotions. The *Freeman's Journal* described their ordeal:

> You entered at a low door at the south west corner of the north gable. Before you were corpses of two women, the wife and she who was to have been a bride yesterday. They were bathed in their own blood which had been scattered upon the door post and upon the walls.
>
> When the jury was shown the room to view the bodies, the sight of these women, who had comely features, gashed now with the strokes of the axe with which they had no doubt been stricken, had evidently an appalling effect. Scarcely a word passed. They looked on in silence.
>
> It was otherwise when they came to the back room. When the sheet was lifted off the grandmother, still clasping the youngest child closely to her side – and the three little girls, their bodies thrown promiscuously one over the other in the corner, and all still in their nightdresses, the jury were quite overpowered. Many of them sobbed aloud. All were in tears.
>
> The ghastly wounds inflicted on the heads and faces of the children could not disguise the fact that they were beautiful.[4]

This scale of the savagery of the attack on the defenceless Marshall family, particularly the women and the children, was now clear for all to see. This was an act which was so terrible that it appeared to have been driven by hatred or revenge and showed no pity for the poor victims. This was surely no simple burglary gone wrong; it was much more than that. Could the person responsible have been insane? Why else would anyone have used that much violence against young children?

The principal witness on the first day was PC Charles Trevener. He told the court he had last seen the Marshall family at 11.00 on Saturday when he passed by their home. Mr Marshall came out of his workshop to speak to him, and the children were playing in the front garden. PC Trevener then went on to describe how he met a man in a felt hat and tightly-buttoned dark old coat heading towards the Marshall cottage at 03.00 am on Sunday morning. Finally, he gave a harrowing account of what he'd seen inside the Marshall cottage (see pages 47–48).

The Coroner released the bodies of the deceased for the funeral. The inquest was then adjourned until Friday 27 May to enable the police to prosecute their investigation. At the next hearing the jury would hear evidence from the doctors who had conducted the post mortem examinations.

---

1   Coroner Frederick Charsley was born in 1821 in Beaconsfield, Buckinghamshire. He was a solicitor by profession. He served as coroner for South Bucks for a number of years. He died in Brighton in 1892 aged 71, leaving £73,391 to his wife Fanny Kenyon. When Charsley's son Frederick was killed aged 43 in a riding accident in 1899 at Stoke Park, the inquest into the fatal accident was conducted by Mr Fells, the mid Bucks Coroner, at the request of the South Bucks coroner Mr G. A. Charsley due to the family connection. The first witness at the hearing was another family member, Dr Robert Stephen Charsley who practised in Slough.

2   *Bucks Advertiser*, 28 May 1870.

3   Occupations and ages obtained from the 1871 census for Denham.

4   *Freeman's Journal*, 26 May 1870.

CHAPTER 17

The Big Breakthrough

On Tuesday, 24 May, Thomas Dunham got cracking with his enquiries. There was a lot to do. Many lines of enquiry are followed by the police in cases like this, but tip-offs from the public are always vitally important in giving the police a breakthrough. This was to be the case in the hunt for the Denham murderer. Dunham was about to be visited by a man with crucial evidence that would put the Superintendent on the trail of John Jones.

Events that had occurred in Uxbridge the day before had not gone unnoticed by this witness, but once news of the murders spread his suspicions were seriously aroused.

The witness in question was Charles Coombes. He was bricklayer who lodged in the Bell Yard in Uxbridge. Little is known about Charles before or after the murders. Although we know much about Coombes's evidence, we know hardly anything about him as a person. He does not appear on the 1871 census or other statutory records of the period. He seems to have disappeared into the mists of time. It's clear, though, that Coombes was an often unemployed bricklayer, who had to live in cheap lodgings. At the time of the murders he was working for a local builder.

To understand what Coombes knew we have to go back in time. He had been lodging at Bell Yard for twelve months, and knew a number of the regulars who also lodged there in landlady Mrs Charlotte

The lodgings at Bell Yard, Uxbridge,
where John Jones and Charles Coombes stayed

Balham's premises.[1] One of the men that he had become acquainted with was a man he only knew as 'Jack'. This was a man who could only ever afford to sleep in a common lodging house, dressed poorly and never had any money. Coombes was wary of him, as well as to some of the stories he had told him.

Charles Coombes gave vital evidence at the inquest and the trial which was widely reported in the newspapers. His evidence was so strong that Dunham dropped everything in order to follow his leads.

The *Bucks Herald* gave a very detailed account of the evidence that Coombes gave at the inquest, which had been hurriedly arranged for the Tuesday (24 May) and then again on Friday (27 May).

> 'I knocked off work at 2pm last Saturday. I arrived home at about 3pm and went down to the lodging house. I saw a man I knew as John Jenkins who had lodged there before. I saw him there 10 weeks ago when he lodged there for 4-5 nights and was taken away for stealing stockings from a garden and had to serve two months.
>
> I did not know what Jenkins' job was or how he made his living. He used to go out at nights. He said he used to make his living before we were up. I saw him in the kitchen at the lodging house and he said he was back from 'that two months' [imprisonment].

When he came on the Saturday I heard him ask if there was room for him which there was. He said he would be out late. He said he had no money but he soon should have, for he was going to see his brother.

When he was there 10 weeks ago, he used to get up at 3-4 am and come back at 6-7 am. He once told me he sold a pair of wheels for 4 shillings and 6 pence, but did not say where he had got them. 10 weeks ago he slept in the same room as me, six of us in one room in single beds.

When he came on Saturday he had no carpet bag, no box of clothes and no money. I saw him on Saturday. He said 'Hello Charlie'. I said 'Hello John so you've got back'. There were several others there at the time. He did not have any food or beer. I left to go to the Queens Head for beer, he did not come with me. He did not say where he was going, only that he was going to see his brother and that he would have money before long. I went to bed at 11pm, and prisoner was not there.

He was in another room in the lodging house with a man called Phil, and a militia man called Carter.

On Sunday morning I went to the kitchen. A man named Dan came into the kitchen and said, 'You won't know the blacksmith (the name that the prisoner was known by), because he has dressed up like a gentleman. He's got a watch chain, carpet bag and a suit of good clothes'. I think he came home early Sunday morning.

At 10am (Sunday) he came into the kitchen. I said, 'What's been up?' He was wearing a black coat, black tie, nice white shirt, boots with false button holes and cracked across. On Saturday night when I had seen him he had a dark cloth coat which he had before the two months and a fustian jacket to cover it, and a very narrow brimmed hat.

 On Sunday morning he had a straw hat on but he bought a cap on Monday and destroyed the straw hat which had a black riband on it. [Charles Coombes was recalled by the Coroner and stated that the hat the prisoner wore on Saturday was destroyed in the kitchen on Monday morning.]

The neck tie shown to me was the neck tie worn on Sunday morning and was the murdered man's. I think it was the chain produced. The prisoner wore that or one like that on Sunday.

He said he had been to his brothers who had given him the clothes and watch. I went to Mrs Balham the landlady who lives in the cottage close by and I said, 'There is something wrong by that fellow, for it don't stand to reason that a brother would strip himself of clothes and a watch. You will hear something in the course of a day or two.'

*John Jones as he appeared
the day before and after the murders*
Illustrated Police News

She said, 'Oh botheration, it's all right, his brother has given 'em to him.'

He wanted me to have some beer on Sunday at dinner time but I would not. Others had been with him having beer and he paid for it with a shilling. The night before he had not got a farthing.

At the missus's house the prisoner was having dinner, some rump steak which he had brought in and some plum pudding which had been made and cooked by the missus. I had some of his steak on his urging me but I did not want it. I got some beer on his giving me the money in the afternoon and after that he said he should stop in the lodging house and go to bed for Mrs Balham locked it up on Sunday afternoon.

He said he was going out at night to fetch a pony & trap which he had bought. He said it was 'as pretty a trap and pony as ever you saw'. I again told the missus something was wrong.

I did not see him again until the Monday morning. Then I saw the prisoner coming out of a public house with two girls. He came over to me and asked if I had any bacca. He then said, 'Shall I go and pawn this watch?' and asked me to go with him, but I refused and went to work.

At night he went to the Queens Head with me. While there he lent a lodger a sixpence. A man came in and said, 'Have you heard of the murder?' The prisoner cocked his head up and said, 'Has there been a murder then?' 'Yes of seven persons'. The prisoner at once asked me the way to the back where he went into a closet. We then went home and went to bed.

In the morning he came into my room and asked for bacca. He asked for breakfast. I told him he could share mine but he did not touch it. He had gone when I returned from work for breakfast.

I asked a fellow worker about the murder and whether anything had been lost. I told him about the man coming back with the clothes, watch and money and he advised me to see the superintendent, to whom I went afterwards.'

The Coroner asked about the pony and trap, and Coombes replied saying he believed that prisoner was going to take Marshall's pony and trap and drive away.

The Coroner asked, 'Did he say what he did or where he came from?' Coombes replied, 'He told me 10 weeks ago that he had stolen as many horses as there were in Uxbridge and that he had stolen his father's pony which he had sold for £14 and that his father had claimed it on his writing home to tell his father where it was.' The carpet bag, the witness added, had been left with the landlady. The Coroner told him that he had acted well in giving his information and that he had given his evidence in an open and straight forward manner.[2]

During the subsequent jury trial, further evidence from Mr Coombes was related in a newspaper report. He told the court the following:

> I saw him come to the house on Sunday morning. 'Why John, I don't know you.' He said, 'I have been to see my brother' I said 'You have no brother round here'. He said 'Yes I have'.

> I last saw him at Mrs Balham's at 5am on Tuesday morning. He told me he was going to Reading. I heard of the murders at 8pm Monday night.

> I went to Supt Dunham on Tuesday morning and told him what I knew. I remember being at the Queens Head, Uxbridge with the prisoner and Jem the blacksmith. A man came in and asked if we had heard about the murders. [3]

Coombes was an ordinary working man who was used to living in a common lodging house and who often lived hand to mouth. He knew that John Jones (alias John Jenkins) was a thief and a man that lived on his wits, going out in the middle of the night to steal things. He knew him to be penniless. He had just been released from prison and he could not afford to pay for his lodging on the Saturday night. He told Coombes that he was going to get money from his 'brother'. Coombes did not believe this assertion.

On seeing Jones at Bell Yard on the Saturday afternoon having been released from prison, he was dressed normally, in scruffy old clothes. He had no bag and no possessions apart from what he stood up in. By the following day, the Sunday, Jones was dressed like a gentleman with a fine suit of clothes, a carpet bag, and a watch and chain. A man that had nothing hours earlier was now buying people beer and eating rump steak. How had he come into such possessions if not by foul play?

Later, on the Monday morning, Jones had asked Coombes to come with him to the pawn shop with a watch and chain. Jones was now very flush with money. Coombes must have initially thought that Jones had simply been out on a burglary job.

By the Monday evening, Jones was in the Queen's Head pub with Coombes, still with enough money to lend to other lodgers, when a man came in to announce that the murder victims had been discovered. The news immediately altered Jones's behaviour.

Coombes, having put two and two together by the Tuesday morning, had to inform the police what he knew about Jones. The *Illustrated Police News* reported:

> Charles Coombes' suspicions arose, and he told his employer he could not rest till he went after the man, as he suspected that he had committed the murders. His master[4] volunteered to pay his expenses.[5]

Another newspaper, later reporting proceedings before the magistrates at Slough, commented on Coombes's evidence:

> The clerk of the court asked Coombes, 'How do you know if he pawned the watch?' 'I went to the pawn shop with him. He told me to stop outside'. Clerk: 'Did he spend any money?' Coombes: 'He was along with two girls all Sunday night and early Monday morning. I said to my chap, 'I wonder if Jack has got anything from that place where the murder took place?'[6]

Coombes was quoted by another local newspaper mentioning Jones being with two girls:

> I saw the prisoner the next morning at about 7 o clock with two girls, one of which was Jane Davis,[7] come out of the public house.[8]

The girls mentioned in these reports were to provide evidence of erratic behaviour by Jones. They gave evidence of him being in possession of a pistol. The *Freeman's Journal* gave details of Jones's manic behaviour on the Sunday evening:

> The Landlord of the Bell Tavern, in Bell Yard, observed a man named Jack [John Jones] enter his house on Sunday evening at 5pm. His manner and appearance was singular. He ordered a quantity of ale for himself but also for every other person in the bar.
>
> Shortly before the house closed, he called in three young women, the names of two of them were Elizabeth Selwood and Susan Burton.[9] After treating the women to a quantity of ale he accompanied them to Chequers Yard.

All the other inmates had retired to rest, but before they could get to sleep, they were alarmed by hearing the strange man slipping down the stairs in his stockings and trying their rooms.

When asked what he wanted he said, 'She won't get me a pot of ale.' One young woman said she would go and get ale from a landlord in the neighbourhood.

The woman returned with the ale and handed it to the strange man who took it and drew a new bright steel barrelled pistol from his coat pocket, and holding it in front of her forehead said, 'I can do for the whole lot of you. I can do for the whole lot in the house'. The man then went upstairs. A dozen times in the night he was heard slipping down the stairs trying every door.

The scene in the room with one of the women and the man appears to have been a dreadful one. He frequently stood over her with the pistol and threatened to shoot her. She states that she was afraid he would carry out his threat to execution.[10]

The Spectator was much more direct in its reporting of Jones behaviour in relation to these women in the night:

He passed the night in a brothel, where again his bloodthirstiness broke out. He threatened the inmates of the house with a loaded pistol, declared that he 'Could do for them all', and throughout the night kept menacing his companion with death till she was nearly dead from the alarm.

The thirst for killing of which we have spoken had clearly obtained possession of him for he had no quarrel with anyone in the house, a row would have involved the greatest risk to himself and yet he tried every door of the rooms occupied by the girls, pistol in hand. The man was drunk with bloodshed and his actions were almost of a lunatic.[11]

Jones's behaviour on the Monday was also significant. The *Freeman's Journal* continued their report:

In the morning the man left and returned to Mrs Balham's where he had breakfast. He shortly left and went to the Bell Tavern where he ordered and drank during the day, eight pots of six penny ale. While at the house he treated several people then asked the landlord for a newspaper, lit a pipe went into the tap room and sat until evening.

A little after 8, a young lad entered the pub and said a whole family were murdered at Denham. The stranger put his pipe and paper down on the table and hung down his head. He trembled violently while the boy recited all the details of the murder and he became greatly agitated.

He went and asked the landlord for a timetable of the Great Western Railway. The landlord handed him the timetable but he trembled so violently that he could not read. He said to the landlord. 'I want to go to West Drayton. I want to go to Brentford. I want to get to Reading. I don't know the name of the place I want to get to. I want to get to the place where there is a large waterworks'.

He read the stations from Uxbridge to London to him. He said 'Yes, West Drayton, Brentford or Southall will do. I must be away in the morning'. He said he would leave by the 9.39 train. He then left the house and went to Balham's Lodging House where he slept.

A little after 6am, he rose and asked Mrs Balham for tea. After taking it he invited her husband out for rum. Balham and the man went into a pub where they drank. Both men then parted. He went to Uxbridge Station where he took the 7.15 to West Drayton.

Susan Burton states that she was in the company of the stranger and he appeared to have very tight boots.[12]

Jones's agitation on hearing the news of the murders was significant. Why would he have been SO affected by the news? Also, why did he have to leave Uxbridge in such a hurry? An interesting observation by Susan Burton that Jones's boots were tight leads one to believe that he may have been wearing someone else's footwear.

Supt Dunham must have listened to Charles Coombes's statement with great joy and relief. His evidence was not simply an excellent lead, he had more than enough evidence to justify the arrest of the suspect John Jones.

Another key piece of evidence was that the old clothing that Dunham had recovered from the scene had been identified by Coombes as that that he had seen Jones wearing on the Saturday. The local newspaper reported it as follows:

Supt Dunham gave evidence to the inquest. The Coroner said the old cord trousers (produced by the superintendent) were almost unmistakable, black patches on white giving a marked appearance.

The witness (Dunham) showed blood covered boots with pieces of brain still attached, a fustian waistcoat, billycock hat (deerstalker hat), old neckerchief and worn blue smock, all found in the murdered man's room which the prisoner had been seen wearing previously. Near the clothes was a hammer. No watch was found. Two boxes were broken open, items taken, and others spread around.

He took the clothes to Uxbridge lodging houses. Charles Coombes came to Supt Dunham and identified the old coats from the house as being worn by the man who had lodged there.[13]

Far more evidence was to emerge in the days ahead which all pointed to Jones's guilt. The question now was where was he? He had told Coombes that he was heading for Reading. There was no time to delay. The suspect had a head start. Dunham was now very much the pursuer. Jones would be feeling the heat sooner than he thought.

---

1 Charlotte Balham or Bollam. She was the 'Mrs' to Jones, and the landlady at the lodgings in Bell Yard. The 1871 Census for Bell Yard, High Street in Uxbridge lists Benjamin Bollam (or Balham) as head of the household. He was 65 years old, a labourer and licensed lodging house keeper, married to Charlotte Bollam (or Balham), aged 52.

2 *Bucks Herald*, 4 June 1870.

3 *Bucks Herald*, 23 July 1870. Some newspapers state that Coombes and Jones were drinking in the Bell Tavern when the news broke about the murders at the Marshall cottage.

4 *Bucks Advertiser*, 28 May 1870. The report stated that Charles Coombes had identified his employer: 'I worked for Mr Stacey for about a fortnight'. Mr Stacey was George Stacey, owner of George Stacey & Sons, Ironmonger & Iron founder of 52 High Street, Uxbridge. He was 66 at the time of the murders. He lived from 1805 to 1879. He left £500 in his will to his two sons. The Stacey family did not enjoy happy times from 1879 to 1888. In October 1880, George's son James Alfred Stacey committed suicide. The *Bucks Herald* of 30 October 1880 reported that 'He was found dead in his bedroom and had shot himself in the temple with a revolver. The deceased was 36 years old and was to have married on Saturday to a young lady residing in the town. He was thought to be insane at the time he destroyed himself.' Later, in 1888, his brother Frederick appeared at a bankruptcy hearing with the company

5 *Illustrated Police News*, 28 May 1870.

6 *Shields Gazette and Daily Telegraph*, 26 May 1870.

7 Jane Davis was a 21-year-old unmarried needlewoman, described as a lodger at Chequers Yard, Uxbridge in the 1871 Census.

8 *Kentish Gazette*, 31 May 1870.

9   Elizabeth Selwood, Susan Burton and Jane Davis were probably prostitutes. No trace of Selwood or Burton has been found in any records for around this time. It's possible that they were 'friends' of Jones, but it seems more likely that they would only have been interested in him when he was looking respectably dressed and appeared to be flush with money. *The Spectator* described the premises as a brothel.

10 *Freeman's Journal*, 26 May 1870.

11 *The Spectator*, 28 May 1870.

12 *Freeman's Journal*, 26 May 1870.

13 *Bucks Herald*, 4 June 1870.

CHAPTER 18

In Hot Pursuit

Supt Thomas Dunham was not a man to hide away in his office and let others do his dirty work. He was a copper who had worked his way up through the ranks, dealing with all types of crimes as he learned his trade. The local papers of the period are full of coverage of his many tussles and escapades with the local villains across Buckinghamshire, but more of this later.

And so it was, on hearing the statement of Charles Coombes, that he knew Jones had set out from Uxbridge for the Berkshire town of Reading. Not knowing what John Jones looked like, he took Coombes with him on the dash to Reading on the Tuesday.

A 35-mile journey commenced. On arriving in the town, the Superintendent visited Reading Police Station where, quite by chance, he was assigned a single local officer to help him on his enquiries round the town to find the killer. Today, a bus-load of armed and 'kitted up' officers would have been on the case. Not so in Dunham's day.

Drawing the short straw that day from Reading Borough Police[1] was 25-year-old Detective William Hounsell Toulman. He was originally from Bothenhampton, Dorset, where he had been born in 1844. Before joining the Reading Police he had worked as an agricultural labourer.[2] He married Margaret Eatwell in the town on 14 May 1866.[3]

William Toulman and Thomas Dunham

When Dunham and Coombes arrived in Reading, a town of almost 40,000 souls[4] lay before them. They had no clue as to where to look for Jones. This could also have been a wild goose chase; Jones could have changed his mind about Reading. He could have stayed on the train and gone to Bristol. No one knew for certain.

Hoping for the best, Dunham knew that Jones would probably have headed for a cheap lodging house. It was a big task, but Dunham might have to search all the lodging houses in Reading to find his man. This job could take all day and night. It was likely to be a long day.

A stroke of luck was to play a major part in proceedings. As Dunham visited Supt James Purchase in his office, Toulman just happened to be there, purely by chance. The *Reading Mercury* described what happened next:

> Coombes proceeded with Supt Dunham, of Slough Police, to Reading. They went to the Borough police station and communicated with Supt Purchase, and PC Toulman (who happened to be in his office), having heard the description of the man, at once remembered that he had seen a man answering the description pass over High Bridge, in the direction of Silver Street.

Supt Dunham, PC Toulman, and Coombes then proceeded to Silver Street.[5]

Good old-fashioned police-work on the part of William Toulman had been key in tracking down the suspect. His local knowledge of all the known lodging house 'trouble spots' would have pointed to the Oxford Arms in Silver Street kept by Abraham Lock.

We shall never know for sure, but the instant discovery of Jones's location may have made all the difference. Jones would never have thought that the police could have been on his tail so quickly after having such a head start.

---

1   Reading Borough Police existed between 21 February 1836 and 1968, when it amalgamated with other forces to become part of Thames Valley Police. History of the Thames Valley Police Booklet: www.thamesvalley.police.uk/museum_booklet_a4.pdf

2   1861 Census for Bothenhampton, Dorset.

3   St Giles Church Reading parish records showing marriage between William Hounsell Toulman and Margaret Eatwell.

4   Census population numbers for the town of Reading, Berks in 1871. According to the 1871 Census, the population was at that time was 39,497, having doubled in 30 years since 1841

5   *Reading Mercury*, 28 May 1870.

CHAPTER 19

A Dramatic Arrest

The search of Reading inns and lodging houses was not without risk. Supt Dunham had been warned at Uxbridge that Jones was in possession of a pistol, so he needed to be on his guard. (Jones was in fact seen in the lodging house with a pistol, but more about this later.)

Dunham later told the jury at Jones's trial that he arrived at Reading at 5.00 pm, and that newspapers carrying reports of the Denham massacre got to the town at 9 o'clock.[1]

In the modern age, newsworthy stories are transmitted around the world in a matter of seconds via the internet or mobile phones. In 1870, news was obtained by the masses by and large through reading newspapers. The murders were only discovered late on the Monday. The matter had to be reported and then printed, before being transported by train. This all took time, so it is no surprise that the papers were only arriving in Reading late on the Tuesday evening. All things considered, this was quite good going.

The timing of the news arriving in Reading was significant in that no one in Reading could have known about the Denham murders at the time the inns and lodging houses were being searched. And so it was, that on the early Tuesday evening, Dunham, Toulman and Coombes arrived at the Oxford Arms Inn at 10 Silver Street, Reading.[2]

Dunham, especially, must have felt a tinge of excitement and

Silver Street, Reading, in 1891

nervousness on entering the premises, not knowing whether they had come to the right place. The Oxford Arms Inn was the right place.

The premises were notorious with the Reading Constabulary as well as the local magistrates. It would be referred to by the police of today as a 'hot spot' for crime and disorder. The local newspapers were full of regular appearances at the local court by victims or perpetrators coming from that address. Local police officers would have been very familiar with the premises. It was known for fights, assaults, drunkenness, threatening behaviour, assaults on the police, thefts, counterfeit coins and robberies.[3]

The two policemen had the following description of the suspect: 5ft 7ins, Scotch accent, sallow complexion, dark beard cut short, dark eyes, brown hair and a moustache.[4] This was all very well, but the description was not very specific. It was vital therefore that Charles Coombes should be with them to enable a swift and positive identification. He would need to identify Jones before he was able to escape, or worse still, draw a firearm on them. In this instance, seconds could count.

Jones had escaped from Uxbridge where he knew the heat would be on and the town swarming with police. He may have felt safe in Reading. He had not given anyone a forwarding address, although he had told Coombes that he was heading for Reading. He may have expected that he would not have said anything, believing that he was his friend.

In any event, Jones would still have been on edge. It was still only two days since the murders and he could not have slept much. He would be in fear of capture and the hangman's noose. He may have intended to lie low for a bit. One thing is for certain - he now had nothing to lose, so if anyone attempted to arrest him, shooting them dead would not add to his sentence as he would already be heading for the gallows if he were to be captured. He would not hesitate to shoot the intrepid pursuers given the chance in order to escape. This was a man capable of the most extreme violence. It was unlikely that he would 'come quietly' to the station.

And so it was that the trio entered the 'Tramps' Kitchen' at the Oxford Arms Inn. The *Bucks Herald* described how on entering the premises Coombes pointed out the prisoner.[5]

A positive identification had been made by the witness, so an arrest could be made as long as it could be effected quickly. The *Morning Post* later reported Superintendent Dunham's evidence at the trial, in which he described how he seized his suspect:

> We were in private [plain] clothes. The prisoner spoke in an angry way. I seized him quickly because I had heard the prisoner had a pistol in his possession – that he had been showing one in the house [i.e. the doss house in Uxbridge]. I was anxious to secure him. He was quite sober. He had had a drink but was not drunk.
>
> I put handcuffs on the prisoner. He said, 'I have not murdered man, woman nor child, but I know who did. I stood by but never murdered anyone myself.'[6]

Finding the clothing belonging to Emmanuel Marshall being still worn by the suspect was more vital evidence to prove that Jones was involved in the murders. The pieces - and there were many -

CAPTURE OF JONES AT READING.

Charles Coombes points out suspect John Jones while Supt Dunham and
Detective Toulman arrest the murderer in the Oxford Arms, Reading.
Illustrated Police News

were starting to fall into place.

The comment 'I have not murdered man, woman nor child' was made before he had even been told of the reason for the arrest. If he was going to claim that he had not been near Uxbridge or Denham as a defence, how would he have known about the murders as the newspapers had not yet reached Reading?

Dunham knew he was holding a strong hand at this point and he would have been completely convinced that he had the right man. The suspect had denied murder, but he was now implicated. The evidence would soon start to stack up against him. Dunham knew that he was on to a winner.

There had been concern that Jones had a pistol that he might want to use on the officers. Significantly, the pistol found on the suspect when he was arrested was one of a pair owned by Emmanuel Marshall. One had been stolen from the cottage and was now in Jones's pocket. Its twin had been left in the house and was now in police possession. Dunham later confirmed that both pistols were of the same make and model.[7]

Tuesday, 24 May had been a long but satisfying day for Thomas

Dunham. He had 'felt the collar' of a seven-time murderer, and had avoided being shot or ill-used by the suspect. It was a good day's work.

---

1 *Bucks Herald.* 24 July 1870.

2 The pub dated from at least the eighteenth century. In 1903 the renewal of the licence was objected to by the justices as it was '...frequented by thieves and persons of bad character'. Despite this, the pub survived until 1959 when it was demolished. Reading Museum Website (www.readingmuseum.org.uk)

3 One particular landlord in the late 1850s named Samuel Plowman had been regularly assaulted by customers at the inn. One of his assailants was Dennis Jennett, who was described as 'a familiar face', 'who has appeared few times less than half a hundred before the bench' (see the *Berkshire Chronicle*, 1 May 1858). Another incident involved the theft of a stuffed owl in a glass case (see *Berkshire Chronicle,* 7 April 1855). All in all, it does not sound as if the Oxford Arms was going to win many stars on TripAdvisor.

   It is interesting to note that Detective Toulman would later be involved in more incidents at Silver Street and the Oxford Arms. In January 1874, a newspaper stated that he went there to arrest a suspect named 'Barry' in connection with a murder of one Joseph Grimes in Wiltshire, a case which was later referred to as the Purton Murder (see *Lloyd's Weekly Newspaper*, 25 January 1874). On another occasion, Toulman arrested a man called Henry Duckett for breach of the peace and assault on Harriett Bloomfield at the Oxford Arms. He found Mr Duckett had a 'fighting attitude', shouting and swearing, and had his face covered in blood. He was fighting with others who tried to intervene. Bloomfield was insensible for two hours. Duckett was later given six weeks' imprisonment with hard labour for his troubles (see *Reading Mercury*, 24 June 1876).

4 *Bucks Herald,* 26 May 1870. The description of a Scotch accent may have been mistaken for a Birmingham accent.

5 *Bucks Herald*, 4 June 1870.

6 *Morning Post*, 23 July 1870.

7 *Bucks Herald*, 24 July 1870.

CHAPTER 20

Taken Into Custody

John Jones must have known the moment he was detained by Dunham and Toulman that the game was up. At that moment, the once small-time criminal was in the big league. He knew that his life was now hanging by a thread. The police had already found a lot of evidence and had plenty more to find, which was going to prove beyond a reasonable doubt that he alone had been the man responsible for seven deaths. The death penalty was firmly ensconced in the statute books, and would not be abolished for almost another 100 years.

The only small crumb of comfort he could draw was that public executions had been abolished two years earlier, in 1868, with the passing of the Capital Punishment Amendment Act. Convicted murderers would now only swing on the gallows within the confines of the prison in which they were being held, and following the execution the bodies would be buried within the grounds of same gaol. Press and witnesses were still permitted to attend, although executions were no longer the great public spectacles that they used to be.

The first execution following the Amendment was carried out by Public Executioner William Calcraft on 13 August 1868 at Maidstone Gaol, when 18-year-old Thomas Wells was hanged for the murder of Edward Walshe, the stationmaster at Dover

Reading Police Station c1970

Priory Railway Station. Calcraft had also carried out the last public execution in the UK, when he hanged the Fenian terrorist Michael Barrett in front of Newgate Prison on 26 May 1868 for his part in the Clerkenwell Outrage the previous year. We will hear more of William Calcraft later in this book.

Arriving at Reading Police Station with the prisoner safely in handcuffs would have been a relief to Dunham and Toulman. This was a huge prize for them both and for the reputation of the Bucks Constabulary. They must have been elated to have got their man.

John Jones had safely been arrested in Reading, but the hard work was about to start. Dunham was going to have to build his case against Jones so that the evidence would convince a jury of his guilt. Countless witnesses were going to have to be interviewed and evidence obtained, but that was for another day. For now, Dunham needed to establish exactly who he was dealing with, and he then needed to get him back to Slough in one piece in order to take him before the magistrates. Neither task would be as simple as it sounded.

Once back at Reading Police Station it was arranged for the Deputy Governor, Robert Walter Boyce, to come and look at the prisoner:

> The Deputy Governor of Reading Gaol, Mr Boyce, looked at him in the cell and recognised him as John Jones and asked him, 'What have you been up to now?' The prisoner acknowledged the recognition. He had served 18 months in Berkshire County Gaol up to last January.[1]

Jones had in fact been held at Reading three times in the past, firstly in 1866 after being convicted of stealing a pair of leather riding reins, then again the same year for stealing a barrow from Reading Cemetery, and finally in July 1868-70 for stealing a lamb and a ewe (see Chapter 5 for the details). He had been released after his latest sentence on 8 January 1870.[2]

---

1   *Bucks Herald*, 4 June 1870. Deputy Governor Robert Walter Boyce had been born in Middlesex around 1825. His work in the prison service took him around the country. At the time of the Denham Murders, he held the post of Deputy Governor at Reading Gaol. By the 1881 Census he had been appointed Governor at Usk Prison in Monmouthshire in Wales. (Usk Prison is still operational and currently houses Category C prisoners, mainly sex offenders. It was built in 1844). He later moved to York Castle, where he became the Governor of the prison there. He died in York in 1887 at the age of 62 (see *York Gazette*, 12 February 1887). York Prison had been rebuilt in 1825; by 1900 the building became a military prison before it was finally closed in 1929

2   *Staffordshire Sentinel*, 28 May 1870.

CHAPTER 21

Jones at Reading

At Reading Police Station, a number of officers were deputed to guard Jones while arrangements were put in place to transport him back to Slough.

The local newspaper covered the story and additionally reported on Jones's demeanour at the station and what he said in relation to the murders:

> He was taken to the police station and placed in a cell where he was guarded by Police Sgt Charles Forbes,[1] PC Charles Johnson,[2] and PC George Leaver.[3] He was double handcuffed and closely watched. He stoutly refused to give his name except that it was 'Jack' and as he was visited by a large number of persons he began to grow impatient, and at last lay flat on the floor of the cell to prevent people seeing him.

> He made but very few remarks with reference to the murders, but in the course of the time that he was in the lock up he said – 'If they don't hang me, I'll hang myself, because I shall always be pointed at as the man who was charged with the murders. People will say, 'There goes that man that killed those 7 people'; and I'll never walk about England no more.'

> He also said, 'I did not murder them but I know who did, but I won't split till tomorrow.' He was very much excited at times and looked wildly about.

> When captured, the prisoner was wearing the trousers and boots of the murdered man.[4]

The journalist for the *Reading Mercury* was not too pleased with the association of a seven-time murderer and the town of Reading. It must have lowered the tone of the place:

> It has been remarked as incomprehensible that Reading should have been selected by the supposed murderer as a hiding place, and it is also unaccountable that he should have communicated his intention of coming here to the man Coombes.
>
> Reading will unfortunately be hereafter indirectly associated with perhaps the foulest tragedy, we suppose that has ever been perpetuated in this country. The supposed murderer was cleverly captured here on Tuesday.[5]

During his arrest, the police needed to recover the clothing that Jones was found wearing. This would prove to be damming evidence as far as Jones was concerned. A Midland newspaper reported on his clothes being removed, as well as his behaviour at the police station:

> He was captured with the murdered man's clothes, so police have provided him with other attire. He now wore a white overall and this was covered in blood, his own, for in the morning in his cell, when he could not have what he wanted, he threw himself on the ground in the most furious outburst of temper like an ungovernable animal, and made his nose bleed.[6]

While Dunham was in Reading, not only did he have to find and arrest the suspect at great personal risk, but he also had to visit Lyons & Hayes, Wardrobe Dealers in Union Street, to recover more evidence that was going to build an even stronger case against Jones. On getting to Reading, Jones had sold some of Marshall's clothing to a secondhand shop. The *Bucks Herald* reported the evidence of Margaret Lyons, the wife of the shop owner:

> Margaret Lyons,[7] wife of secondhand clothes shop keeper of Reading, said 'I identified the coat produced [belonging to the murdered man] and that man [the prisoner] brought it into my shop on this day week. The prisoner was accompanied by a man named Wooderton who carried a waistcoat. The prisoner said he wanted a 'slop', and on me telling him that I had not got one he offered to sell me the coat and waistcoat for 8 shillings.
>
> I offered him 4 shillings for them and afterwards gave him 4 shillings

and six pence. The prisoner was wearing the coat at the time, and on my buying it, he took it off. I had previously asked his name and he gave it as John Groves of Uxbridge. About an hour later Supt Dunham came in and I gave him the coat and the waistcoat.'[8]

Dunham was able to discover the evidence of the murdered man's clothes because a man called James Wooderton, who lodged in the Oxford Arms, had recounted how he had met Jones in the kitchen of the lodging house on Tuesday 24 May. The two men later went drinking in Reading, and afterwards Wooderton accompanied Jones to a

Margaret Lyons buying Marshall's clothes from Jones in the secondhand shop in Reading.
Illustrated Police News

secondhand shop where he sold the coat and waist-coat. Marshall's clothes could therefore be identified by Wooderton as the same garments sold by Jones to Mrs Lyons.

The clothing could be identified, and the pawn ticket for the watch was more evidence waiting to be collected by Supt Dunham which would also connect Jones to the murders. Even at this early stage the evidence connecting him to the murders was huge, although there was still more to come. At this point, Jones had admitted knowledge of the crime but was trying to pin the blame on two unknown men.

A further 'key' piece of evidence was provided by another lodger at the Oxford Arms, Harriett Willis. She gave evidence of the key that

James Wooderton had said had been thrown in the cupboard at the lodgings. The *Bucks Herald* gave details of her testimony:

> An aged widow who described herself as working in the Oxford Arms, tramp ward, said a man came into the home on a previous Tuesday, holding up the key produced, said 'Who owns this?' but no one answered. She found the key among the bones and rags. She knew the key by some white paint on it.[9]

Another newspaper gave details of Willis handing the key in:

> The key to the Marshalls' house was found in cupboard in a lodging house where Jones had stayed and was captured by a woman called Willis who took it to Reading Police Station and gave it to Insp Townsend.[10]

Harriett Willis[11] later identified Jones in court. This key found by Willis and seen being deposited by Wooderton was important, as it was the one to the Marshalls' Cottage. The police would check the key against the lock on the door to see if it fitted. It did. The *Bucks Herald* again gave more details, this time from witness Superintendent Jervis[12] of Buckinghamshire Constabulary:

> Supt Jervis of the Bucks Constabulary, produced the lock of the front door of Marshall's house, and the key fitted exactly. On the lock too was some paint of the same colour as that on the key and it looked, the witness said, as if the lock had been painted with the key in it.[13]

The paint on both key and lock, and the fact that the former unlocked the door of Marshall's cottage, proved beyond doubt that Jones was in possession of the key of the door to the crime scene. He claimed that two men committed the murders. If this was the case, why would they have given him the key to the cottage? It made no sense, other than the fact that he locked the door himself after having committed the murders and had not disposed of the key.

The other main puzzle in the suspect's behaviour was the story about the two mysterious men who had, according to Jones, committed the murders. Most people in his position, facing a likely death penalty, would have been singing like a canary to Supt Dunham. His refusal to cooperate with the investigation was in itself more damning evidence.

1   Sgt Charles Forbes was born at Walcot in Shropshire in 1832. The Census of
    1871 shows him as married and living at 8 Trinity Place, Reading. He was used
    to dealing with violent 'customers' and his name appears very regularly in the
    local newspaper, dealing mainly with public order cases involving drunks. The
    Reading Mercury of 22 April 1865 gave details of three of his cases, all of which
    ended up at the Reading Borough Magistrates' Court on 19 April. In the first
    case, while arresting a drunk called William Newton, the prisoner gave him a
    violent blow to the head and threatened to cut his throat. Newton was sentenced
    to three days' imprisonment. Case number two involved another drunk, William
    Blake, while case three related to one Jane Young, who was also drunk. She
    kicked off nearly all her clothing, was violent in her manner and struck Forbes
    while using foul language. It was necessary to procure a truck in order to
    remove her to the police station. She was sentenced to seven days' imprisonment.

2   PC Charles Johnson was born in Wantage, Berkshire in 1843. He does not
    appear to have been so prolific an officer as some of his colleagues according
    to contemporary news reports. One incident he dealt with was an old-fashioned
    offence: the *Reading Mercury* of 19 April 1873 reported that John Law and John
    Davis were charged with lodging in an outhouse and not giving a good account
    of themselves. PC Johnson found them asleep under some hay in Mr Smith's
    shed at the back of the gaol. Each was sentenced to one month's hard labour.
    The 1881 Census records Johnson as married and residing at 23 Essex Street,
    Reading.

3   PC George Leaver was 25 years of age and single. He was born in Brightwell,
    Berkshire. In common with other Reading Borough Police officers, he would
    have been used to dealing with violence from the inhabitants of the town on a
    regular basis. In 1869, though, he dealt with a less serious offence when he
    arrested a boy called Charles Wicks for stealing some broccoli. Wicks was
    sentenced to seven days' hard labour (*Reading Mercury*, 15 May 1869). The
    Census of 1871 shows PC Leaver living at the Police Station, London Street,
    Reading. He was still a Reading police constable in 1881. At Christmas of that
    year, a mob armed with sticks refused to disperse despite being begged to go
    home; Leaver was struck on the side of the head. One of the mob, George
    Josey, kicked the officer on the leg and was given one month imprisonment
    (*Reading Mercury*, 31 December 1881). Leaver left the force shortly afterwards
    and became a publican. In 1891 the census shows him and his wife Rosehannah
    at the Fox & Hounds in Hampstead Harris, Berkshire. Come the 1901 Census,
    Leaver had returned to Reading and was the landlord of the Cathedral Beer
    House at 67 London Street. He died on 1 September 1904, leaving £89 to his
    wife. It's likely that policemen who had served 25 years dealing with drunks and
    ruffians and who could 'look after themselves' would be ideally suited to
    working as publicans.

4   *Reading Mercury*, 28 May 1870.

5   Ibid.

6   *Staffordshire Sentinel*, 28 May 1870.

7 Margaret Lyons (née Hayes) is shown on the 1871 Census residing at 19 Union Street, Reading, in the centre of the town, not far from Reading Railway Station. 29-year-old Margaret was living with her 30-year-old husband, Martin Lyons. They had married in Reading in 1867. She was born in Ireland, he in Reading. They were still at the same address in 1881, and Margaret was still there in 1891, although her husband was absent, living as an inmate at the Cholsey Lunatic Asylum in Berkshire. Her brother William had, by 1891, moved into the shop at 19 Union Street and they ran the business together as an antique & wardrobe dealers for the next 20 years, before being declared bankrupt in 1902 (*Reading Mercury*, 7 June 1902).

8 *Bucks Herald*, 4 June 1870.

9 Ibid.

10 *Bucks Herald*, 26 May 1870. Inspector John Townsend (1825-1902) was born in Easthampstead, Berkshire near Bracknell in 1825. He joined Reading Borough Police in 1846 and retired in 1870 when his heath began to fail. After Townsend had completed 23 and a half years service, Reading Town Council were looking to appoint a Serjeant-at-Mace as the previous incumbent had just died. The Council committee agreed that Insp Townsend had served the police force for almost a quarter of a century with diligence and fidelity and that all of the officers were agreed on his appointment. He was to be paid a sum of £38 and 8 shillings per annum.

Policing Victorian Britain was a rough job and Townsend had several violent incidents to deal with according to various articles in the *Reading Mercury*. One report, on 13 September 1862, entitled 'Disturbances in Alfred Street' gives a flavour of the period as it describes a public order problem following a dispute in the town. 'The crowd gathered in great force and those that looked on 'must have numbered several hundred. A posse of policemen, under Inspector Townsend, were assaulted with missiles, and had their hats knocked off with old kettles, sticks, etc. The policemen drew their staves, but wisely refrained from using them, and the crowd gradually drew off.'

Another *Reading Mercury* story from 11 February 1860 and entitled 'Escape and capture of two convicts' relates an exciting story. Two convicts, John Brown and Robert Bevill were being moved from Dartmoor Prison to Chatham. They were being conveyed by train with eleven other prisoners and were all dressed in prison uniform covered in 'arrows'. The prisoners were in two batches and were being guarded by only three warders. The men were chained together, but both had somehow slipped their handcuffs. Three miles after leaving Reading Station, while the train was travelling at 30 MPH, they opened a door and leapt to freedom. A police search began and the following day, Insp Townsend saw two suspicious characters in High Street, Reading. He grabbed the collar of both men and charged them with being the escaped convicts. Townsend then held onto Brown who made 'desperate resistance and used fearful epithets, saying he would not be taken by one man'. At the police station, Brown was to be found wearing a brown slop frock, underneath which was a woman's old cloak and a shirt. When this was removed, his Dartmoor prison suit was visible. Bevill was also wearing his prison garb under a smockfrock.

On being interviewed about their escape and the luck of avoiding serious injury jumping from the speeding train, Brown stated that 'it shook every bone in my body'. They stated that they had hidden in the woods initially but had then come across John Silver's cottage near Woodley, where they had stolen the clothing that they had been found wearing. On appearing in court Brown 'laughed heartily' when Insp Townsend described the dresses he wore over his prison suit.

John Townsend and his wife Jane lived together for more than thirty years in Reading at number 5, 9 and also 11 Eldon Street (source, Census records 1871, RG10,1284, schedule 23, page 39; 1881, RG11/1308, schedule 68, page 37; 1891, RG12/996, schedule 95, page 19; 1901, RG13/1150, schedule 97, page 14). Ex inspector Townsend died on 2 December 1902 leaving £1,253 in his estate (Probate register, London, 3 January 1903, page 347).

11 Harriett Willis is shown on the 1871 census as head of the household at 19 Silver Street, Reading. She was a 58-year-old widow, working as a charwoman. Her probate record shows that at the time of her death on 4 April 1885, she was living at Hawk Court, Silver Street, Reading, a spinster who left £152.

12 See Appendix E for details of Supt Jervis's career.

13 *Bucks Herald*, 4 June 1870.

CHAPTER 22

An Extraordinary Journey

The police had their man, but they now had to return him to the jurisdiction of the area where the offence had occurred. This meant conveying him from Reading back to Slough. There were no private security services in those days responsible for transporting prisoners between police stations, courts and prisons. This was a job for the police. In theory this should have been a simple process, but the local constabulary were going to be severely tested during Jones's transportation.

With no time to lose, arrangements were made involving two cab journeys as well as a trip by rail. The *Reading Mercury* takes up the story:

SCENE OF REMOVAL OF THE PRISONER

It was only natural when the fact became known that such a desperate and depraved a character as the man Jones was in Reading, that immense excitement and intense indignation be aroused. Crowds of persons assembled at the police station, and towards 6 o'clock it was estimated that the concourse numbered 1000. The arrangements for the removal of the wretched man were ably carried out by Supt Purchase. Sgt Josey and a number of policemen were dispatched to the Great Western Station, and Mr Peach, the superintendent at the station, provided a second class carriage for the prisoner and Captain Drake, the Chief Constable of Bucks, and Supt Dunham.

This carriage was shunted till the train arrived and then it was attached to the rear of the train without any obstruction or confusion.

Reading Great Western Railway Station
Neil Watson collection

Shortly before 8 o'clock, a cab drew up to the police station and the prisoner was quickly placed inside. The crowd was then so great that the horse could barely move, and some of the spectators gave expression to their feeling by shouting out, 'Burn him!' and similar remarks. A number of policemen walked on each side of the cab and it was with difficulty that the station was reached.

Arrived at the station, the execrations of some of the people in the crowd became louder, but owing to the judicious arrangements, the prisoner was conveyed to the carriage, and the train shortly afterwards moved away.

The train arrived at Slough at 8.55, when the prisoner was removed to the police station, in the care of Captain Drake and Supt Dunham. Hundreds of people had assembled at the station.[1]

The *Illustrated Police News* gave more information about the journey and police numbers:

Capture of the prisoner was leaked, and that he was going to leave Reading by the 8.10pm GWR train. 1000 people assembled. Jones was taken to the station in a fly, a posse of 16 police constables were on duty there at. He was booed and hissed by the large concourse that had been assembled. He was taken through the goods station and placed in a 2nd class carriage in the charge of Supt Dunham, the Supt of the Uxbridge Police and Captain Drake the Chief Constable of Bucks Police. The carriage was afterwards shunted onto the 8.10pm train, and as the carriage passed the station the prisoner received the hearty excrations of the crowd outside.[2]

The *Bucks Herald*[3] added that Supt Job Denson was also involved in accompanying the prisoner on the train.

The excitement of the night did not diminish on the evening of this extraordinary journey.

Slough History Online contains an article which was allegedly told to the author by the son of Supt Dunham, James Alfred Dunham. (This information was not recorded at the time so is open to speculation as to its veracity.) It does, however, sound possible. The report mentions the arrival at Slough and the problems of containing the safety of the prisoner:

> Jones was brought to Slough by railway, and the news having spread through a wire the Superintendent had sent to his wife, a crowd gathered at Slough Station, and so obviously intended to do the prisoner a mischief that a constable was dressed up in his coat, and distracted the attention of the crowd, whilst Jones was smuggled out another way. When the crowd discovered how they had been tricked, they rushed off to the police station, and it was impossible to get Jones to the cells, so chains were fetched, and he was chained to the leg of the heavy table in the kitchen of the Superintendent's house until the crowd dispersed.[4]

The serious public order situation is supported by a report in the *Morning Post*, which stated the following:

> Several thousand assembled outside Slough Station. The greatest indignation was displayed by the populace when the police and their prisoner stepped therefrom. He was hooted and yelled at on all sides and it was with the greatest of difficulty that the police, who were assisted by Mr Harper the Slough Station Master,[5] could get their prisoner through the booking office and into the cab. There were a large number of brick makers in the crowd and many struck at the prisoner as he got into the fly. One blow struck him on the nose causing blood to flow. At length he was got into the fly which was rapidly driven to the police station.[6]

This was policing at its most exciting. Dunham had much work ahead in terms of routine statement taking and court appearances and the like, but keeping his prisoner healthy and alive was his number one priority. His problems of transporting Public Enemy Number One were not over yet.

1   *Reading Mercury*, 28 May 1870.

2   *Illustrated Police News*, 28 May 1870.

3   *Bucks Herald*, 26 May 1870.

4   Slough History Online. Taken from chapter 12 of Alfred G. Hailstone's 'Buckinghamshire Constabulary Centenary 1857-1957', available at www. sloughhistoryonline.org.uk/asset_arena/text/pdf/sl/sl/sl-sl-max_chapter12-d -02-000.pdf

5   William Harper was employed by the Great Western Railway for 26 years. He joined in 1845 as a 23-year-old porter at Reading. His subsequent postings were as follows: 1865 to Aldermaston; 1867 to Hungerford; 1867 to Slough; 1871 to Wantage Road. He resigned on 26 November 1871. He received £300 from the GWR fund on his retirement. Information from Register of Inspectors, Booking Constables and Booking Porters. Great Western Railway). The 1881 Census shows William as a retired hotel keeper. He died on 30 September 1888, leaving £1,222.

6   *Morning Post*, 26 May 1870.

CHAPTER 23

The First Magistrates' Court Hearing At Slough

The days following the discovery of the murders were busy ones for everyone concerned in the case, none more so than Supt Dunham, who must have been running on adrenaline that week. He could have had very little sleep. His mind must have been racing with all the evidence he was going to have to uncover and all the witnesses he had to manage. With Jones safely in custody, his initial court appearance would determine if there was a case to answer, and there surely was. The first week saw both the Magistrates' hearing as well as the first day of the two-day inquest.

In 1870 Slough Police Station and the Magistrates' Court were adjoining buildings in William Street. Slough History Online states the following about the buildings:

> In June, 1850, it was proposed at the Bucks Quarter Sessions that a Sessional Court should be held at Slough, but the motion was lost by 16 votes to 8. On 6 August following, however, the Bucks Petty Sessions were first held at Slough, in the Mechanics' Institute. Three years later, it was announced that the magistrates were about to have 'a spacious room built in connection with the present Police Station (in William Street) wherein to hold the Weekly Sessions'. In 1864, a new Police Station was built in the High Street with a Court Room, in which the Petty Sessions, formerly held every Tuesday, were held twice weekly.[1]

Interest in the murders was at fever pitch, and large crowds of people assembled outside the police station and court house, some climbing on to window sills, in order to get a look at the murderer.[2]

The local newspaper reported details of the magistrates themselves:

> The Magisterial enquiry took place at Slough on Wednesday. Sir Robert Bateson Harvey (chairman),[3] Captain Farrer[4] & Edward John Coleman[5] were on the bench. The Prisoner was charged with seven murders. The Clerk asked the prisoner his name, he replied 'John Jones' in a gruff voice.[6]

Jones must have been suffering from a lack of sleep since the murders in the early hours of the Sunday morning. The enormity of his situation must have been weighing him down as well. He was now living in fear of the gallows. This all added to the rough picture that presented itself at his first public appearance in the courtroom at Slough. One local paper described his unflattering appearance:

> Prisoner John Jones is rather under medium stature, his countenance is repulsive but not remarkably so. His eyes are keen, though sunken, and suggest much cunning. He has an unpleasing appearance aided by the fact that his hair is cut short, suggesting of the manipulation of the prison barber. He has a haggard expression. Admission to the court was denied to the general public.[7]

A different reporter also mentioned his appearance in court:

> The suspect is 5'7', has a Scotch accent, sallow complexion, dark beard cut short, dark eyes, brown hair & moustache, painters cap, white smock and stripped trousers.[8]

It's surprising to find Jones being described as having a 'Scotch' accent. Being from the Birmingham area, his 'Brummie' accent may have confused the reporters. The *Staffordshire Sentinel* added to the unflattering descriptions of Jones:

> He is described as most unprepossessing appearance, his head indicating a thoroughly animal organisation.[9]

Worse descriptions were to come in reports by the *Shields Gazette*. They did not hold back on a character assassination of the suspected murderer:

> Prisoner is in appearance, a true type of the worst class of tramp or haymakers, so called. He stands 5 feet 6 inches, sallow completion, small eyes without a spark of intellect, and a short thick jet black beard and moustache. He is one of the most repulsive looking characters ever seen, but he assumed an air of indifference. He stood handcuffed in the dock next to two policemen.[10]

This was Jones's first appearance at Magistrates' Court. In consequence of the short amount of time which had elapsed since the crime and the arrest and transportation back to Slough, only two of the many witnesses gave evidence to the court that day. Supt Dunham and Charles Coombes both gave details of their evidence. Their job was to convince the court that there was a case to answer. Once that end was achieved, Dunham would be free to continue collecting evidence against Jones. The prisoner was duly remanded in custody until the following Tuesday.

Supt Dunham was the first witness. He described the discovery of the seven bodies and the clothing that had been left behind at the scene. He also produced items found in Jones's possession, as well as a shoe he had been wearing that had blood on it. Jones interrupted Dunham's evidence to tell the court that he had had a nose bleed that morning. The Superintendent told the court that he knew both Emmanuel Marshall and his elderly mother. He also spoke of going to the lodging house kept by Abraham Lock in Silver Street, Reading, and how he apprehended Jones who was in possession of a loaded pistol. On being arrested and handcuffed, Jones told the officer: 'I never murdered anyone, but I know who did.'

As previously stated, this comment from Jones was a crucial admission. He could have denied all knowledge of the murders, but this comment absolving himself of blame, but apparently knowing the real culprits, was damning. More evidence regarding this and other matters will be heard later.

A small but important piece of evidence regarding the boots worn by the deceased and subsequently Jones was given by Supt Dunham, later repeated at the inquest:

PORTRAIT OF THE PRISONER

Supt Dunham was the first witness called and his first deposition taken on first examination and repeated to the inquest with additions were read over to him. To these depositions the witness now added that he found the murdered man's pockets were turned inside out and he felt the stockings which were on his feet, and these were without grit, a fact which proved to the witness's mind that the deceased boots were taken off his feet after he had ceased to move. The Chairman asked the prisoner if he desired to question the witness, but he replied without a moment's hesitation in the negative.[11]

Charles Coombes was then sworn in and told the court of seeing Jones first wearing his old clothing and later appearing with a new set of fine clothes, and having money when he had none the day before. He also told the court of Jones pawning a watch. He added that he had seen the Superintendent on Tuesday morning and had given him all his information.

On having the case remanded, Jones turned round, stooped and picked up his cap which he had placed on the floor when entering the dock and, putting on a hideous smile, shouted to the witness, who remained in the witness box, 'Goodbye Charlie.'[12]

Before Dunham apprehended Jones, the police had been desperate to find the perpetrator of the murders and anyone with the slightest suspicion falling on them could expect to be arrested on suspicion of murder. It's interesting to note that another person named Robinson had been detained in connection with the murders, with the *Bucks Herald* mentioning this arrest while reporting on proceedings at the Magistrates' Court:

> A male called John Robinson who lived at Silver St, Windsor [this is an error, and should have read Reading], was arrested in connection with the murder, but he was not implicated and was released. He was lately discharged from the 63rd Foot. He had been drinking in a pub in High Wycombe and knew a good deal about the murder. He had been in Uxbridge on the Monday and had left suddenly. He was not implicated however and was released on Wednesday night there being no evidence against him.[13]

With Jones now remanded to prison, the first legal hurdle had been negotiated. Dunham had successfully begun the busiest week of his life. He still had the inquest to attend and lots more evidence to assemble, but it had been a productive 24 hours. His last job of the day was to ensure that Jones was safely delivered to Aylesbury Gaol.

1   Slough History Online (www.sloughhistoryonline.org.uk).

2   *Bucks Herald*, 28 May 1870.

3   Magistrate Sir Robert Bateson Harvey, 1st Baronet of Langley Park (1825-1887) was an English Conservative Party politician who sat in the House of Commons in two periods between 1863 and 1885. He was educated at Eton College and Christ Church, Oxford. He was a Captain in the 5th Buckinghamshire Rifle Volunteers and then in the Royal Buckinghamshire Yeoman Cavalry. He was a JP and Deputy Lieutenant for Buckinghamshire.

4   Captain William Frederick Farrer (1810-1872). The family home was a fine mansion at Brayfield House, Cold Brayfield, Buckinghamshire. He also lived in London, Cheltenham and Bath. He married Frances Ricarda Parry Jones in 1834. He was a land owner and J.P. owning a number of farms. His son William was born in Clarges Street, Mayfair and later joined the Royal Horse Guard Blues. Captain Farrer was involved in the provisional committee of the Bedford and Northampton Railway in 1845. He sat on the Buckinghamshire Assizes as well as the Slough, Bucks Petty Sessions. He was part of the committee which

purchased a site in Slough for the new Police Station and Petty Session Court. He died 21 April 1872 at his home, 31 Pulteney Street, Bath leaving £16,000 in his estate.

5   Magistrate Edward John Coleman, who was born in 1834, bought Stoke Park in 1863 from Lord Taunton for £95,000 (around £10 million in today's money). He was a coalmine owner and also a broker on the London Stock Exchange. He retired at the time he bought Stoke Park. A staunch Tory, he became a magistrate for Buckinghamshire in 1870 and High Sheriff in 1879. Prime Minister Benjamin Disraeli was a close friend and supported Coleman's application for membership of the Carlton Club in St James's, to which all prominent Tories belonged. Coleman ran into financial difficulties in 1884 ending up in the Bankruptcy Court. He died shortly afterwards in 1885 on the Isle of Wight. His probate record shows him leaving £69,055 in his will. Stoke Park is now a luxurious Country Club

6   *Bucks Herald*, 26 May 1870.

7   *Bucks Advertiser*, 28 May 1870.

8   *Bucks Herald*, 26 May 1870.

9   *Staffordshire Sentinel*, 28 May 1870.

10 *Shields Gazette and Daily Telegraph*, 26 May 1870.

11 *Bucks Herald*, 4 June 1870.

12 *Bucks Herald*, 26 May 1870.

13 Ibid.

CHAPTER 24

An Attempted Lynching

When the first court hearing at Slough ended and the case was adjourned, this resulted with Jones being held on remand at the County Gaol which was situated at Aylesbury almost 30 miles to the north. Having already had problems with transporting Jones from Reading by train, the police must have had concerns for the safety of their suspect.

One newspaper reported the journey:

> When the exam was over, Jones was taken to a cell at the back of the station to await a quiet moment for the removal to Slough Station where he was to proceed to Aylesbury Gaol. At 1.30pm he was put into a cab and was driven towards the station with Chief Constable, Captain Drake and Supt Dunham attending. The 1.35pm train for Aylesbury was due when the police reached the station.

> A dense mass of people, principally of working men, crowded the platform opposite the doors and made a desperate rush whenever the door was opened. Captain Drake and his officers had to stand some rough work.[1]

The *Bucks Herald* reported further details regarding the crowds at Slough Station:

> At the station, there were hundreds of navvies working on the line. 'Tear the ------- to pieces'; 'Lynch him, lynch him'. The mob went to the booking office, people were jumping fences and there were several attempts to lynch him. When the train left, the police told the

mob that he had gone. He had been shut in the ticket office. Jones was put on another train. On the journey he told police that he would give them the slip. They arrived at Aylesbury at 4pm. There was a small crowd at the station. He was hissed and hooted. He was put in a fly with Captain Drake, Supt Denson, Supt Jervis and other officers to the County Gaol.[2]

The *Morning Post* gave more details of the excitement at Slough Station, with information on those under whose supervision Jones was placed:

> The murderer was driven through Slough to the down station of the Great Western Line, where at the time of the arrival of the party of police with their prisoner, but few persons were about. The prisoner was strongly handcuffed, and dressed in the suit of clothes provided by the police, was taken into the booking office. Upon the fact of the prisoner's arrival at the station becoming known, crowds rushed to the spot.

> Many people clambered round the windows, while others endeavoured to get through the doors leading from the platform to the booking office, which were kept closed by the police and the porters of the railway company. By the time the 1.35pm down Aylesbury train arrived at Slough it was quite apparent that the police would experience considerable difficulty in getting the murderer into the train.

> A dense mass of people, principally working men, crowded the platform opposite the doors and made desperate rushes whenever there seemed the slightest intention of opening them. At last the train ran into the station, and an effort was made to get him into a compartment which the officials at Paddington had been telegraphed to reserve. So great was the violence of the crowd, that it was found impossible to get the murderer into the train, and in their efforts to effect this object, Captain Drake and his officers had to stand some rough work.

> In the meantime the greatest excitement prevailed, the passengers in the train sharing in it as well as those on the platforms. It being found morally impossible to get the prisoner into the 1.35pm Aylesbury train, the crowd, seeming as if they wished to rush at and ill treat him, he was retained in the booking office.

> While this was going on, the up Gloucester goods train reached Slough and the down Windsor train was run up to the platform with a couple of empty carriages attached to it. The people were cleared from the platform by the police and railway officials, aided

ATTEMPT TO LYNCH THE PRISONER AT SLOUGH STATION

*The scene at Slough GWR Station with the mob trying to get to the prisoner.
The station was full of navvies trying to do harm to Jones. How typically British
that the person at the front of the queue in trying to assault him was an old lady
armed with an umbrella.*

Illustrated Police News

by Mr Harper, the Slough station master. The last two carriages of the
Windsor train were suddenly detached, the Windsor part went on,
and the murderer was rapidly run into the compartment of a second
class carriage, Captain Drake, and Superintendents Denson, Sargent
and Jervis being with him.

As quickly as possible, the Gloucester goods engine was hooked on
to the carriage in which the prisoner was seated, and at once ran out
of the station. While the police were getting the murderer into the
van the crowd again broke into the station, surrounded the train, and
yelled and hooted to their hearts content, till the train left at 1.57pm
for Taplow, when the other train had just arrived, and into which the
prisoner was quietly transferred and taken to Aylesbury.[3]

The *Windsor & Eton Express* gave vivid further details of the
pandemonium at the station:

It was with the greatest difficulty that the police and railway officials
protected him [Jones]. Violent blows were struck at his face as soon
as he came onto the platform. The police superintendents warded

off several blows from the prisoner, but in doing so received several themselves. To save his life they were obliged to run him back into the booking office, but so desperate were the efforts to get hold of him, that the windows were broken and the door shattered to pieces. The prisoner shouted out, 'If I am guilty they will hang me, but don't let them knock me about'.[4]

Pleas were made to the mob to desist in their behaviour and that if he was guilty he would be punished according to the law. Volunteers were asked for to guard him to the carriage door. This was met with a general cry of 'Yes we'll take care of him if we get hold of him'.

The incident at Slough Station was clearly a very serious public order situation, with the police being heavily outnumbered by the unruly mob. There are no reports of arrests during the incident; the police were probably happy simply to have gotten away with their prisoner still in one piece.

---

1   *Bucks Advertiser*, 28 May 1870

2   *Bucks Herald*, 26 May 1870.

3   *Morning Post*, 26 May 1870.

4   *Windsor & Eton Express*, 28 May 1870.

CHAPTER 25

The Inquest
(Second Day)

The adjourned inquest got under way on Friday 27 May. Once again the Swan Inn was filled to capacity, and large crowds continued to gather outside.

The coroner Mr Frederick Charlsely told the court that since the first hearing on Tuesday a man had been apprehended and charged with the murder of the Marshall family. The prisoner (John Jones) was currently in Aylesbury Gaol but he would not be present at the inquest. The *Bucks Herald* explained the reasoning behind the Coroner's decision:

> The Coroner, Mr Charsley, said normally when a person is charged with a crime it was usually desirable for them to be present to hear the evidence. In this case it was not necessary, and added the reason being that there is a lot of ill feeling against the prisoner and it was not advisable to remove him from the gaol.[1]

In fact, the Chief Constable had advised the Coroner that it would be hardly safe to bring the prisoner to the inquest. At the same time it prevented any chance of him escaping.

The first witness to be examined was Superintendent Dunham. He largely repeated the evidence he had given previously at the committal hearing:

Supt Dunham gave evidence on the condition of the bodies. The Coroner, on the old cord trousers [left at the scene] stated that they were almost unmistakable if they were seen once, and the jury concurred, the black patches on white giving them a very marked appearance. The witness showed blood covered boots with pieces of brain still attached, a fustian waistcoat [a heavy cotton cloth worn by working men in the 19th century], billycock hat [deerstalker], old neckerchief and a worn blue smock, all found in the murdered man's room which the prisoner had been seen wearing previous to the murder. Near the clothes was a hammer. No watch was found, though a stand with a watch-key on it was in the room. Two boxes were broken open, and some of their contents had been abstracted, and others were spread about the room.

The witness then said he went to various lodging houses in Uxbridge with these clothes. Charles Coombes came to me and identified the old coats found in the house as those which a man who had lodged there had worn. I at once took the witness with me to Reading and we searched several lodging houses. We arrived at the Tramps Kitchen in Silver Street, Coombes pointed out the prisoner, who was sitting on the other side of the room, against the wall. I had been advised at Uxbridge that Jones had a pistol. I seized Jones by the throat. Before I reached him, and before a word was said to him, he exclaimed 'I never killed man, woman nor child!'

The witness—'When I had seized him, a constable with me [Detective Constable Toulman] seized his arm, exclaiming that the prisoner was drawing a pistol from his trouser pocket. It was loaded with slugs but was not capped, the caps being in his waistcoat pocket. I handcuffed him and charged him with the murder of Emmanuel Marshall and others, and he said, 'I did not do it but I know who did.' I said 'Why, you scoundrel, you have the murdered man's boots on, and his trousers too,' and the prisoner replied, 'I know that.'

'He had a white slop on over his trousers and witnesses will speak to the trousers, boots and shirt worn by the prisoner being the property of the murdered man. I found keys of drawers upon him, a new portmonnaie [wallet] with 5s. 6d. in silver in it, as well as a token piece. The pockets of the deceased man's trousers had been turned inside out.

'The prisoner refused to give his name at Reading. I said to him that he had spent two months in Coldbath Fields Prison under the name John Jenkins. He said 'That's my --- name'.'[2]

The witnesses who gave the most disturbing evidence on the

second day were the doctors who had performed the post mortems on the seven bodies. Four doctors had been involved in the examinations.[3]

Dr John Spencer Ferris, who was 28 years old, gave his opinion on the bodies. Each victim, he said, had received a lethal blow to the skull so violent that the skulls were able to be pulled apart:

> I was called in on Monday at Denham, at the house of the Marshalls, whom I well know. I was called at half past seven pm. I saw in the front room the bodies of Charlotte Marshall, the wife, and Mary Ann Marshall, the unmarried sister, of the deceased man. Charlotte Marshall was lying with her head against the wall; her skull was covered in blood and the wall close by was smeared with blood.
>
> Mary Ann Marshall was lying with her feet on Charlotte, and her head the other way. Her head and face were covered with blood.
>
> In the back kitchen I saw the body of the grandmother, Mary Marshall, with her arm round the body of the youngest child [Gertrude], both dead, and the heads of both were covered with blood. In the fireplace were the bodies of Mary and Thirza, one on the other, both the heads again covered in blood.
>
> I went out into the foundry, and by the side of the forge I saw the body of Emmanuel Marshall, completely covered with a sack. He was lying on his face, with his legs towards the back of the forge. Directly on moving the sack I saw two large wounds on the back of the head, and on turning him over I found his face completely smashed in ... On the back of Marshall's left hand there was a severe bruise and his right finger was grazed. There was no wound or bruise on the body or other limbs. The front of the face and the clothes in front were covered in ashes as if the body had been dragged along the forge.
>
> There were four facial wounds, one over the nose, one over the left eye, and a deep one on the chin. The upper and lower jaws, even to the bone under the eye, were completely smashed in. On the head the hair was matted with blood, and ashes were on it.
>
> On the scalp there were five wounds, one on the left side of head, one behind it, an inch and a half long, another small one behind that, on the back of the head a large one, on the right side a long lacerated wound.
>
> There was a fracture of the base of the skull from right to left, to such extent that the skull could be pulled in half. The scalp wounds were probably produced by a poker, and the smashing of face and fracture by a sledge hammer or the back of an axe.

Injuries to Thirza (aged 6):

On her there was no fracture or bruise of limbs or body but there was a wound in the scalp and protrusion of brain, and blood was oozing from the right ear, behind which there was a small cut. The face was uninjured.

On removing the scalp, an open space measuring 4 by 5 inches was discovered. In fact the whole right side of the skull was smashed, to the right side of the spine. The whole injuries on the child were produced probably from one blow of a sledgehammer.

Injuries to Mary (junior) (aged 8):

Had no bruise or fracture of body or limbs, but on the head was a semi-circular wound 5in. in length, which almost completely cut off the right ear, a small wound above the right ear, other wounds on the back of head, and near them a 'starred' cut. Three of them were made by a poker but the starred cut could not have been made by any instrument yet found.

There was a wound on the right side of the face, and both jaws were broken. Inside the skull there was a punctured wound corresponding with the starred cut on the outside, and the base of skull fractured across, dividing the skull in half.

Injuries to Gertrude (aged 4):

The body had blood coming from the nose, mouth and ears, but she had no injuries whatever to body or limbs. All the bones on left side of the head were completely smashed in – the temple bone alone being intact. Many fragments of bone were detached and there was much blood on the brain. All the injuries were probably done to this body by a sledgehammer.

Injuries to Mary (senior) (aged 77):

The examination of the body showed a graze to the right knee, but no other injury to the body or limbs. On the head was a bruise over the right eye, and contusion on left, a triangular wound on the right temple, a wound 3 inches long on the right side of head, behind the right ear a wound, all deep and lacerated. Blood was oozing from the left ear. There was a fracture across the base of the skull, so that it could be pulled in half. Much blood was on the brain.

Injuries to Mary Ann (aged 32):

No injury was on the body or limb. There was a slight cut on the upper lip, a wound an inch in length outside the left eye, the teeth of the upper jaw were knocked into her mouth, a wound an inch and a quarter long was down the parting of the hair, a wound three inches long was on the right side of head, and these appeared as if done with a sharp axe. There was a large quantity of blood between the brain and the skull, a large starred fracture on the right side of the skull, and inside a large amount of blood again, and a fracture at the base, so great that the skull could be pulled in half. Several pieces of bone were detached.

Injuries to Charlotte (wife):

On the body no injuries were done to body or limbs. On the face the left upper eyelid was bruised, and there was blood oozing from the left ear. There was a jagged transverse wound an inch long over the right ear, a wound three inches long at the back of the head, another the same length on the middle of the head, a fourth jagged, on the left side of the back of the head, much blood under the scalp, and a fracture at the base of the skull, right across, so that the skull could be pulled in half. The injuries were done by a sledgehammer, or by the back of an axe.

The Coroner —Are these injuries the cause of death in each case?

Dr Ferris] — They are.[4]

Dr George Housman MacNamara[5] deposed to having assisted the last witness, his partner, in the post mortem examinations, and corroborated the evidence already given.

Charles Coombes, whose tip-off to Superintendent Dunham had resulted in the arrest of Jones, was examined next. He described his relationship with the prisoner, and the events over the previous weekend when Jones had mysteriously absented himself from the Uxbridge lodging house on Saturday night and returned on the Sunday morning wearing a new suit of clothes and flush with money.

Sarah Alderman,[6] the keeper at the Dog & Duck public house in Denham, which was about half a mile from the Marshall home, provided important testimony which placed Jones close to the scene of the crime. At 8.00 am on the morning of the murders he knocked on her door demanding alcohol. Why would he have been in such a hurry to have an early Sunday morning beer? What would he have been doing between 3.00 am, when he was seen by Constable Trevener, and 8.00 am, when he entered the pub, still in the vicinity of the Marshalls' house? Was the drink to steady his nerves? She stated:

On Sunday morning last, about eight o'clock, a man came to my house and asked if I could draw a pint of beer. I declined to draw it until half past twelve, and he said he was a traveller from Wycombe, and could claim it. I drew it and he stayed about ten minutes.

He was dressed in dark clothes, and had a straw hat with a black band on it, and had a carpet bag in his hand full of some things. He paid for the beer with a shilling taken from a purse. The purse was like that produced [that found on the prisoner].

He did not drink all the beer and said he had been late the night before drinking currant and all sorts of wine. He did not appear as if he had been drinking, but he seemed very tired. The man wore a hat exactly like the one I have seen on Mr Marshall, whom I knew very well.[7]

Mary Ann Sparke,[8] the sister of Mrs Marshall, was then called to give evidence. She appeared overwhelmed with grief. She was able to identify the clothes and footwear worn by Jones when he was arrested – his shirt, collar, necktie, the boots and the trousers – as being those belonging to Emmanuel Marshall. Furthermore, she said the chain which had been pledged was similar to the one worn by her sister.

Prison Warder Daniel Love was called next.[9] He was not only able to identify the old clothing left by Jones at the scene of the murder, but was also able to give details of an alleged conversation with Jones where he made threats to kill a person near Uxbridge:

Daniel Love, warder of Berkshire County Gaol, Reading, said he knew 'Jenkins' as alias Reynolds, Owen and Jones, and identified the jacket found in Marshall's room as one given to Jenkins on leaving gaol in January last, when his sentence of 18 months imprisonment expired. He served that time for stealing a ewe and a lamb from Abingdon. The blood covered boots also found in Marshall's room were given to him on being discharged.

When the prisoner was discharged, he asked the way to Uxbridge, and said he knew a man there who had got some money and he would have it, and rather than have another 18 months he would murder him. Witness told him not to do such a thing as that. He believed that prisoner's name was Owen as one day he cut the name 'J. Owen' on a piece of soap, and when it was found so he remarked that that was his proper name.[10]

A pawnbroker's assistant named James Weston[11] was next in court. He was able to identify Jones as the man who had entered his shop the day following the murder and pawned a silver watch and gold chain. This was also significant, as Jones had no property and not a penny to his name on the Saturday. The shop was Joseph Butcher's Pawnbrokers at 155 High Street, Uxbridge. The newspapers reported Weston's evidence as follows:

> James Weston stated that on Monday last, a man came to his employer's shop and offered the silver watch and gold chain produced in exchange for 25 shillings. The man gave his name as George Wilson of Reading. The witness asked the man if the property was his own, and he answered sharply that it was. The witness told him that it was his duty to ask that question.
>
> The man said he had been on a 'bit of a spree' at Uxbridge, and the witness told him they did not take things from people on a spree. He said, 'Oh, do lend me something on it as I have to get back to Reading to see my father.' The witness lent him 15 shillings on the watch and chain.[12]

The first officer on the scene, PC Trevener, was recalled to give further particulars to the court, which were recorded by the *Bucks Herald*:

> The witness produced a blacksmith's sledgehammer, covered in blood, found by him near the bodies of the murdered women; also a large woodman's axe, found near the bodies of the three children and the grandmother, also covered in blood, back and edge, and apparently used both ways; and in the forge, near the body of Emmanuel Marshall, the upper part of a broken poker, and near the entrance of the forge the lower part. The handle of the poker was covered in blood, and the second part was lying in a pool of blood. The witness held up the different implements to show the coroner and the jury.
>
> He identified the hat found at the house as the one worn by the man he had met on the Sunday morning about 3 o'clock. The coats also found at the house he identified as being worn by the same man, for he looked at the man to see whether he had concealed anything under the coats, and so he had taken particular notice of the coats.[13]

The *Herts Advertiser & St Albans Times* gave a few extra details about the murder weapons:

Newspaper article in the Buckingham Advertiser of 21st May 1970, showing what is supposedly the axe used in the murders.

The head of the sledgehammer appeared to weigh four or five pounds. The handle was short, not more than a foot in length, if so much. The blood was still visible...

The axe had a handle about two feet six inches, or from that to three feet long. The head was massive; the edge appeared to be blunt. It had probably been used to chop wood.[14]

---

1 *Bucks Herald*, 4 June 1870.

2 Ibid.

3 Dr John Spencer Ferris, Dr George MacNamara, Dr Cornelius Fox, and Dr Pratt.

4 *Bucks Herald*, 4 June 1870.

5 Dr George Housman MacNamara M.R.C.S. was born in Ipswich circa 1825. At the time of the Denham Murders he was a 46-year-old widower with three children, living at 59 St Andrews, Uxbridge, close to Dr Ferris. He was still living at St Andrews in the 1881 census, and his 21-year-old son Hugh Winkworth MacNamara was shown as a surgeon. When Dr MacNamara died at Kingsdown House, Box, Wiltshire, (a nursing home) in 1899, his estate was worth £6,552. One of the beneficiaries of his estate was none other than Dr John Spencer Ferris, who had been with him at the Denham Murders.

6 Sarah Alderman was aged 33 at the time of the murders and married to Joseph Alderman, the beerhouse keeper of the Dog & Duck, Uxbridge Road in Denham. According to the 1871 census she was born in Denham. The pub was situated on the road from Denham to Uxbridge.

7 *Bucks Herald*, 4 June 1870.

8   Mary Ann Sparke was the sister of Emmanuel Marshall's wife, Charlotte. By the time of the 1871 Census she was living with her father, Loyal Sparke, at 63 Waterloo Road, Uxbridge. Also living with them was two-year-old Francis Marshall, who had survived being the eighth victim of the massacre as he had not been at home on the day of the murders. On 29 August 1880, Mary Ann married Metropolitan Police Constable Michael Pennifold at St John's Church, Uxbridge. By the time of the 1881 Census she was living with her husband and father at 19 Rockingham Street, Uxbridge. Also present was 12-year-old Francis. The couple had at least three children. A daughter named Gertrude Charlotte Pennifold was born and baptised on 29 November 1881. This child must have been named after two of the victims of the murders. Sadly, Gertrude only survived for eight hours. A son was born later, in 1884. The child was delightfully named Michael Loyal Sparker Pennifold, so commemorating both his father and grandfather. Sadly, PC Pennifold died in 1900 at the age of 51.

9   Daniel Love was 28-years-old at time of the murders. He had been born at Silchester in Hampshire. In the 1871 Census he was living at 7 Devonshire Place, Reading, and was described as a prison warder. By 1881 he was a clerk living in Easthampstead, Berkshire. He appears to have had an unhappy time. By 1911 he was living in Southsea but listed as 'General labourer out of employment, ill health on club'. He was recorded as having been married for 42 years, but had in fact separated in 1880 and had no children. It's not known why he left Berkshire Gaol. He died in 1917 in Portsmouth aged 76.

10   *Bucks Herald*, 4 June 1870.

11   James Weston was an assistant pawnbroker to Mr Butcher, pawnbroker of Uxbridge. On the 1871 Census he was listed as living at 155 High Street, Uxbridge, aged 31 years, employed as a 'pawnbroker manager'. He was born in Great Missenden, Bucks. He married Emma Butcher on 19 October 1868 at Hillingdon Parish church. The bride's father was none other than Mr Joseph Butcher, pawnbroker, who owned the business. By the 1881 census James Weston was still at 155 High Street, Uxbridge, listed as a pawnbroker. He was recorded as retired ten years later, residing at 'Claremont', Cornwall Road, Uxbridge, aged 52. By the 1911 Census Emma had died and James was residing at 2 Cowley Road, Uxbridge, age 72. He died on 6 January 1923 at that address, leaving an estate worth £6,225 5s 1d to his son James Butcher Weston, a tobacconist.

12   *Bucks Herald*, 4 June 1870.

13   Ibid.

14   *Herts Advertiser & St Albans Times*, 28 May 1870.

CHAPTER 26

The Coroner

The coroner was a legal/medical post which had existed over many centuries. At the start of Queen Victoria's reign, the first Births and Deaths Registration Act of 1836 was passed, prompted by public concern and panic caused by inaccurate 'parochial' recording of the actual numbers of deaths arising from epidemics such as cholera. There was also growing concern that, given the easy and uncontrolled access to numerous poisons, and inadequate medical investigation of the actual cause of death, many murders were going undetected.

It was the job of the coroner to ascertain the identity of the deceased, the place of death, the time of death and the cause of death. The verdicts that a jury could arrive at were accidental death, natural causes, an open verdict, suicide, manslaughter or murder.

Although it appears quite clear from all the evidence we have heard that a verdict of unlawful killing would be returned on all the victims, it was possible that the verdict in relation to Emmanuel Marshall could have been one of suicide, with all the others being murder.

However, evidence given by the doctors of the post mortem clearly proved that it was impossible for Emmanuel Marshall to have killed himself after having killed the others.

At the end of the hearing Mr Charsley addressed the jury members, summing up the evidence:

> It pointed to one person and one person only as being the murderer.
> He went over the circumstances which had been detailed before
> them, and left it to the jury to say whether the deceased people had
> been murdered, and if they were satisfied that the prisoner's identity
> had been established.

> In conclusion, he gave the police great credit for the way they had
> acted in the difficult position of having to search out a crime when
> the murderer had obtained so long a start.[1]

While the jury was deliberating, a new piece of evidence emerged.
The *Bucks Herald* gave the details:

> A vehicle was driven to the door and Supt Dunham announced that
> a key had been found concealed in the Tramps' Kitchen at Reading
> where the prisoner was apprehended, and this key proved to open
> the front door of the house where the murders were committed. This
> key had been seen in the prisoner's possession at Reading.[2]

The jury did not need to deliberate long:

> Almost at once they returned a verdict of wilful murder in each case
> against John Jones alias John Jenkins and the Coroner delivered
> over his warrant to Capt Drake, the Bucks Chief Constable, for the
> prisoner's delivery in the due course of law to take his trial.[3]

Jones's life was now in great danger. The criminal case had been
committed for trial and the coroner's inquest had given Jones's
name as the person responsible for the terrible crimes, where the
only sentence could be execution by hanging. The police had got
their man. It was now just a question of compiling all the witness
statements to build a rock-solid case.

The Chief Constable must have been very happy with his officers.
The investigation and arrest, as well as successfully getting Jones to
Aylesbury still in one piece, was a great piece of police work. The
next job would be the public order operation involved in policing
the funeral.

Denham was about to be swamped with people wanting to be part
of one of the most heartbreaking funerals ever to be seen in England.

1   *Bucks Herald,* 4 June 1870.

2   Ibid.

3   Ibid.

CHAPTER 27

The Funeral

The funeral of seven lost souls from one family was always going to be a big event. The small village of Denham was going to experience a momentous day as thousands of people flocked to the South Buckinghamshire settlement. The remaining family members had a harrowing day in store.

The *Worcestershire Chronicle* of 1 June 1870 gave details of a final visit from a relative:

> Many persons, including ladies of high position, had previously come from all parts of the country to Uxbridge, and expressed an intense desire to be allowed to enter the cottage and see the bodies, but the police very properly forbade any intrusion by strangers on the premises. A very old man, said to be the brother of the woman of 77, was admitted, with a few other relations of the deceased, to take a last look at the bodies of the murdered family.

The funeral was held on Friday 27 May. It was widely reported around the country, and people flocked to Denham Parish Church. One newspaper reported the following:

> The weather on the day of the funeral was fine. It drew together more thousands that we would like to compute. The village was crowded from all directions but chiefly from the direction of Uxbridge. Streams of visitors from an early hour of the afternoon knew no cessation. There was a continuous flow on foot, horseback and in hundreds of vehicles of all descriptions, from chariots of the rich to the humble

The funeral at Denham Parish Church
Illustrated Police News

cart of the costermonger.

The funeral started at 5pm. The coffins were supplied the night before, and the bodies deposited in them and lodged in the front room and were brought out one by one and placed on trestles in front of the house. The coffins were made of elm, each bearing the name of the occupant. There were forty pall bearers all suitably attired.

A large detachment of the Bucks Police was joined by many of the Metropolitan Force from Uxbridge who had been brought to the place, and a body of them led the procession. Admiration was shown for the arrangements of the Bucks Constabulary under the direction of Chief Constable, Captain Drake assisted by Supt Dunham, several inspectors and 50-100 officers joined by a considerable number from Uxbridge.[1]

Other papers gave different accounts. One national publication, the *Pall Mall Gazette*, stated:

FUNERAL CORTEGE – An immense concourse had assembled to witness it. People lined both sides of the road from the scene of the massacre to Denham Churchyard, ¾ mile distant. Crowds came by vehicles from all parts of the country. All was silent decorum. It was a plain funeral service. Expenses were paid by two leading inhabitants of Uxbridge who expressed a wish to do so. The crowds were silent and bareheaded. The Police were six abreast, and the crowds fell back. There was a melancholy line of seven coffins. The grandmother, Marshall his wife and sister had black palls, the children had white drapery.

A dense throng of vehicles followed. Old Mrs Marshall was buried first with her husband who as the headstone told, died in 1860, in the 68th year of his age. Mr & Mrs Marshall were buried in the middle; sister and eldest child buried on the right; two youngest buried on the left.

All blinds in Denham were drawn yesterday and all the shops half closed. The stated intention of the landlord is to pull down the old cottage in which the massacre took place and build another a few yards distant.[2]

The *Royal Cornwall Gazette* gave further details:

People came from Iver, Slough and Windsor. 600 - 700 people arrived by vehicles and train. The coffins were borne by men from the neighbourhood. There were 36 pall bearers. The bodies were removed at 4.40, the procession was taken by Supt Dunham and 20 local police four abreast. Coffins were removed in the following order. Grandmother first then Emmanuel Marshall, his wife then his sister, then the children.

The chief mourners were Mr & Mrs Sparkes [parents of Mrs Marshall; sic], Mr & Mrs Spooner [brother-in-law and sister of Mrs Marshall], Mr Sparkes junior and Miss Sparkes [brother and sister of Mrs Marshall; both sic]. There were four graves, three were side by side and the other for the grandmother nearby. Mr & Mrs Marshall were buried together. The sister, Mary Ann, and eldest child Gertrude were buried together. The two other children were buried together. The burial service was conducted by Rev Joyce and Rev Shepherd, curates. A brass plaque on each coffin showing the name, age and date of death, but no mention as to the cause.[3]

The *Bucks Herald* noted a sad comment made during the service by the local clergyman, the Rev Charles Joyce:[4]

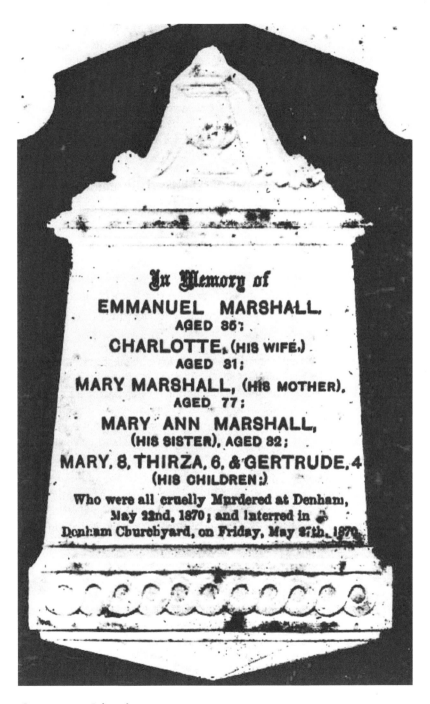

Ornate memorial card
Thames Valley Police Archives

The Rev C. Joyce gave a touching sermon in the old church. He mentioned only last Sunday a member of the family was asked for the last time in church [Mary Ann's marriage banns]. How little the congregation knew that the one called, lay with the dead. How on the morning the bells which were to have pealed merrily, rang a funeral knell. The doors which were open to receive a bride, received instead a corpse. During the whole of the sermon, scarcely a dry eye could be seen, everyone present was deeply overcome by the excellent sermon.[5]

The *Bucks Advertiser* gave further details of the undertaker:

The coffins were made and the whole arrangements of the funeral were under the direction of Abraham Jones of Iver,[6] and were carried out in a way that which was very creditable to him.[7]

The *London Standard* commented on the funeral, highlighting the infamy that the murders had conferred on Denham. It also indicated the feelings of the family in relation to wild rumours that had been circulating:

As the cortege passed along to the churchyard, the inhabitants of the cottages by which it passed were in most cases affected to tears. It required the services of 30 policemen to keep clear space for what portion of the ceremony conducted over the graves... Thus ended a scene extraordinary in itself, happily unprecedented in its nature and one which will render the churchyard of Denham celebrated until the end of time.

The deceased leave behind them two sisters who state as follows; Our brother went to Australia about 15 years ago. We used frequently to hear from him till about 5 years ago since, when he stopped writing and we have long ago come to the conclusion that the poor fellow is dead. The description of the prisoner is not at all like him, and such a statement as has appeared in the papers is very hurtful to our feelings, and we hope it will be contradicted.[8]

The press reported on disturbing behaviour by ghoulish souvenir hunters:

A morbid desire to possess a memento of the horrible crime has shown itself very prominently among the visitors to the cottage of the murdered family in Denham. A fir tree has been nearly stripped and many loose articles abstracted in spite of the precautions of the police.[9]

1 *Bucks Advertiser*, 28 May 1870.

2 *Pall Mall Gazette*, 28 May 1870.

3 *Royal Cornwall Gazette*, 4 June 1870.

4 Rev Charles Joyce M.A. was a 35-year-old curate of Denham Parish Church at the time of the funeral. He was born in Ireland. He was shown as the curate in Denham in both the 1861 and 1871 census returns. By 1881 he had married Maud and moved away from the parish to become the rector of Fulmer, Bucks. He was later to become the High Sheriff of Buckinghamshire's chaplain. It's unlikely that he would ever have had a more emotionally charged funeral to conduct in his years of ministry as that of the Marshall family. He was also the foreman of the inquest jury held at the Swan Inn

5 *Bucks Herald*, 4 June 1870.

6 The census returns for Iver show Abraham Jones residing there from the 1841 to 1891, initially listed as a carpenter. By 1851 he was described as a master carpenter, employing one man. At the time the murders took place he employed five men, and at the height of his success, in 1881, he was listed as a builder, employing fifteen men and one boy. He died in 1895 aged 81.

7 *Bucks Advertiser*, 28 May 1870.

8 *London Standard*, 28 May 1870. The evidence in the case was to prove without question that the brother of Emmanuel Marshall had nothing whatever to do with the murders (see Chapter 11).

9 *Bucks Herald*, 4 June 1870.

CHAPTER 28

The Committal Hearing
at Aylesbury Gaol

In the normal course of events all judicial cases, whether they be Magistrates' Courts, Crown Courts (then known as Assize Courts) and Coroners' Courts are held in public buildings so that the general public can attend and observe justice being done, the only bar to attending being the available seating and space in the public gallery.

It was against this knowledge that the committal hearing for John Jones was moved from the local magistrates' court at Slough to Aylesbury Gaol. This was a highly unusual move, and one which was to cause anxiety among the magistrates.

It was, however, an indication of how seriously the authorities viewed the security of the prisoner, and their fear that he would be killed or maimed by the mob.

In modern times, remand prisoners now routinely 'appear' in court via video link. This means that prisoners are saved from having to appear in person at courthouses for case management hearings and the like. Prisoners still have to appear in person for actual trials, however. This development saves both the courts and prisons money in transportation and security costs. It also means that a chance of escaping is removed.

Jones was a desperate and dangerous man. Moving him around

the country was full of potential dangers for both the prisoner and the police.

The second hearing was duly held at the Bucks County Gaol, at Aylesbury, without fear of public order disturbances, on Tuesday, 31 May 1870. The Chairman, Sir Robert Bateson Harvey, was on the bench, as were Mr John Bramley-Moore,[1] Rev H.H. Way and Mr Edward John Coleman.

The *Derby Mercury* gave details of Jones's preparations for his appearance in court:

> The prisoner was brought into the magistrates' room in the prison in the custody of two stalwart gaolers. He had in his hand a roll of foolscap paper, which is said to be a written statement. The week's imprisonment had rather improved his appearance. He looked much cleaner, less callous, and exhibited something approaching deference to the magistrates. There was much interest to see the prisoner. Many of the neighbouring gentry were present, including a couple of ladies, who were accommodated with chairs behind the magistrates. There was also present a well-known artist from the celebrated Exhibition of Madame Tussaud.
>
> The prisoner employed himself all day in writing out what he called a statement of facts, which was to the effect that he himself was entirely innocent of the murder, but that he knew who had committed it. He described the murderer minutely, even to the clothing worn by him and admits that he accepted 50 shillings and the clothes which he wore when arrested not to betray the perpetrator of the crime.[2]

Before the hearing commenced, Sir Robert addressed the court to explain why the case was being held behind the secure walls of the County Gaol. His words were reported in the *Bucks Herald* of 4 June 1870:

> I should like to make a few remarks upon the extraordinary circumstances under which the bench has met here today. It has been mentioned in the public prints that we were afraid to meet in Slough in consequence of the strong feelings of the people of the district against the prisoner, and the belief that attempts would be made to injure him.
>
> That is not the reason for our meeting here, and my opinion is that we could always rely upon the efficiency of our police and upon the certainty that Capt Drake, the Chief Constable, would take care to

provide the necessary extra assistance to prevent any such attempt being made. But we meet here because the Coroner has issued a warrant of committal, and so taken the prisoner from under our control. I felt very strongly on this matter and it was only because I feared that justice might be thwarted if I did not go on with the evidence that I consented to attend. I feel that some explanation is due for the unusual course adopted by the Coroner on this occasion.

These comments appear to conflict with the views of the Coroner. Sir Robert appears to indicate that the normal procedure should have been followed, and that Jones should have been allowed to appear in an 'open' court. The prisoner should have been allowed to take his chances with the mob.

The Coroner would later respond to Sir Robert's demand for an explanation. In a letter to *The Times*, he wrote:

In your impression of today, I observe that the chairman of the magistrates who on Tuesday finally examined the man John Jones alias Jenkins, remarked that he felt some explanation was due for the course of action the Coroner adopted in issuing his warrant of committal.

My duty as defined by the Statute 'de Officio Coronatoris, 4th of Edward I.,' was immediately upon the finding by the Coroner's jury of a verdict of murder against the man Jones to issue my warrant for his commitment to the county gaol. I did this and placed it in the hands of Capt Drake, the Chief Constable.

In ordinary cases it is right for a party apprehended on suspicion to be allowed to be present at the inquest, but in this case the Chief Constable gave me what I could not but feel to be sufficient reason for not doing so. – namely, that after what had already occurred it would be hardly safe to bring the prisoner to the inquest. The course adopted by the Chief Constable in placing my warrant in the hands of the Governor of the county gaol had the effect of preventing the recurrence of the scenes which occurred outside the police court and at the railway station on the prior hearing before the magistrates, and while I fully believe that we could rely on the efficiency of our police, there is no doubt that an attempt would have been made to carry the threat of the populace into execution, and the resistance, though successful, would probably have been attended with serious consequences. All this had been avoided by the adjourned hearing at the county gaol at Aylesbury.[3]

THE CELL-AYLESBURY

The witnesses for the prosecution were then examined by the court, most of whom had already been examined at the inquest or the earlier magistrates' hearing.

A useful prosecution witness was Henry Salter,[4] who picked up Jones in Hanwell and gave him a lift to Uxbridge. He was able to give evidence of Jones's clothing, and to the fact he had no money. He also told the court about Jones's evasiveness about the 'brother' that he told him he was going to get money from. However, Salter was not the most convincing of witnesses in relation to his identification of the suspect in the courtroom. The *Bucks Herald* gave the details:

> I am a carman to Mr Carter, a carrier. On Saturday week, 21st May, I was driving from Acton to Uxbridge, along the turnpike road, when a man who wore these clothes [those left in the murdered man's house], came up to me close to the gates at Hanwell Asylum and asked me to take him up for a lift to Uxbridge.
>
> He told me after he got up that he had no money. I put him down at the Green Man, Uxbridge about 10 minutes to 6 in the evening. He rode about 6 miles with me. He said coming along that though he had no money, he had a brother near Uxbridge from whom he should obtain some. I asked him where his brother lived, but he made a laugh of this and said, 'That's a question I shan't answer'. He said he should not go to his brother until after dark. He also said he had been moving round the country, had spent money in his time, and had been 'rackety cove'.[5] When I put him down he thanked me for the ride and said he should make his way into the town. The Green Man is a little way out of the town.
>
> I did not have much to say to the man, for another man got up after the prisoner had rode for about two miles, and the man principally talked to him for the rest of the journey.
>
> Clerk: Do you know who he was?
>
> Witness: Yes.
>
> Did you put him down in the same place?
>
> Yes.
>
> What was the name of this man?
>
> Sydney.
>
> Did the prisoner tell you that he had ever been out of the country?
>
> No Sir.
>
> Should you know this man again?

THE PRISONER AND THE CARRIER.

Yes.

Look around and see if he is here.

The witness then began a careful survey of those present, first of all directing his gaze especially and for some moments among the magistrates, as if he expected to find the prisoner taking down depositions. So impressed was he that the culprit was at that end of the room that the clerk energetically requested him to 'look around'. He looked around accordingly, but too rapidly, for again his gaze became fixed on the bench.

A general titter, in which the prisoner joined suddenly, awakened the elderly witness to the fact that was still on the wrong track and for a third time he commenced his survey, taking the bench as his starting point. The witness then turned his eyes to the far right and without at all looking at the prisoner who was behind him, pointed, amid much laughter, to one of the country newspapers reporters, who had a beard covering the lower part of his face and was sitting in a shaded place.

The witness was asked if he was sure that he saw his passenger of Saturday week, and he at once owned that he had made a mistake. He was looking towards the same group again and was pointing out one of the London reporters as the man when... The prisoner said, 'Look at me and see if I am not the man?'

The witness at once exclaimed with a look of delight: Yes you are the man. Bean't you the man who rode with me to Uxbridge?

Prisoner: Of course I am.

The witness then formally identified the trousers, coat, hat and boots found in the house, with the murdered bodies, as those worn by the prisoner when riding on the Saturday in question.[6]

The first officer on the scene, PC Trevener, now deposed to evidence he gave before the Coroner. The prisoner showed no emotion when the sledgehammer, the woodman's axe, and the poker were exhibited to the magistrates. Mr Bramley-Moore asked the witness specifically about the sledgehammer:

Magistrate: Is the handle on the hammer the usual length – it looks to me very short?

Witness: Yes sir, it is a sledge hammer and I have often seen the deceased man using it.

Supt Dunham: I have frequently seen Marshall working with it. He could not afford to keep a man, so that he no doubt shortened the handle in order that he might use it himself. He was a very hard working, industrious man.[7]

Quietly, the prisoner said he had no questions to put to PC Trevener.

Elizabeth Simpson was the next witness. She was a near neighbour of the Marshalls', who clearly kept herself to herself. Little is known about her but she was to provide very important evidence to the court in proving Jones's involvement not only in the disposal of the Marshalls' belongings, but in the murder itself. She testified to seeing Jones coming out of the Marshalls' property on the Sunday morning at 7.00 am:

Elizabeth Simpson, a married woman, wife of a groom and living in Denham, stated:

I live in a house about 100 yards from that lately occupied by the Marshalls, of whom I did not know much. On Sunday 22 May, I went out at about 7 o'clock to look for a key which I had dropped in the road on Saturday night. When I came to the turn of the road which gave a view of the Marshalls' house, I saw a man come out of the gate. The man was dressed respectably. He wore a dark coat and he carried a carpet bag of a greenish colour.

I overtook him as he got to the Uxbridge Road which is about the same distance from the Marshall's house one way as my house is distant from the other. The man said it was a fine morning and asked me if I was hurrying for the train. I said I was not but that I was looking for my key I had lost on the previous night.

Magistrate's clerk: Should you know the man again if you were to see him?

Witness: I think I should know his side face.

The clerk: Just look round the court and see if he is here?

The witness began timidly to look round, but before she had half scanned those present she pointed to a gent, whose beard was somewhat like that of the prisoner and said, 'That's him, I think.' The man became uneasy creating some little amusing sensation in which the prisoner took part.

Clerk to witness: You have not half looked round – look again.

She then closely scanned the faces and looked behind her. The prisoner was one of a group of people who had crowded behind him and about him, but as there was no prisoners dock, there was nothing to distinguish him from the rest of the audience. He was not handcuffed, and the warders were sitting down apart from him.

As soon as the witness caught sight of the man she exclaimed pointing directly at him, 'That looks like the man' and asked if he might be turned to her so as to present his side face. She said, 'That's the man, only his face had more colour in it than it has now.' The prisoner met her gaze and stared at her for a moment or two during her hesitation and smiled when she pronounced him to be the man.

Clerk: You said he had more colour in his face. Did that appear to be natural or flushed from the heat?

Witness: I should think it was from exertion.

The Bench: How far did he walk with you?

Witness: About ¾ of a mile. I thought he was Mr Marshall until I came to part with him, and I spoke to him as if I had been speaking to Mr Marshall for I told him I had seen him and the 'missus' go in on the previous night. He told me he was nearly running over a man and his wife on the previous night, and that a drunken man had threatened to throw his wife and a lad with them into the cut, that he [the prisoner], had interfered and asked her why she did not go home with her husband and was told by her that she was afraid.

He had told her that he would go a long way to save a woman and offered to go with her. The prisoner said he asked the husband to go quietly with his wife, and the drunken man said 'Who are you?' to which the prisoner replied 'A man', that the drunken man struck him, that he knocked the drunken man down and that he met a policeman, to whom he recounted the tale.

While the prisoner was walking with me, Mr & Mrs Arnold[8] passed us and I asked the prisoner if he found my key, to leave it at The Plough, which is near Marshall's for I still thought it was Marshall to whom I was speaking. The prisoner said he did not know the people I met for he was a stranger, and I at once said I thought he was Mr Marshall as I had just seen him come out of the Marshall house. He said the family had gone on an excursion at half past 5 in the morning. He asked me if Mr Marshall kept any man.

Questions were put to the witness by the prisoner:

Prisoner: Now missus, did I say that I lighted upon a man at the canal bridge?

Witness: Yes you did.

Did I say that there was another man besides the drunken man there?

Wait a bit, let him [the clerk] write it down.

Didn't I say there was another man there?

No, you said you knocked a man down.

I said there were three other men there.

Not to me.

Yes I did.

You said that a man came up at the time.

Now mind your answer, for remember, my life depends upon this. Did I say there was another man there?

No you did not say so.

Might I have said to you without you hearing?

No you could not have said it without my hearing.

Didn't I say that there were two men with me?

No, you said when you knocked the man down, his wife laughed, but did not let her husband see her.

Didn't I say that she had a child with her besides a lad?

No.

Clerk said to prisoner: Have you any other questions?

Prisoner: No that will do, it doesn't matter.

Witness: It doesn't matter perhaps, but it is the truth.[9]

This last statement from Jones, saying that he had two men with him, was significant. He had cautioned Elizabeth Simpson that her answer could save him from the hangman's noose. She denied that he had mentioned him being with two men. Jones tried to lay the blame for the murders on two other men, who had then given him the clothes from the Marshalls' cottage. This was his attempt to introduce the 'men' into his evidence but this tactic fell at Simpson's flat denial.

John Smith[10] was called next. He was a minor but still significant witness whose evidence placed Jones in the area of the scene of the murder at about the right time, and also of being in possession of a large amount of cash as well as a watch:

John Smith, coal dealer living at Denham turnpike [about a mile from Marshall's home], said: My house is between Denham and Uxbridge and on Sunday morning, a little before 8 o'clock, I was sitting outside my house when the man I identified as the prisoner came by. He had said something to a woman tramp which attracted my attention. He was passing me but he looked back and was holding in his hand the purse produced [that found on the prisoner]. He said he had been to see his brother who had given him £20 and his sister who had given him a watch and chain, which he showed me.

The watch was at 10 to 8 and that produced [the one pawned] is like the one shown to me by the prisoner. There was a locket and chain. The prisoner said that he was without the price of a night's lodgings the night before and he should sell the watch, for he could not tell the time by it now he had it, and he should spend the money. He asked for £2 for the watch and chain, but I told him I had watches enough.

He then wanted me to go to Uxbridge drinking, saying he had plenty of money and he had for the purse, was 'pretty nigh full' and he had £19 19s 9d. I went up the road to fetch my horse that had strayed up towards Uxbridge, and the prisoners walked with me talking. He pulled some money out of his waistcoat and also out of his trouser pockets. I was talking to him 10 minutes. I never saw him before that morning.

Clerk to Prisoner: Any questions to the witness?

No sir.

Clerk to witness: Did you notice his clothing?

Yes, I noticed that his shoes were cracked.

The trousers, black coat and silk necktie belonging to the deceased man and which the prisoner then wore were produced, but the witness could not swear to these.[11]

John Smith was followed by Thirza Spooner (née Marshall), the sister of victim Emmanuel Marshall. She was a licensed victualler, who lived in The George public house in Iver.[12] She repeated the evidence she had given at the inquest regarding the property of Mary Ann Marshall. She was also questioned by the magistrates about Emmanuel Marshall's brother who had gone to Australia:

> Clerk: Did you ever see the prisoner before?
>
> Witness: Not to my knowledge.
>
> Clerk: Had Mr Marshall ever had men working for him?
>
> Witness: Yes sometimes.
>
> Bench: Have you ever seen Mr Marshall's brother who went to Australia?
>
> Witness: Yes.
>
> Bench: Does he have any resemblance to the prisoner?
>
> Witness: No, none whatever. He was taller and fairer than the prisoner.[13]

The final two witnesses at the committal hearing were James Wooderton and Harriett Willis, both residents of the Oxford Arms, the lodging house in Silver Street where Jones was detained by Supt Denham and Detective Toulman. Both gave vital evidence regarding the key to the Marshalls' house which potentially placed Jones at the murder scene. The *Bucks Herald* report gave details of Wooderton's evidence:

> I am a smith living in Reading. I was lodging at Silver Street, Reading on Tuesday 24 May. When I went to the kitchen of that house about half past 12, I saw the prisoner there. I never saw him before. The prisoner asked me if I would show him where the Gaol was, as he wanted to see someone, and he would stand some beer. Shortly after that he took a key from his pocket and offered it to a women in the room. She said 'I don't want the key. If I carry it, someone will think I want to rob their house'. No one would have the key.
>
> I said, 'Throw it into the cupboard along with the rags and bones.' I took the key from him and threw it in. He then took a pawn ticket out of his pocket. It was for a watch and guard for 15 shillings. He put the ticket in his pocket again. We then went out shortly afterwards, and when we got nearly to the bottom of the street, I said, 'Have you got 2d, because let us have a pint before we go further.' He said, 'Yes, I will

go and sell my coat for more.' He offered it for sale but no one would buy it. We had the beer and I offered to show him where the gaol was, and he said he would not go.

We then went into another public house where the prisoner took off his coat and waistcoat and a young woman mended a hole under the arm of his coat, while he handed the waistcoat to me, saying he would sell them for more money. I said this is the best way you are going to sell your coat. I took him to Mrs Lyons and she purchased the coat and waistcoat.

I then took him to the pawnbroker's shop, where he purchased a slop. We then returned to our lodgings. We were out from about half past 12 to about 5 o'clock. We had something to eat and he was taken into custody about half past 5.[14]

While Wooderton described the key being thrown into the cupboard, Willis found the key and handed it to the police. She also identified John Jones:

Harriett Willis,[15] an aged widow who described herself as working in the Oxford Arms tramp ward, said a man came into the home on a previous Tuesday, holding up the key produced, saying 'Who owns this?' but no one answered. She found the key among the bones and rags. She knew the key by some white paint on it.

The witness was told to look round and see if the man was present. She looked round the apartment and after regarding several faces she came to the prisoner when she exclaimed, 'I see him fast enough', whereat the prisoner laughed heartily.[16]

Another newspaper gave details of the key being handed to the police at Reading:

On Thursday a woman named Willis opened the cupboard and found the key and took it to the Reading Police Station, where Inspector Townsend has now got charge of it.[17]

As was mentioned in Chapter 21, Supt James Jervis produced the above key, together with the lock from the door of the Marshalls' house. The key fitted the lock, as reported by the *Bucks Herald*:

Supt Jervis of the Bucks Constabulary produced the lock of the front door of Marshalls' house, and the key fitted exactly. On the lock was some paint of the same colour as that on the key and it looked, the witness said, as if the lock had been painted with the key in it.[18]

Towards the end of proceedings the clerk of the court read out the charge. Once again the *Bucks Herald* reported what was said:

> The Clerk then read the charge against the prisoner, that of feloniously, with malice aforethought, killing and slaying the seven deceased persons, and after the usual warning being given, the prisoner was asked if he had anything to say in answer to the charge. The prisoner in a firm and rather determined voice replied 'Not a word sir.'

> The prisoner, waiting till after his answers had been recorded asked the magistrates, 'Can't I claim the 5 shillings and 9 pence which was taken off me?'

> No notice was taken of the question put by the prisoner and when he was asked to sign the statement and if he could write, he replied, 'No, I cannot', but notwithstanding that he afterwards wrote his name in a very good hand. The commitment for the trial at the next assizes was then made out, the prisoner was then removed to his cell.

> He shows the utmost hardihood. He has prepared a wild statement which is no secret, even though found with the murdered people's property upon him, yet he is innocent of the murders as the clothes were given to him by the REAL murderer, who he professes to describe minutely, even to the clothing worn by him, and who, he alleges, gave him £2, 10 shillings, and the clothes which he wore when arrested not to betray him.[19]

This murder was a very high profile case which the whole country would have been following in all the local and national newspapers. The authorities were determined that a trial would take place, and that there was not a chance of Jones avoiding justice by escaping or by taking his own life:

> Since his committal, the prisoner has been closely watched, night and day, and a strong man, belonging to Aylesbury has been engaged especially to sit in his cell at nights.

> We understand that he has expressed the intention of avoiding a trial at the assizes if he possibly can, but proper precautions have been taken to prevent his carrying his purpose to execution.[20]

Jones's case had now been committed to the Assizes court at Aylesbury. It would be another seven weeks before the trial began, as the prosecution prepared its case. Jones was not going anywhere. He had several weeks to prepare a defence. The fact that he had not given the names of the 'real murderers' was not helping. The prosecution had a large list of witnesses. So far, Jones had no one to call to speak up for him. His prospects of saving his skin were looking decidedly thin.

---

1   As a young man John Bramley-Moore (1800-1886) went out to Brazil to engage in commerce, and lived for several years in Rio de Janeiro. He married Seraphine Hibernia Pennell in Rio in 1830. On his return to England in 1835 he settled at Liverpool as a merchant. In 1841 Bramley-Moore was elected by the town council as an alderman, an office he held for the next 24 years. He was the Chairman of the Liverpool Docks. One of the docks was named after him. Bramley-Moore was elected Lord Mayor of Liverpool in November 1848. He was later returned to Parliament in 1854 as Member for Maldon. He lost his seat in 1859, but then represented Lincoln from 1862 to 1865. For many years Bramley-Moore was chairman of the Brazilian Chamber of Commerce in Liverpool, and lobbied the government to reduce the duties on coffee and sugar. In 1863 he made a speech in Parliament on the subject of the relations of England with Brazil, for which he was decorated with the Order of the Rose by the Emperor Pedro II of Brazil. In 1877 whilst visiting England, the Emperor paid him a visit at Gerrards Cross. He was a magistrate for Lancashire and later Buckinghamshire. He was chairman of the Bank of Egypt and a director of the London and North Western and North Staffordshire Railway. Some years before his retirement from business, Bramley-Moore went to live at Langley Lodge, Gerrards Cross, Buckinghamshire. He built a free reading-room in the town. In November 1886 he was staying in Brighton when he died suddenly in the arms of his faithful valet, Clark who had served him for 27 years. He passed away on 19 November 1886, aged 86, and was buried in Liverpool. Flags flew in Liverpool at half mast on his passing. (Obituary, *Bucks Herald*, 27 November 1886.)

2   *Derby Mercury*, 8 June 1870,

3   *The Times*, 2 June 1870.

4   Although I cannot be 100% certain, I suspect that Henry Salter was born in Cowley and lived in Wood End Green, Hayes. The 1871 Census for a male of this name appears there aged 38, and is described as a 'labourer in brickfield'. The same Henry Salter died in 1913 in Uxbridge.

5   'Rackety Cove'. Rackety is described in a Victorian Slang glossary as 'Illicit occupation or tricks'. Cove is slang for 'a man'. It could be deduced to mean that in the context of the conversation that Jones had with Henry Salter, that he was someone who made his living by criminal means.

6   *Bucks Herald*, 4 June 1870.

7   Ibid.

8   The Arnolds are likely to be William and Ann Arnold. He was a 60-year-old

gardener living at Denham Place Lodge, Denham at the time of the 1871 census. However, according to Elizabeth Simpson's inquest testimony she was overtaken by two men, one of whom was Thomas Arnold, the son of William who was actually sitting on the inquest jury at the time she gave her evidence. See *Daily News*, 25 May 1870..

9 *Bucks Herald*, 4 June 1870.

10 John Smith is shown in the 1871 Census as living on Uxbridge Road, Denham. He is shown as a coal dealer, aged 24 born, in Beadwell, Gloucestershire. His wife was listed as Sarah Smith.

11 *Bucks Herald*, 4 June 1870.

12 Probate record: £100 to Thirza Spooner of Iver, widow, aunt and guardian of Francis William Marshall.

13 *Bucks Herald*, 4 June 1870.

14 Ibid.

15 Harriett Willis is shown on the 1871 Census living at 19 Silver Street, Reading. She was listed as the head of the household, a widow aged 58 years, and a charwoman born in Swallowfield in Berkshire. The *Chelsea News & General Advertiser* of 4 June 1870 described her as 'an eccentric looking old lady'. She died on 4 April 1885. Her probate record showed her living at Hawk Court, Silver Street, Reading. She left £152.

16 *Bucks Herald*, 4 June 1870.

17 *Bucks Herald*, 28 May 1870.

18 *Bucks Herald*, 4 June 1870.

19 Ibid.

20 Ibid.

CHAPTER 29

Francis William Marshall – The Surviving Child

The Marshall family were all but wiped out on 22 May 1870 by John Jones. The only crumb of comfort was the survival of the Marshalls' only son, Francis William Marshall. He had been baptised in Denham Parish Church on 21 November 1868.[1] He was the youngest of four children, and at the time of the murders was a toddler of around 18-months-old. He was not at home in Denham at the time of the murders as he had been sent to stay with his grandfather, Loyal Sparke, in nearby Uxbridge.

It's not clear from the newspaper reports whether this was a short term arrangement, just for the wedding of Emmanuel Marshall's sister, or whether it had been going on longer than this. In any event he was safely away from Cheapside Lane on the fateful night.

It's hard to know how much he would have known about what went on regarding the murders. He had been robbed of both parents, his grandmother and three sisters in one night. Fortunately, he did not suffer the trauma of being sent to an orphanage following the murders as he was kept by the relatives who were already looking after him. It not known when he was told about the terrible events in Denham, or what emotional scars it left him with.

Emmanuel Marshall left £100 in his estate, which was passed to his sister Thirza Spooner (née Marshall).[2] She was the landlady at The George public house in Iver. Although Francis does not appear to ever have lived with his aunt Thirza, it may be that the money from the estate was passed to the family who looked after him. The probate record listed her as 'guardian' of Francis.

The *Tower Hamlets Independent* notes in its pages the following with regard to Francis:

> A Member of Parliament has, it is stated, intimated his intention of providing for the youngest child of the Marshall family, who was not at his parent's house at the time they were murdered.[3]

At first, Francis stayed at 63 Waterloo Road, Uxbridge[4] with his grandfather, Loyal Sparke, a 57-year-old machinist. Also living there was his aunt Mary Ann Sparke. In 1880, Mary Ann had married policeman Michael Pennifold in Uxbridge.[5]

By the 1881 census they were all living at 19 Rockingham Road, Uxbridge,[6] and by 1891 at 6 Montague Road, Uxbridge, with Michael Pennifold now listed as the head of the house.[7] He and Mary Ann had had two children, one of whom was the wonderfully-named Michael Loyal Sparker Pennifold. His grandparents lived in the house, but were by now in their seventies.

Sadly, Francis William Marshall did not appear in the 1891 census, as he had passed away five years earlier, on 29 December 1886, aged only 18 years.[8] The death certificate revealed that he died at home at Rockingham Road. He had been employed as a merchant's clerk. His uncle Michael Pennifold was the informant of the death. Interestingly, the death had been certified by Dr J.S. Ferris, the same man who had completed the post mortems on Francis's family in 1870.

The cause of death was recorded as 'Phthisis'. This name, together with another archaic name, 'consumption', have fallen out of use, as its modern title is tuberculosis, or TB. This condition was, and still is, a killer. Today it kills a few hundred people in the UK each year.[9] Around the world it is still a huge problem in developing counties.

In Victorian Britain the disease was one of the biggest causes of mortality. The infection was typically passed through the air when infected people coughed or sneezed on other people. Poverty and city dwelling were a large factor in one's chances of contracting the condition.

The disease attacked the lungs of the patient. Sufferers would have a wasting disease, and would develop a hacking cough as well as being consumed with fatigue. TB affected the rich and poor, the young and old. Many famous people fell victim to TB, including the likes of Robert Louis Stevenson, Keats, Shelley and D.H. Lawrence.

It's very sad that Francis Marshall should have survived the attentions of an axe-wielding murderer only to die from TB, a condition that is now treatable.

Francis's 'stepfather', PC Michael Pennifold, may have outlived Francis but he also died at a young age, passing away at 51 in Uxbridge in 1900.[10] PC Pennifold had joined the Metropolitan Police on 14 October 1872 as warrant number 56028,[11] and had been posted to X Division. He retired in October 1897.[12]

---

1 Denham Old Parish Record, Baptism no. 406. 21 November 1868.

2 Probate Record, 7 June 1871.

3 *Tower Hamlets Independent*, 4 June 1870.

4 1871 Census.

5 Parish Register for Marriages, 1880.

6 1881 Census.

7 1891 Census.

8 Death certificate. Registered on 30 December 1886 at Hillingdon.

9 Public Health England: Tuberculosis in the UK, 2014 report.

10 Death Register.

11 Metropolitan Police Attestation Ledgers (National Archives: MEPO 4/352).

12 Metropolitan Police Leavers Book (National Archives: MEPO 4/340).

CHAPTER 30

The Trial Begins
at Aylesbury Assizes

The Buckinghamshire Summer Assizes were opened on Wednesday 20 July 1870 by the Hon. Sir William Fry Channell.[1]

Twelve cases had been put together for the Assize to consider. They included charges of wounding, arson, housebreaking, false pretences and attempted murder. John Jones was number 6 on the list. His case was going to be the trial of the year, if not the decade. No one had been tried and convicted of seven homicides at one time before.

The first business was to empanel a Grand Jury[2] and a Foreman.[3]

The job of the Grand Jury was to determine whether there was a case to answer against each prisoner. In order for cases to proceed to trial, the Grand Jury had to return a bill of indictment, i.e. a true bill. This was effectively them checking to ensure that there was sufficient evidence to justify prosecuting the accused.

In delivering the Charge to the Grand Jury, Baron Channell spoke particularly about the Jones case:

> There is one crime of great magnitude, which will require your attention, but which, I think, will not make any considerable demand on your time. It is the case of the man Jones, charged with the wilful murder of Emmanuel Marshall, and, I am sorry to say, of six other persons, some older, some younger. Now, that a brutal murder was

Aylesbury Assize Court in the town's Market Square

committed, will admit of no doubt in your minds.

Plunder seems to have been the object.[4]

The judge then drew the Grand Jury's attention to several points they needed to consider:

1.   Emmanuel Marshall could not have murdered the family and then have killed himself.

2.   Jones was discovered wearing the boots of the victim, Emmanuel Marshall.

3.   When apprehended, Jones told Dunham before anything had been said to him 'I have never murdered anyone'.

4.   The clothing found at the murder scene belonged to Jones.

5.   A watch and chain were stolen. Jones pawned a watch and chain.

6.   A key which Jones had tried to get rid of in Reading was found to fit the Marshalls' door.

7.   Jones was seen in the vicinity of the murders at the time the crime occurred.

8.   He was seen by a neighbour coming out of the Marshalls' house, saying the family had gone on holiday by the early train.

He continued:

Left: Acton Tindal, Clerk of the Court, and Right: Judge Baron Channell

If all or the chief of the circumstances are made out to your satisfaction, your object will not be to enquire as to the mode in which the murder was committed – of which there is no doubt – but whether there is evidence to warrant you in putting the prisoner on trial for the murder. If these circumstances are made out, or the principal of them, there can be no difficulty on your parts in returning a true bill.[5]

His Lordship then remitted the Grand Jury to their duties.

*

It's quite strange for the modern reader to comprehend, but on Wednesday, 20 July, on the day that the Assize began, Jones had not organised a defence and he had no legal representation, a situation which is unthinkable in today's modern legal framework. The *Bucks Herald* reported events on the Wednesday in relation to Jones's wishes about being represented:

Jones was brought into court and placed in the dock. The learned baron [i.e. Mr Justice Channell], addressing him, said, 'John Jones, you are not sent for your trial now; but you are aware that you have been committed for trial on a charge of wilful murder by a verdict of the coroner's jury, and the depositions, which are relied upon to substantiate the charge, are now before the Grand Jury. I wish to know if you have any counsel?'

Jones - No Sir.

Judge - You are not bound to have the assistance of counsel, but if you wish it, you will get it. Do you desire to have counsel?

Jones – Yes, Sir.

Judge – Do you wish to be defended by any counsel in particular?

Jones – No, Sir.

Judge – So you leave it to the court, to select counsel for you?

Jones – Yes, Sir.

Judge – Then I will see that the papers shall be put in the hands of some learned counsel to defend you. I sent for you to know your wishes, so if you desire to be defended by counsel it would not be well for the necessary papers to be put in his hands at the last moment. I will put the papers into the hands of counsel at once, in order that he may look over them, and prepare himself for your defence.

Jones – Thank you, Sir

Baron Channell first offered the case to Mr George Lathom Browne, but he declined it. He then offered it to Dr Abdy, recently appointed Recorder of Bedford, by whom it was accepted.

A copy of the depositions were supplied to Mr Abdy during the course of the day.[6]

It therefore transpired that the defence barrister was given less than 48 hours in order to take instruction from his client, read the statements and prepare a defence. It was a tall order. There appears to be no record of what was said between Dr Abdy and his client. John Thomas Abdy[7] was a very able barrister, but he must have realised that trying to successfully defend John Jones was going to be beyond even his capabilities.

On Thursday the Grand Jury returned a true bill of seven counts of murder against John Jones.[8]

*

On Friday 22 July, Jones was brought back to the Assize Court in Aylesbury town square to face trial for the wilful murder of the Marshall family. A large crowd had gathered outside the Court House. The *Berkshire Chronicle* described them as a mob:

Barricades were set up at the court house approaches; Streets in front of the court was thronged with an eager and excited mob, and a large force of the County Constabulary were placed in front of it to preserve order.[9]

The *Morning Post* recounted Jones's arrival at court:

The prisoner arrived at the courthouse in the prison van from the county prison, and on being recognised by the crowd who thronged the approaches to the building, was greeted with loud groans.[10]

The jeering crowds must have given Jones a feeling of foreboding. It was if he had been found guilty before the trial had begun.

The court building appears to have been in a chaotic state as spectators clambered for space in the courtroom:

So great was the application for admission to hear the proceedings, that it was necessary to admit by order of the High Sherriff. Sides of the dock were provided with seats for reporters. Doors of the court opened at 9am and such a rush was made by the parties who had long assembled outside as was never seen on any similar occasion.

Barriers were placed on the staircase and these were jealously guarded by policemen. Every place was crammed with a dense mass of people and the hall outside the court house was also thronged. The heat was very intense, which towards the close of the trial became almost insupportable.[11]

The *Oban Times and Advertiser* added a few colourful details:

The court, which is a small and old-fashioned building, was crowded, though the admission of the public was by ticket. The galleries were exclusively occupied by ladies.[12]

Mr Justice Channell entered the court a little after 9 o'clock, followed shortly by the prisoner, who was placed in the dock.

Jones stepped to the front, and folding his arms, assumed a determined and resolute air.

The prisoner was charged with seven separate indictments, namely with the murders (of the seven Marshalls), at Denham on 22 May last. To each indictment he pleaded not guilty. The charge for the murder of Emmanuel Marshall was proceeded with. Before the proceeding commenced, his lordship ordered the prisoner to be accommodated in a chair in the dock.[13]

At the start of proceedings the Crown was ready to prove its case against John Jones. They had a host of witnesses and a large number of exhibits to persuade the jury of the defendant's guilt. The Crown had two eminent barristers, Mr Peter Frederick O'Malley[14] and Mr William James Metcalfe,[15] to prosecute the case.[16] By request of the court, Jones was defended by Dr Abdy and Mr J.W. Cooper.[17] Thomas Dunham was also prepared, despite the distraction of having to testify at the Assizes the day before in an unrelated arson case.[18] He had all the witnesses ready, and the trial was going to produce much damning evidence to prove Jones's guilt.

Mr O'Malley began by outlining the case for the prosecution:

> In May, Marshall lived at a place called Cheapside in the village of Denham, about two miles from Uxbridge. The house is a solitary place, the nearest house being 100 yards from it, and there are two or three other houses near, in one of which lives a woman called Simpson.

> Emmanuel Marshall, a blacksmith by trade, lived in that house with his family, and he was in the habit of occasionally employing tramping smiths when he had pressure of business. The prisoner Jones is by trade a blacksmith, travelling round the country looking for work. The Marshalls were seen alive on the Saturday evening, but nothing seems to have attracted notice until the Monday evening. There were wild rumours that Marshall killed his family then killed himself. The position of the body and the wounds proved that he could not have killed himself.[19]

Before calling his first witness, Mr O'Malley told the jury the main thrusts of the evidence that would go to prove that John Jones was the murderer of the Marshall family:

> 1.   There was no doubt that the inmates of the house were savagely and barbarously murdered. Their heads were beaten in or smashed by a very heavy instrument.

> 2.   The clothing found at the scene of the murders was identified as belonging to John Jones.

> 3.   At 3am Jones had been seen by a policeman near the scene of the crime wearing the same clothing that he identified as being found at the murder scene.

> 4.   On his return to the lodgings in Uxbridge, Coombes and Balham

saw him in a different suit of clothes than what he arrived in.

5.   He later had possession of a watch and chain and a locket that he offered for sale.

6.   The watch sold belonged to the murdered man.

7.   Jones was found in possession of a pistol in his pocket which was one of a pair belonging to Emmanuel Marshall, the other being found in the cottage and would be produced.[20]

O'Malley then told the jury it was their duty to find Jones guilty as after hearing the evidence they would have no doubt as to his guilt:

> You will take all the facts which will be laid before you into your attentive consideration, and while you care that justice shall be done to the prisoner, it will also be your duty to see that a murderer does not go unpunished, and I think that when you have heard the evidence you cannot be of any other opinion that the prisoner is the man who committed these savage and atrocious murders. He will be defended by counsel, but after you have heard the evidence, I do not think you will have any doubt that the prisoner is the man who committed the murders.[21]

There seemed little doubt in the mind of the prosecutor, as well as the newspapers generally, that Jones was the murderer; by the time the day was out, the court would decide whether this was to be the case. It was going to be a highly charged and exciting day.

---

1   Sir William Fry Channell (1804–1873), judge, was born at 22 East Lane, Bermondsey, on 31 August 1804. His family came from Devon and had naval connections. His father, Pike Channell, was an officer under Admiral Nelson at Copenhagen. On leaving the navy he became a merchant and lived at Peckham. His mother was Mary, stepdaughter of William Fry. Channell's only education was at private schools, including the Reverend Martin Ready's school at Peckham, and he often complained about his lack of formal education. He remedied the defect by private studies, and had a good knowledge of the English classics. Channell was articled to a solicitor called Tustin. He was called to the Bar in the Easter term of 1827 and had a busy practice, both at the Surrey sessions and on the home circuit. In 1834 he married Martha Hawkes, the couple having a son, Arthur Mosely Channell, who would also become a barrister of the Inner Temple. In 1856 Channell acted as Commissioner of Assize on the Spring and Summer Circuits and Winter Gaol Delivery. On 12 February 1857 he was appointed by Lord Chancellor Cranworth to succeed Baron Alderson in the Court of Exchequer and was knighted. A Conservative, in 1852

he issued an election address at Beverley but withdrew on finding how corrupt the borough was. Channell remained on the bench until January 1873 when severe asthma prevented him from going on circuit. He died on 26 February 1873 at his home at 2 Clarendon Place, Hyde Park, London. As a judge, Channell was conscientious, careful and learned, and very harsh in sentencing (*Oxford Dictionary of National Biography*).

2   They were: Caldon George Du Pre , John Hale, Edward Lowndes, James Trevor Sr, Thomas Chapman, William Duncan, Walter Caulfield Pratt, Lawrence Hall, Henry Rudyerd, Richard Howard Vyse, Charles Pole Stuart, Richard Purefoye Fitzgerald, S.W Jenney, R. Rose, J. Carson, E.C.S. Thompson, C. Morrell, J.E. McConnell, R.H. Hussey, G. Jackson, Joseph Bailey and Joseph Lowndes. (List of jurors reported in the *Bucks Herald*, 23 July 1870.)

3   The foreman was Caldon George Du Pre, who served as MP for Buckinghamshire from 1839 to 1873. Caldon G. Du Pre (1803–1886) was the son of James Du Pré of Wilton Park, Beaconsfield. He was an officer in the 1st Life Guards and became a JP and Deputy Lieutenant for Buckinghamshire. His 'town address' was 40 Portland Place, London. The 1861 Census lists him as a 58-year-old magistrate and landed proprietor, born in St Georges, Middlesex. He was living with his father James. There were 12 servants 'living in' at the time of the census. He was a very wealthy man. Probate record shows Du Pre as Late of Wilton Park, Beaconsfield, Bucks, who died on 7 October 1886 at 3 St Albans Place, Haymarket. He left £356,544 in his will.

4   *Bucks Herald*, 23 July 1870.

5   Ibid.

6   Ibid.

7   John Thomas Abdy LL.D was the son of Lieutenant-Colonel James Abdy. He was born in Fort St George, Madras, India on 5 July 1822. He was educated at the Proprietary School, Kensington and later Trinity Hall, Cambridge, where he graduated as Senior in the Civil Law in 1844. In January 1850 he was called to the Bar by the Inner Temple. In 1854 he was appointed Regius Professor of the Civil Law at University of Cambridge, holding that office until 1873. He was Lecturer on Law at Gresham College, London, and a magistrate for Hertfordshire and for the borough of Cambridge. In 1870 he was appointed Recorder of Bedford, and the following year was promoted to be County Court Judge of Circuit No. 88. The year after the Denham Murder trial he was living with his wife Marian and their family at The Grange, Welwyn, Hertfordshire. He was then aged 48 and was listed as a barrister at law and judge. He died in Rottingdean, Sussex in 1899, when his address was given as 69 Cornwall Gardens, South Kensington. He left £11,416 in his will.

8   *Maidstone Telegraph & West Kent Messenger*, 23 July 1870.

9   *Berkshire Chronicle*, 23 July 1870.

10 *Morning Post*, 23 July 1870.

11 *Bucks Herald*, 23 July 1870.

12 *Oban Times and Advertiser*, 30 July 1870.

13 *Morning Post,* 23 July 1870.

14 Peter Frederick O'Malley QC (1804-74) was born in Ireland and educated at Trinity College, Dublin. He was called to the Bar in 1834 and became a Queen's Counsel in 1850. In 1858 he succeeded to the leadership of the Norfolk Circuit, and was appointed to the Recordership of Norwich the following year. He married Emily Rodwell in 1839; their eldest son Edward Loughlin also followed a career in law, becoming Attorney General of Jamaica in 1876. In later years O'Malley twice ran unsuccessfully as a Conservative candidate for the borough of Finsbury. In 1874 he died suddenly from heart disease at his home in Lowndes Street, London, sitting by his fireside having just returned home from a case. In his will he left £25,000 to his wife, beside whom he is buried in Holbrook, Suffolk. His obituary praised his skills as an advocate, remarking on 'the fluency of his oratory and the earnestness and zeal with which he supported the interests of his clients.' (See *Bury and Norwich Post*, 15 December 1874; *Norwich Mercury,* 23 December 1874.)

15 William James Metcalfe QC (1818-1892) was born in 1818 at Fowlmere, Cambridgeshire, son of William Metcalfe, clerk of holy orders. He was educated at St Johns College, Cambridge. He obtained a B.A in 1842 and an M.A in 1845. He was called to the bar in 1845 at Middle Temple, London. Between 1866 and 1874 he was the Recorder of Ipswich. He then took over as Recorder of Norwich in 1874 following the death of Peter Frederick O'Malley (source, page 399 *Alumni Cantabrigienses*). Both Metcalfe and O'Malley prosecuted the Denham Murderer. In 1878 he was made a Queen's Counsel. Between 1879 and 1892 he was Judge of County Courts, Bristol. Metcalfe was married 3 times. On 13 May 1848 he wed Georgiana Emily Austin at St George the Martyr in Middlesex. He gave his occupation as 'esquire' and his address as 10 Kings Bench Walk on the wedding certificate. Georgiana died in 1855 and he married again on 22 November 1859 at Holy Trinity, Brompton, to Agnes Mary Vaughan. His occupation was given as barrister and his abode as Inner Temple on the wedding certificate. Agnes died on 26 March 1874 at Dover Street, London, aged 38. His final marriage was to Evelyn Maud Goodwin in Brighton in 1878. The 1881 census showed that William was living, aged 62, at 107 Whiteboys Road, Westbury on Trym with his 24 year old wife Evelyn (Census RG11/2502, schedule 101, page 9). His residence at the time of his death was at 8 Manilla Road, Clifton (Census RG12/1969, schedule 49, page 10). William died in the robing room at the Guildhall Court, Bristol, on 8 December 1892 of heart disease. He was buried at the Arno Vale Cemetery in Clifton with a huge attendance of people including the Mayor of Bristol in his stage coach and many members of the legal profession. One floral tribute from the High Bailiffs office was marked 'In remembrance of our beloved Judge.' William and Evelyn's son Frederick Evelyn Metcalfe went on to make a name for himself in the legal profession. He later set up E. F. Metcalfe and Company, Solicitors of 73 Queen Square, Bristol. Metcalfe Solicitors still exists in Bristol at 46 Queen Square.

16 The barristers were earning additional fees by conducting other cases at the Assize before the main event of the Crown v Jones. They were on opposing sides in the private case of Henry Wyatt v Mr James Pettit. Mr Metcalfe was successful in winning the case for the plaintiff. In another private action, that of Simons v

Barry, Mr O'Malley acted for the defendant. This case was settled out of court. In a final private case of Coote v Merry, Mr O'Malley successfully defended his client in a case over a disputed £98. (Details reported in the *Bucks Herald*, 23 July 1870.)

17 William Cooper (1811–1877) was a successful barrister who worked with all of the other 'Denham lawyers' over the years. He regularly appeared with or against Mr Abdy, Metcalfe and O'Malley in prosecuting or defending clients. Two cases of interest in which he collaborated with Mr Abdy were high profile murder trials. In August 1869 at Norwich Assize they unsuccessfully prosecuted Mrs Mary Ann Langford for murdering her husband and child. The case was known as the 'Lynn Poisoner' (*Bedfordshire Times*, 17 August 1869). In another unsuccessful prosecution, Martha Hughes was acquitted of manslaughter of her child in Luton at Bedford Assize in March 1865 (*Bedfordshire Mercury*, 18 March 1865). Born at Norwich, he attended Oxford University where he obtained a B.A. He was then called to the Bar at Lincolns Inn in 1831. He married Anna Marsh at Erpingham, Norfolk on 15 February 1832. During his career, he was the senior barrister practising at the Middlesex Sessions (*Ipswich Journal*, 22 September 1877). He also went on the Norfolk Circuit, practised at the Central Criminal Court and was standing counsel to the Treasury and the Great Northern Railway Company. His career also included appointments as a Commissioner in bankruptcy and Recorder of Ipswich where he succeeded William Metcalfe. His brother, Carlos Cooper esquire, Judge, became the Recorder of Thetford and the Norfolk Court of Record. William lived at 10 Bernard Street and 98 Wimpole Street, Bloomsbury, London (1861 Census, RG9/166, schedule 96, page 30, and 1871 Census, RG10/339, schedule 125, page 30). He was also a writer of plays and poems. Cooper died on 17 September 1877 at his home at 25 Great Russell Street, London, aged 66. When his probate record was listed he left £1,000 to his widow Anna (Probate London 11 January 1878, page 314). Following his death, Judge P.H. Edlin addressed the Middlesex Sessions with words about William Cooper. He described his qualities thus; kindly; an honourable character; without pretensions to eloquence; effective speaker; shrewd; and that he would never condescend to give fictitious colour to the facts in order to obscure the truth.

His son Alfred Cooper (1839–1908) became an eminent surgeon. He was a consulting surgeon in west London and to St. Marks Hospital and among his clients was Edward, Prince of Wales. Later in his career his made friends with many noble people. Through his friendship with the Duke of Hamilton he was introduced to the Duke of Edinburgh. When the Duke became Duke of Saxe-Coburg of Gotha he appointed Cooper as his Surgeon in Ordinary. In 1874 he was present at the marriage of the Duke in St. Petersburg, as medical attendant to the then Prince of Wales, the present Majesty. He was later knighted by King Edward VII. Through his connections with the Russian Court, he received from the Czar the honour of knighthood of the Russian Order of St. Stanislas (source: www.findagrave.com/memorial/43757078).

18 On 21 July, the day before Jones's trial, he had also been a witness in a case of arson which had taken place a month before the massacre of the Marshall family. He was therefore called to give evidence to the Aylesbury Assize in the

prosecution of a 26-year-old pipe maker called George Newbury, who had been charged with setting fire to a stack of oats valued at £120 belonging to Mr John Goodwin Ive of Langley Marish. Giving evidence to Baron Channell, Dunham told the court that he had spoken to George Newbury at Slough Police Station, and was told that he 'wished all the ricks in the neighbourhood had gone up in smoke, with the farmers in the midst of them.' He added that they would not give him work when he asked for some. Dunham's testimony helped the case, as Newbury was found guilty and was sentenced to seven years' penal servitude. It's hard to know how much thought Dunham gave to this case as he waited patiently for the main event to start on the Friday. (Details of case reported in the *Bucks Herald*, 23 July 1870.)

19 *Bucks Herald*, 23 July 1870.

20 Ibid.

21 Ibid.

CHAPTER 31

The Evidence

The opening submission having been given, Mr O'Malley called his first witness, Superintendent Thomas Dunham of the Buckinghamshire Constabulary. Dunham must have been happy that the day of the trial had finally arrived. He would have lived and breathed this case for two months. This day was the culmination of a lot of determined police work.

It must also have been emotional for him. He had been at the scene of this terrible crime. He had seen the effects of the axe and the sledgehammer on the Marshall family members, both young and old. He would have felt the indignation of discovering Jones in Reading still wearing the boots of the victim. Also, here was a man who had been armed, who could in other circumstances have threatened Dunham's life by shooting him with Marshall's pistol. This was a case that Dunham had to win.

Supt Dunham gave his evidence, beginning with his visiting the scene and finding the battered bodies. He stated that the women were all dressed in their nightclothes and that their beds had all been slept in. All the victims had received terrible injuries to their heads. There were signs of a great disturbance in the outer smithy part of the house. Emmanuel Marshall had put up a terrible struggle. He had been dragged along the floor. He was also wearing clean stockings with not a trace of grit on them, concluding that his boots had been removed after death.

Dunham told the court that the bedroom used by Mr and Mrs Marshall was next to the smithy, and that any noise from the workshop could easily be heard in that bedroom.

He went on to describe the clothing found in the room, which included a pair of cord trousers which had been repaired on the seat and on one of the knees with blue cloth, making them highly memorable. The boots found left behind were saturated with blood.

The bedroom was in great disorder. Boxes had been forced open and the watch stand was empty. He then gave evidence of obtaining the watch that he produced to the court from the pawnbroker, James Weston. Charles Coombes had come up to him in the street, and as a result of what he told him they travelled to Reading, to the Oxford Arms.

Dunham then related evidence of the arrest at 5pm, whereby Jones had said before anyone had said anything to him, 'I have never killed man, woman nor child, but I know who did'. The superintendent pointed out that the news of the murder had not reached Reading at this point.

Cross-examined by Dr Abdy, Dunham added a further very significant comment made by Jones, though he could not be sure of the exact wording used by the prisoner. He told His Honour, 'I think he said, 'I stood by when the murder was committed'. This is my impression, but I will not swear that he said it.'

This comment is hugely frustrating for the modern reader. Was Jones saying he was in the house at the time the murders were committed? If he was in the house when the family had been killed, this would have been enough to have made him part of the offence. Any modern detective would have interviewed Jones using a video camera in an interview room with his solicitor present. He would have made contemporaneous notes of the interview, and he would have asked Jones to clarify what he meant.

In none of the reports of the investigation in the newspapers or elsewhere do we ever see any police questions being put to Jones about the identity of the 'real murderers'. He does not appear to have been interrogated on the facts in any organised or methodical way.

The Police and Criminal Evidence Act of 1984 (PACE) regulates the way modern police forces gather evidence. It deals with all manner of procedural situations, as well as regulating interviews and dealing with the identification of suspects. In 1870, PACE was still over a century away from appearing on the statute books, so suspects were dealt with in a way that is alien to the modern police officer.

What is frustrating about this case is that we never hear any 'explanation' from Jones. What was he doing in Denham? Had he worked for Marshall? Who was his 'brother' that he allegedly obtained the fine clothing from? Why did he flee from Uxbridge? There were so many searching questions that could have been asked of him, especially as the weight of circumstantial evidence against him was so huge.

Apart from the lack of questioning at the police station, Jones did not enter the witness box at the trial in Aylesbury. Had he done so we would surely have had a much clearer picture of his version of events.

What the modern reader may not know is that throughout the 19th century, defendants in criminal cases were not allowed to give evidence in their own defence. Indeed it was only after the passing of the Prisoners' Counsel Act in 1836 that defendants were given the right to be fully defended by a lawyer. In 1870, John Jones had the right to be defended by counsel, but no right to enter the witness box as a competent witness. This appears to us today as an absurd situation but in the 19th century it was the norm. It amounted to a huge infringement of the prisoner's capability of defending himself. It meant that Jones was never able to tell the court his side of the story.[1]

Next to give evidence was the first police officer on the scene of the murder, PC Charles Trevener, who went to the cottage and found Charles Alderman there. He locked the door and left a man named West outside.[2] He told the court that he found the bodies as well as the sledgehammer, axe and broken poker, which he produced to the

173

court. He then stated that he had seen Jones in Denham at 3.00 am on the Sunday morning (around the time that the family had been murdered). He had particularly noticed the glass buttons on Jones's coat.

Elizabeth Simpson was the next witness. Her home was 100 yards from the Marshall house and she had seen Jones coming out of the property. She said he was respectably dressed. On asking him about leaving their house, Jones told her: 'The man at that house and his wife, his mother and his children are all gone for a holiday.' Mrs Simpson continued: 'I said I dare say they are gone to London, and he said I dare say there are. The man I was talking to was a man with a dark beard. I have since seen that man, to the best of my knowledge at the prison. I went to see him in prison with Mr Dunham and PC Trevener.'

A fresh witness, 26-year-old agricultural labourer Charles Alderman,[3] told the court how he broke open the door of the Marshalls' house. The ever-detailed *Bucks Herald* reported the following:

> On 23 May at 7pm he went to the house of Emmanuel Marshall, seeing no one about, he broke open the door. He saw the dead bodies on the floor. He sent for PC Trevener. Nothing was touched till he came.[4]

A lot of the witnesses who had given evidence earlier at the Magistrates' and Coroner's hearings again gave their sworn testimony at the trial. The evidence given was usually the same as what they had already said previously, so does not bear repeating here. With some witnesses, however, certain points were elaborated on.

Charles Coombes, who was instrumental in the arrest of Jones, gave his evidence to the court. He was followed into the witness box by the keeper of the lodging house in Uxbridge where Jones had stayed. Charlotte Balham of the Bell Yard told the court that he could not pay for his lodgings:

> I keep a lodging house in Uxbridge. He came to me on 22 May and asked for lodging. I went to the kitchen later and asked for the money. Other lodgers gave me the money. He said 'You won't have anything

off me today mother.' He said he was going to see his brother that night.

Next day he brought a beef steak and asked me to make a pudding for his breakfast.

On Monday evening I told him about the murders and he said it was a very shocking thing. He later asked for the carpet bag he had left in my possession and told me that he was going away for 2-3 weeks. The prisoner has lodged with me several times and his conduct has always been very well in the house.[5]

Sarah Alderman told the court that Jones had paid for a beer with money taken out of the same purse that had been produced in the court. The other witnesses, whose evidence we have heard before, were then examined by the court. John Smith told the court that he had seen Jones on the road, and that he showed him a lot of money. He said that his brother had given him £20. He was also in possession of a watch and chain.

Elizabeth Selwood was reported as having said the following:

Said she was in the prisoner's company the Sunday before she heard of the murders at Denham, and she changed a sovereign for him. He took the money out of a purse like the one produced [in court]. He had a watch and chain with him; the chain was like the one produced. He had with him a pistol, also like that produced. He passed the Sunday with her, and left at half past six o'clock on the Monday morning.[6]

Other witnesses gave their evidence. Henry Salter, the carman who gave Jones a lift on his cart, recognised the clothing found at the murder scene as that being worn by his passenger. James Weston, the assistant pawnbroker, told the court that he bought the watch and chain offered by the prisoner which he had subsequently given to the police. He paid him 15 shillings. Jones had identified himself as George Wilson of Reading.

James Wooderton stated that he had seen Jones disposing of the key in Reading, which later proved to be the door key at the murder scene. He was also present when Jones sold a coat and waistcoat to Mrs Lyons, who then appeared to confirm that she had bought the clothing for 4 shillings and sixpence.

Harriett Willis from the Oxford Arms stated that she had found the key in a cupboard in the premises. Supt James Jervis produced to the court the lock on the door of the Marshalls' house, as well as the key which fitted it.

Mary Ann Sparke, sister of Emmanuel Marshall, identified the shirt, collar and trousers which had belonged to her brother and were found being worn by the prisoner. She also identified the knife found on him as belonging to her brother as well. She added that she had found at the house one of the pair of pistols belonging to Emmanuel Marshall; the one produced in court which had been found on the prisoner was identical.

Thirza Spooner told the court that the watch produced by the police was similar to one owned by Marshall, although she could not swear to it. She could, however, identify the chain.

Daniel Love, prison warder, identified the jacket produced in court which had been found at the murder scene.

Dr Ferris told the court that he had examined the bodies 40 hours after death and gave particulars of the injuries. These were consistent with having been struck with the weapons found at the scene.

---

1   The issue of prisoners giving evidence at their own trials was only finally resolved by the passing of The Criminal Evidence Act, 1898. This finally allowed defendants to enter the witness box and made trials fairer to both the defence as well as the prosecution. (Ronald D. Noble, *The Struggle to Make the Accused Competent in England and in Canada*, 1970).

2   This man was almost certainly 53 year old wheelwright David West, a neighbour of Mr Marshall who lived in Cheapside Lane (1871 Census, reference RG10/1398, schedule 133, page 23).

3   Charles Alderman was born in Chalfont St Giles, Bucks. He lived at Yew Tree Cottage, Denham, at about the time of the murders. He had married Emma Turner on 19 October 1862 in Denham and the couple had three daughters before Emma tragically died on 8 August 1869. Charles is listed in the 1871 Census as a 27-year-old Agricultural Labourer. He married Ann Cooper on 31 July 1887.

4   *Bucks Herald*, 23 July 1870.

5   Ibid.

6   Ibid.

CHAPTER 32

Summing Up and Verdict

Once the final prosecution witness had left the witness box, no one was called by Dr Abdy to give evidence in defence of John Jones. Not even Jones himself. You may think it strange that a man who was being tried for seven terrible murders and denying his guilt at the Assize would have wanted to have called some witnesses.

The principle of English criminal law is that of being innocent until proved guilty. The prosecution had to prove its case. The jury had to be sure that he was guilty in order to bring in that verdict. Dr Abdy only needed to put a doubt in the Jury's mind to have the case dismissed.

It was obvious from the Inquest and the earlier magistrates' hearings that the weight of evidence against Jones was massive. Although no witnesses were produced to say that they saw him commit the murder, all the other evidence fitted together like a jigsaw to give the court an understanding of what had occurred.

One wonders what Dr Abdy had concluded when he was given the brief. In his heart he must have known that it was a hopeless case. He does not seem to have tried very hard to break the prosecution case. None of the questions to any of the prosecution witnesses seem particularly searching. All the witnesses seem to have been given an easy ride, which is not generally the case in criminal trials.

As we have seen, in 1870 defendants were not allowed to give evidence in their own defence Newspaper reports have alluded to Jones preparing a statement of fact, but at no time did he ever verbally explain his evidence in any courtroom. Today we can only speculate on the contents of any such evidence.

We can be certain, though, that if Jones had given live evidence at his trial he would have been severely tested by Mr O'Malley, who would surely have cross-examined him on his role in the murder and the existence of the man or men who he claimed had actually carried out the murders.

Mr O'Malley summed up for the prosecution, followed by Dr Abdy's submission on behalf of the defendant. Dr Abdy did what he could for his client, even if his arguments for Jones's innocence were hardly compelling. The *Bucks Herald* gave details of both sets of summing up:

> Mr O'Malley summed up the case against the prisoner. He dwelt upon the fact of the prisoner being a smith, and acquainted with the habits of Marshall, who was also a smith. His theory was that Marshall was met at the door of the smithy and murdered, and that he was afterwards dragged to the side of the anvil and covered up there. His wife, hearing a noise, runs down and sees the murderer covered with blood and is attacked by him and murdered also. Then, seized with desperation and excited by such scenes, he murdered the children and all the household one after the other, as they come down.

> He then traced the nature of the evidence, which he accumulated with crushing weight against the prisoner. There was no doubt in the matter; the jury should do their duty to their country and to God and return a verdict of guilty.

> Mr Abdy addressed the jury for the defence. He made a long and able speech. Points were raised that the prisoner was not seen going in or out of the house. Marshall was found dressed for the day and did not come down in a hurry. The coolness with which he went about mingling with persons in the neighbourhood was incompatible with guilt.[1]

After the advocates had returned to their seats, Baron Channell finally gave His Honour's observations to the jury. Sadly, the judge apparently did not do a good job in projecting his voice as many complained that he was hard to hear. The *Bucks Herald* again reported the details:

> Judge Baron Channell commenced his summing up at 4.15pm and spoke for three quarters of an hour.. He pointed out the most salient points in the evidence. Many observations were inaudible.
>
> The jury were only two minutes in consultation. When they had taken their seats, the Clerk, addressing the foreman, asked him if they were all agreed on a verdict.
>
> Clerk: Do you find the prisoner at the bar, guilty or not guilty?
>
> Foreman: Guilty.
>
> Clerk: And is that the verdict of you all?
>
> Foreman: Yes.
>
> The Clerk then told the prisoner he had been found guilty by due course of law of the charge of wilful murder, and asked him if he had anything to say why sentence of death should not be pronounced upon him. The prisoner replied — 'Nothing'.
>
> Judge Baron Channell assumed the black cap and proceeded to pronounce sentence upon him.
>
> 'John Jones, you have been convicted after a very lengthy and patient trial of the very serious offence charged against you on this indictment. Although the indictment of wilfully murdering Emmanuel Marshall is the only indictment which has been tried against you, there is no reason to doubt from the evidence that you have been guilty of wholesale murder.
>
> The evidence which has been produced is to my mind quite satisfactory to show that you were the perpetrator of these murders. Although I suggested to the jury any points which may possibly have admitted to doubt, yet the short time which they took to come to a conclusion shows that the evidence was quite as satisfactory to them as it was to me.
>
> I hope the Lord will be more merciful to you than you have been to your victims.
>
> You will have the services and attention of the chaplain of the gaol between this and the time of your execution, and the assistance of any other minister of religion who you may require.
>
> I trust you will make the best use of the time which is left to you in this world and that you will endeavour to obtain forgiveness and pardon for the offence which you have committed. I have only now to pronounce the sentence of the court upon you, which is that you be taken from here to the place from whence you came, that you then be hanged by the neck within the walls of the prison, and that you be

buried within its precincts and may the Lord have mercy upon your soul.'

Prisoner (with a wave of the hand) said — 'Thank you my Lord'.

Some of the audience hissed and hooted the prisoner. He looked up calmly and smiled. He attempted to speak to the witness Balham with whom he lodged but was taken below.

His lordship called up Supt Dunham. He said that on the recommendation of the magistrates he would give directions, in accordance with the Act of Parliament empowering him to do so, for a gratuity of £10 to be given to him for his conduct in apprehending the prisoner, and getting up the case. Supt Dunham thanked his lordship and the court was adjourned.[2]

The giving of the jury's verdict is normally the most exciting moment of any criminal trial. In today's court hearings, some juries can be out deliberating for a number of days. In Victorian times, trials were usually very much shorter. When the two minutes of the jury's deliberation was over and they returned their verdict, it was no surprise that a conviction had been achieved. The judge had clearly been of the same opinion regarding the guilt of Jones and he duly passed sentence.

There really was only one sentence for a crime of this magnitude. Jones would hang by the neck until he was dead. No one, perhaps even Jones himself, could argue with the verdict or the sentence.

The *Reading Mercury* noted the timings of the day, as well as the two minute deliberation of the jury. One can only assume that the verdict was concluded by a show of hands or nods of the head.

Thomas Dunham had had a very satisfying day. He had just secured the conviction of, at that time, the worst mass murderer in English criminal history. If this was not enough, the judge was sufficiently impressed with the case to award Dunham £10 as a reward for his work on the case. This was to be his finest hour.

Charles Coombes, however, was not quite so lucky. The *Bucks Herald* reported his plea to the court for money at the end of the trial. He made application to court clerk, Mr Platt,[3] to bring to the attention of the judge his conduct in the case with a view to receiving a reward. Mr Platt confirmed that the judge could not help

Condemnation of J. Jones,

At Aylesbury, for the Wilful Murder of Mr. Marshall and his family, at Denham, near Uxbridge.

The trial of John Jones, alias Owen, for the wilful murders of Emanuel Marshall and six other persons, took place at Aylesbury, on Friday, July 22nd, before Mr. Baron Channell. The Court was crowded.

It will be remembered, that on the 22nd of May last, the house of Marshall was broken into, and a foul murder of the whole family was perpetrated. The prisoner was taken into custody, and was found wearing some of the murdered man's clothes, and it was also proved that he had been dealing with other property stolen from the house.

The Jury, after a patient inquiry, returned a verdict of Guilty. The Judge then passed sentence of Death on the prisoner. The prisoner, who was the only person in court who heard the sentence unmoved, raised his hand and gave a military salute to the judge, and, as he left the dock, said in a loud voice, "Thank you, sir." Disley, Printer, High-street, St. Giles, London

In a dark dismal cell in Aylesbury gaol there now lies
　Bewailing his unhappy fate,
The murderer, John Jones, condemned for to die,
　But his sorrow alas comes too late.
For those wholesale butcheries near Uxbridge town,
　On the 23rd of May last,
And for his fiendish deeds he guilty is found,
　His die on this earth it is cast.

　For those cruel murders so base,
　　Of poor Marshall and his family,
　The murderer Jones, to all men a disgrace,
　　His guilty life ends on a tree.

To all it's well-known how he did those foul deeds,
　And how his victims bodies were found,
How the sad details made each heart to bleed,
　And caused indignation around.
And how those poor souls the murderous wretch,
　By his savage hands strew'd on the floor,
Their brains scatter'd round—they lay still in death—
　Such deeds cause each heart to deplore.

Oh! Marshall, poor Marshall, hard was thy fate,
　In thy prime to be robbed of thy life,

For thy actions gave no one just cause for hate,
　To no one you gave cause for strife.
Yet the wife of your bosom, and little ones dear,
　For whose fate each true is grieving.
Nor thy poor aged mother the wretch would not spare
　But their dear souls I trust are in Heaven.

Poor Granny's grey hairs would his pity not move,
　Nor that poor little dear at her breast,
That poor aged dear, her love it was true,
　For that darling she held close in death.
Would any suppose in a Christian land,
　Such blood-thirsty monsters exist.
Who would wreak such vengeance on a fellow man,
　Or such dreadful crimes could commit.

Now the Denham murderer for death is cast,
　And for mercy must look to his God,
If so great a miscreant for mercy dare ask,
　For crimes, sure to bring it's reward.
The Judge said, John Jones, for your end prepare,
　Your career on earth it is run,
To your offended Maker, your time spend in prayer,
　To repent the crimes you have done.

him. Coombes stated that it would not encourage people to come forward with evidence against a murderer in the future.

Mr Platt replied that every person was bound to give all information to further the ends of justice. Coombes considered that he was harshly dealt with, and had no money to get home to Uxbridge. The money he had been given for attending the Assize was hardly enough for his keep and lodging.

Asked whether he had lived extravagantly, he admitted having to pay some debts in the town which he had paid out of the money. Mr Platt said the witness's expenses were nothing to do with old debts. As he retired, Coombes gave audible vent to his dissatisfaction.[4]

---

1   *Bucks Herald*, 23 July 1870.

2   Ibid.

3   Clerk of the court is likely to be Samuel Eli Platt. According to the 1871 Census, he was a 49-year-old man born in Leeds, living with his wife Ann at Buckingham Road, Aylesbury. His occupation was shown as Law and mercantile accounts.

4   *Bucks Herald*, 30 July 1870.

CHAPTER 33

Awaiting His Fate

It's hard to know the feelings that Jones experienced on the day of the trial. As the trial took place, he paid his full attention to the proceedings, and he made notes of what was being said. It's as if he expected to be cleared of the murder. The *Morning Post* described his behaviour:

> The prisoner, who had throughout the proceedings paid the greatest attention to the evidence, and constantly communicated with his counsel by means of the pencil and paper supplied to him, but who had been very anxious during the short deliberation of the jury, now drew himself up and making a military salute said 'Thank you, sir' with much bravado. He was loudly hissed from the body of the court. As he was descending the steps from the dock to the cells beneath, he stopped defiantly on hearing the hisses and seemed gathering himself for a spring into the crowd; the warders, however, hurried him down the steps and the court was adjourned.[1]

Having had the verdict announced, Jones must have felt anger at his fate. He knew that he had only days to live.[2] It's unknown whether he could see out of the prison van as it transported him the mile back to Aylesbury Gaol. It was to be his final journey anywhere. There was little hope of a pardon in a case like this. The evidence had been overwhelming, and Jones would have to make the most of his last two weeks on earth. As the gate of Aylesbury Gaol clanked behind him, his spirits must have hit at rock bottom.

Jones has been convicted on the evidence presented to the court. Any jury today would probably have come to the same conclusion. The circumstantial evidence was convincing in every respect. Jones had offered no defence other than the claim that he knew who had committed the crime but did not take part himself. This was hardly a credible explanation given the evidence against him.

What was still very frustrating for the police and the family of the victims was that they still did not know the truth of what had happened. Only John Jones could unlock the details of the Marshalls' last moments on that Sunday morning in May. Some murderers confessed in prison before going to the gallows, but Jones never did. It is a feeling of unfinished business.

One can only imagine the terror that must have engulfed his victims, particularly the women of the house, as they were slain one by one by Jones. Once the man of the house, Emmanuel Marshall, had been killed, there was no one to protect the others.

Perhaps this crime of cold-bloodedly murdering innocent woman and children was just too terrible to own up to? Jones had been captured before he could come up with a convincing alibi or excuse. One has to question his mental state. He was a man who was down on his luck, was in and out of prison, and who probably felt life was against him. He had no one, and nothing, in his life.

How could Emmanuel Marshall, a man with a similar trade have everything - a house, respectability and a family - that he did not? How could he have refused to pay him? The feeling of revenge can be very powerful. One can now only speculate as to whether Jones was suffering from any metal condition that made him behave in this way.

Was Jones suffering from schizophrenia? His life in adulthood had been a disaster, and he had ended up tramping the country, never sure of work, food or a place to shelter, living hand to mouth and regularly getting arrested for minor thefts. Victorian life was very hard, especially for the poor. Social Services was a thing of the future, and the threat of the workhouse was ever present. Mental health care was in its infancy.

If we look at the symptoms for schizophrenia we could conclude that Jones ticked a number of the boxes: social withdrawal; hostility or suspiciousness; deterioration of personal hygiene; odd or irrational statements; strange use of words or way of speaking; depression; extreme reaction to criticism; inappropriate laughter or crying; inability to cry or express joy; agitation; paranoia; lack of emotion. One other major symptom is that of hallucinations, or the hearing of voices. We don't know if this was the case with Jones, but so many of the symptoms fit with his behaviour pattern.

A very significant piece of evidence about Jones's medical history emerged when the police were trying to ascertain who he actually was. He had initially given false names to the police and altogether tried to conceal his identity. As a result of these police enquiries, a photograph was taken of the prisoner and forwarded to the Northamptonshire Police. It was reported that after the family had identified him as John Owen they gave details of his life history. Intelligence about a terrible accident that befell him while working was related. The *Saunders's News-Letter* takes up the story:

> He was bound apprentice when he was 15 years of age, in 1847, to Thomas Mason, a blacksmith of Byfield. While there, Mason and Owen were pulling down some iron fencing at the rectory, and while Mason was using a pickaxe, Owen incautiously stooped down, and Mason accidentally struck him on the right side of the head, which nearly killed him, causing a severe wound, the scar of which he carried for years, and is believed to carry now.[3]

The accident at Byfield Rectory must have been a shocking incident. Any similar head injury would be a major concern even today, but in the late 1840s such an injury could easily have proved fatal. John Owen was lucky to have survived such a blow to the head. Twenty years later, the Marshall family would not be so fortunate.

We could speculate about the long term effect that this head injury had on Owen. One can only imagine how badly affected he was, or whether this had any connection with the commission of the crimes in Denham twenty or so years later. Serious brain injury can also lead to irritability, aggression, depression, disinhibition, and denial or lack of awareness.

While Jones awaited his execution, his behaviour continued to interest the newspapers and to test the staff at Aylesbury Goal.

Following his conviction the newspapers were full of the news and no sympathy was being shown to the condemned man's situation. A ballad was printed, lamenting the Marshall family and condemning John Jones. It contained a drawing of Jones in the prison, receiving the counsel of a clergyman as he held his head in his hands.

The handbill, which is held in the Bodleian Library in Oxford, was published in St Giles in London. Although the ballad would not win any poetry prizes, it did express the revulsion which appears to have been shared by the population for a crime as grave as this one. This was no ordinary murder:

> In a dark dismal cell in Aylesbury gaol there now lies,
> Bewailing his unhappy fate.
> The murderer, John Jones, condemned to die,
> But his sorrow alas comes too late.

> For those wholesale butcheries near Uxbridge town,
> On the 23rd of May last.
> And for his fiendish deeds he guilty is found.
> His die on this earth is cast.

> For those cruel murders so base,
> Of poor Marshall and his family.
> The murderer Jones, to all men a disgrace,
> His guilty life ends on a tree.

> To all it's well known how he did those foul deeds,
> And how his victims' bodies were found,
> How the sad details made each heart to bleed,
> And caused indignation around.

> And how those poor souls the murderous wretch,
> By his savage hands strew'd on the floor,
> Their brains scattered round – they lay still in death –
> Such deeds cause each heart to deplore.

> Oh! Marshall, poor Marshall, hard was thy fate,
> In thy prime robbed of thy life,
> For thy actions gave no one just cause for hate,
> To no one you gave cause for strife.

Yet the wife of your bosom, and little ones dear,
For whose fate each one is grieving.
Nor thy poor aged mother the wretch would not spare
But their dear souls I trust are in heaven.

Poor Granny's grey hairs would his pity not move,
Nor that poor little dear at her breast,
That poor aged dear, her love it was true,
For that darling she held close in death.

Would any suppose in a Christian land,
Such blood thirsty monsters exist.
Who would wreak such vengeance on a fellow man,
Or such dreadful crimes could commit.

Now the Denham murderer for death is cast,
And for mercy must look to his God,
If so great a miscreant for mercy dare ask,
For crimes, sure to bring its reward.

The Judge said, John Jones for your end prepare,
Your career on earth is run,
To your offended Maker, your time spend in prayer,
To pardon the crimes you have done.[4]

---

1   *Morning Post*, 23 July 1870.

2   The date of the execution was fixed for Monday 8 August at 8 o'clock.

3   *Saunders's News-Letter*, 25 June 1870.

4   Bodleian Library, Oxford University. Frame 06187. Ballad Work - Roud Number: V12933. Edition Bod14502.

CHAPTER 34

The Hangman – William Calcraft

Once the Judge had sentenced John Jones to death, plans were put in place to have the official hangman, William Calcraft, visit Aylesbury Gaol to perform the execution. It would have fallen to Mr Acton Tindal,[1] the Under Sheriff of Buckinghamshire, to contact Calcraft and make the arrangements for him to attend on 8 August 1870.

Tindal had been present at the execution of murderer William Mobbs at Aylesbury Gaol five months earlier on 28 March when he had been hung by Calcraft. On that occasion, Tindal had taken down a confession to the crime by Mobbs prior to the execution.[2] There was to be no such confession given by John Jones.

William Ong Calcraft[3] is an infamous figure in British legal history. It is widely supposed that he is the country's most prolific and longest serving hangman. It is estimated that he was involved in the execution of about 450 people in a career stretching over 45 years.

Born in Great Baddow, near Chelmsford in Essex in 1800, he was a shoemaker by trade. Prior to this he had worked as a butler to a gentleman in Greenwich and also as a night watchman at a brewery in Liquorpond Street (now Clerkenwell Road), London. He supplemented his earnings by working as a hawker, selling meat pies outside the walls of Newgate Prison, where he had a chance meeting with the official executioner for London, John Foxton.

Foxton, who had served in the role for 40 years, subsequently gave Calcraft a job flogging young offenders for 10 shillings a week. On Foxton's death, on 4 April 1829 Calcraft was appointed as official Executioner for the City of London and Middlesex. He was to go on to be involved in most of the high profile murder cases of the era, often 'performing' his executions before large crowds of people before the executions were moved inside prisons in 1868.

As a side line business, Calcraft would sell parts of the hangman's rope as souvenirs. This sort of transaction gave birth to the expression 'money for old rope'. In addition to these earnings he was also allowed to keep the clothes and personal effects of the condemned, which he could sell afterwards to Madame Tussaud's for dressing the latest waxwork in the Chamber of Horrors. With the advent of rail travel, Calcraft became widely sought after in all parts of the country. He travelled far and wide, even as far as Scotland. He apparently enjoyed the travelling. He was paid a guinea a week as well as a guinea for each execution.

On 28 July 1865 he carried out the last public execution in Scotland when he hung poisoner Dr Edward William Pritchard outside Glasgow North Prison, an event which was said to have been attended by 100,000 onlookers. Dr Pritchard's crime had been to poison his wife and mother-in-law. The doctor eventually confessed to the murders. He had been having an affair with their 15-year-old servant.[4]

A famous double execution was carried out by Calcraft on 13 November 1849 outside Horsemonger Lane Gaol in Southwark, in the case referred to as 'The Bermondsey Horror'. Husband and wife Maria and Frederick Manning were both convicted at the Old Bailey for the murder of Irishman Patrick O'Connor. Maria shot O'Connor, while Frederick finished him off with a crowbar. They then buried the unfortunate Irishman under the kitchen floor. Charles Dickens attended the execution and was appalled by the behaviour of the crowd. He described their behaviour as 'inconceivably awful' in his letter of complaint to the editor of *The Times* on 14 November.[5]

Calcraft used the 'short drop' method of hanging. This method was later replaced by having a longer drop, which would result in death by snapping of the neck rather than being slowly strangled in the method used by Calcraft. Many disliked his method of execution. In one infamous incident, Calcraft struggled to dispatch William Bousfield, a 29-year-old tobacconist who had murdered his wife and three children.

The unfortunate Bousfield had walked into Bow Street Police Station to admit the murders, covered in blood. While awaiting his execution he threw himself on a fire in the prison in an attempt to commit suicide. It was not known whether he would survive long enough for the sentence to be carried out.

At the appointed hour, Bousfield had to be placed on a chair and carried to the scaffold. As he was dispatched, the chair had reduced the length of drop and he managed to swing his legs up back onto the opening of the trap door. A warder then pushed his legs back down the hole, but again Bousfield hooked them up on the scaffold in an attempt to save his life.

It was at this point that Calcraft rushed underneath the scaffolding and hung onto the condemned man's legs in a severe struggle. This had the effect of strangling the man to death. The whole event had taken ten minutes. It was an unedifying sight, and the crowd voiced its disapproval by yelling and hooting. Calcraft may not have been thinking straight that morning, as he had received death threats in an anonymous letter from the Kent Street Roughs[6] stating that he would be shot while on the scaffold, and to put an end to any further executions.

Three of Calcraft's census record entries make interesting reading. In 1851, while living at 1 Devizes Street, Shoreditch, 50-year-old Calcraft was modestly described as 'His Honour – The finisher of the Law'.[7] By 1861 he had moved to 2 Poole Street, Shoreditch, and was recorded rather plainly as a shoemaker.[8] In 1871, the now 70-year-old widowed Calcraft was listed as spending the night of the census at Bedford County Gaol, and was now using the title 'Public Executioner.'[9]

Calcraft eventually retired in 1874 due to old age, and he was

William Calcraft

replaced by William Marwood. He died at Poole Street, Hoxton in 1879.

1　Acton Tindal (1811-1880) was a pupil at Charterhouse School. He became the Clerk of the Peace for Buckinghamshire in 1838, taking over the post from his father. He remained in the position for 42 years. He lived in Aylesbury in The Manor House, Bierton Road, close to the County Gaol (*Chelmsford Chronicle,* 5 November 1880).

2　*Bucks Herald*, 2 April 1870.

3　*Dictionary of National Biography*, Vol 1-20, 22, Page 690. The *Dictionary of National Biography* began in 1882 as an ambitious project spearheaded by George Smith to produce a biographical dictionary of prominent figures from Britain and Ireland from the earliest of times up to 1900. The efforts of hundreds of contributors resulted in a 22 volume alphabetical series containing thousands of biographies.

4　Scotland's People (www.scotlandspeople.gov.uk/Content/Help/index.aspx? 2325).

5   *The Times*, 14 November 1849. Here is part of Dickens' letter describing the mob: 'When the day dawned, thieves, low prostitutes, ruffians and vagabonds of every kind, flocked on to the ground, with every variety of offensive and foul behaviour. Fightings, faintings, whistlings, imitations of Punch, brutal jokes, tumultuous demonstrations of indecent delight when swooning women were dragged out of the crowd by the police with their dresses disordered, gave a new zest to the general entertainment. When the sun rose brightly - as it did - it gilded thousands upon thousands of upturned faces, so inexpressibly odious in their brutal mirth or callousness, that a man had cause to feel ashamed of the shape he wore, and to shrink from himself, as fashioned in the image of the Devil.'

6   Kent Street was a road in a very dangerous area of Southwark. The *Edinburgh Evening Courant* of 1 January 1857 describes the Kent Street Roughs as 'Blackguards and queans [meaning a disreputable woman; specifically a prostitute] in Tooley Street, The Mint, Borough Road and the New Cut. It was a crime ridden area which was renamed Tabard Street in 1877.

7   1851 Census.

8   1861 Census.

9   1871 Census.

CHAPTER 35

The Execution of John Jones

After weeks of huge public interest in the circus that the Denham Murders case had become, the final chapter of the story was about to unfold. John Jones was to meet his maker in Aylesbury Gaol at the appointed time, Monday 8 August 1870 at 8 o'clock in the morning. This was going to be an event that only a handful of people would witness. Although the onlookers would still often crowd outside prisons where a hanging was going to take place, after 1868 the public were no longer able to witness the act of punishment.

Aylesbury had seen hangings taking place before the ban on public executions was made. Up until the execution of John Tawell in 1845, hangings had normally been set up in Market Square in front of County Hall. After that time, two further executions took place - in 1854 and 1864 - outside the new County Gaol.[1]

The last few days of John Jones's life would see people visiting the prison, letters being written and guidance from clergymen. A last chance to tell the truth about the offence was offered to the condemned man, though in Jones's case he never took up the chance to take responsibility for the crimes.

The *Manchester Evening News* described the prisoner's behaviour prior to the execution:

> Owen continued to exhibit the callous and brutal demeanour which has characterised him since his apprehension. Owen recently had

an interview with his wife, and at her earnest entreaty promised to make a full statement of the circumstances connected with the murders. One of the visiting justices attended to receive his confession, when Owen stated that he was passing the murdered peoples cottage on the Sunday morning, he saw two men standing there, who called him, and gave him the money and the clothes which led to his apprehension.[2]

The *Alnwick Mercury* gave more details:

> The Rev Mr Bunbury,[3] the chaplain of the gaol, has been unremitting in his solicitations to bring the prisoner to penitence for his terrible crime, but the prisoner only returned his kindness by curses and foul expressions.

> At length on Thursday last, he said he was a Catholic, and a Roman Catholic clergyman from Wolverton on being sent for visited him. He however only received similar treatment, and the prisoner declared that he did not believe that there was either a God or Devil, Heaven or Hell. At one time he virtually confessed to the murders by saying, 'I am only sorry that I did not shoot Supt Dunham and a ----- Justice of the Peace that once sentenced me as well.

> He was visited lately by his father and wife, neither of whom had seen him for years, but he treated them coldly, and when they shed tears replied to their grief by saying, 'What have you to snivel for?[4]

The *Berkshire Chronicle* added more details about the effect that the Rev Bunbury had on Jones when it reported:

> On Sunday he went to the chapel, and was an attentive listener, until he came to the part of the service where the Rev Bunbury, the chaplain of the gaol, asked the prayers of the congregation 'for a prisoner now lying under sentence of death in the gaol'. The convict then left the chapel and cried bitterly.[5]

It is interesting to note that Jones's wife, Hannah Owen, visited him in the prison. The *Northern Standard* gave details of her visit:

> In a reply to a letter from him desiring to see her, and asking her forgiveness for having left her, his wife paid him a visit on Thursday week, but he only upbraided her with having caused him to leave her. In a fit of remorse he said she might come again next day, when his conduct was much altered and he cried like a child and asked for her forgiveness. She endeavoured to draw a confession from him, but he declared that he was innocent.

> When she left him, he gave her a missal[6] which the Catholic priest
> had left him, inscribed to his wife 'from her affectionate husband,
> John Owen'.[7]

Hannah Owen had not seen Jones for several years. It's not
recorded what she thought about Jones, or whether she thought him
innocent. Whether she thought that it had been worth the journey
to Aylesbury to see him one final time was also open to question.
Hannah had not been very lucky in matrimony. Her first husband,
John Russell, had died only nine years into their marriage. Her
second suitor had abandoned her and then brought shame on her
by murdering seven people. Worse was to come, as she died aged 63
of heart disease at Brailes on 28 March the following year. The death
certificate described her as 'widow of John Owen, blacksmith'.

The *Berkshire Chronicle* gave more details of Jones's incarceration,
and included information about the special arrangements that the
prison took to ensure that Jones did not cheat the hangman's noose:

> He frequently expressed his determination not to 'Dance in the air'
> [i.e. hang]. He tried all manner of excuses to get out of his cell. He
> asked the height of the gallery above his row of cells to the stone floor
> beneath, and indicated in other ways that he contemplated suicide.

> Since then, a stricter watch was kept on him, one warder by day and
> two by night being his constant attendants, and as nothing could
> have prevented him rushing up the steps and precipitating himself,
> could he have once escaped from his warders, strong netting was
> affixed to the entrance of the gallery so that he might be thrown back
> upon his keeper.[8]

Jones was seen by a number of people in his final days. These
included the catholic priest from Wolverton, Mr Blackwell, and
also Mr and Mrs Hunt. Hunt was a preacher and blacksmith from
Weedon near Aylesbury. Mrs Hunt had known the prisoner's brother,
who was reported to have left the country. Jones then spent time
discussing his life with the warders:

> He contented himself with alternately abusing and confiding in
> his guard, whom he has entertained with a history of his various
> incarcerations, boasting proudly of his exploits, and stating that if he
> could get out, there were two (using a horrible expression) he would

like to murder.

Among other things he frequently told his warder that he would make his mother out for a liar, as she had always told him that he would die in his shoes, but he would kick them off 'Just before the job'.[9]

Continuing his strange behaviour, Jones asked for a special sleeping location on his last two nights. The Australian *Sydney Empire* gave the details:

On 6 August, he further sought to show his indifference by asking to see his coffin, and stating that he should like to sleep in it the last two nights of his life.[10]

William Calcraft always arrived at the prisons well ahead of the hanging, in order to prepare for the job at hand. Jones was advised when his executioner arrived at Aylesbury Gaol, and the news was not met with approval, as reported by the *Salisbury and Winchester Journal*:

Calcraft arrived at the gaol on Saturday night, and the prisoner was appraised of his presence. He said he should like to see him at once, but as Calcraft did not then go to see him, the prisoner said, 'Well, if he is not civil when pinioning me I shall give him one in the mouth.' Throughout Sunday he was coarse and flippant in his conversation, had a conversation with Calcraft, and retiring to rest at 9 o'clock soon went soundly to sleep.[11]

With all cases of murder, it would always be preferable to have a confession from the accused, particularly so in a capital punishment outcome. People wanted to know the full facts of what had happened on that fateful Sunday morning. Jones had never admitted the killings, so there was excitement when it was intimated that he was about to admit the offences in the *Illustrated Police News*:

On Thursday and Friday the prisoner was visited by his wife, by whom he was exhorted to make a full statement of all the circumstances connected with the murder. He promised he would do so, and sent a note to the Rev Joshua Greaves,[12] rector of Great Missenden, who is one of the visiting justices of the prison, stating that he wished to make a confession of the facts connected to the murder. Immediately upon receipt of this Mr Greaves hastened to the gaol at Aylesbury, and there in his presence and the chief officials of the gaol, he made a long rambling statement which was so manifestly false that, although it was taken down word for word as it came from his lips, he was not asked to sign it.[13]

Frustratingly, the record of Jones's statement has not survived, but it was clear that he was never going to take responsibility for the murders. The *Illustrated Police News* gave further particulars about his visitors. He had been visited several times by a Mr Shelley,[14] an independent minister from Aylesbury, who tried to obtain a confession. He was also examined by the prison surgeon Mr Robert Ceely, who appears to have attempted an early form of lie detector test:

> Mr Shelley urged upon the culprit on Saturday of the duty and necessity of confessing his guilt if he was to obtain a pardon. He replied that he fully admitted that he had no expectation of mercy from God if he did not confess his sins and ask for a pardon but in the most solemn manner repeated his assertion of innocence and called God to witness its truth. Mr Shelley urged him again that there would be no hope for him if he went into eternity with a lie in his mouth. Mr Robert Ceely, surgeon of the prison said the same, taking him under the gas light to look in his face and feel his pulse. Mr Ceely did so, and told the prisoner that his pulse was very strong, but jerking sometimes as if he was under caution. He replied he could not help that, but it was not from fear or guilt.[15]

On the Sunday night, Jones went to sleep for the final time, knowing the fate that awaited him come 8.00 am the next morning. One of the guards got him to repeat the words of a prayer, after which he recited the Lord's Prayer before drifting off to sleep. He awoke at 3.20 am and had a breakfast of a pint and half of tea, a 2lb loaf and two plates of meat. The *Berkshire Chronicle* continued its reporting of his final four hours:

> He walked round his cell for some time and wrote three letters to his friends, having sent six away the night before. [One wonders who these 'friends' were.] He had seen Calcraft walking in the garden, and on leaving his cell shook hands with him and told him to do his duty.[16]

The *Sydney Empire* took up the story:

On the morning of his execution he ate his breakfast heartily, and spent the remainder of the morning in joking. At three minutes to eight the bell began to toll, and Calcraft met him in the corridor, and the prisoner at once submitted to be pinioned. The procession was then formed, accompanied by Mr. Sheriff Tindal, Mr R.C. Ceely, surgeon, Superintendent Jervis, the warders; and the chaplain reading a part of the burial service.

When the culprit came in sight of the gallows it seemed to absorb his whole curiosity, and after surveying it for a moment, he attempted to go up two steps at a time, but at the request of the warders he walked up in a more orderly manner.

Calcraft then placed him on the drop, put the rope round his neck, and the white cap over his face. The culprit asked to be allowed to make a statement, which was permitted.

The culprit then said, 'My friends, I am going to die for the murder of Charles – What's his name? I forget. Oh! Charles Marshall, But I am innocent.' The execution was then proceeded with, and the prisoner fell two and a half feet. Death was almost instantaneous. After an hour the body was cut down, and an inquest held.[17]

The ever-helpful *Illustrated Police News* gave details of Jones's final words to the hangman, and also mentioned the Chief Warder, Mr Armstrong. The report indicated that journalists were at the prison to record Jones's final minutes:

He walked to the foot of the scaffold with a resolute but by no means a defiant air. Calcraft then pinioned his legs, shook hands with him, which the prisoner seemed to return cordially, and said, 'Good bye'. Calcraft then put on the cap and adjusted the rope. Before the bolt was withdrawn, Owen said to Mr Armstrong the Chief Warder, 'Can I turn round sir, and say a few words?'[18]

If the execution had taken place in earlier years, Jones would have been hung in public. Because of the new Act, only a handful of men bore witness to his final moments.

This list of onlookers and participants did not include Supt Thomas Dunham. Perhaps it would not have been correct for him to have been there to see the hanging due to the effect it may have had on the prisoner. The Constabulary were however represented by Supt Jervis. One extra place was found for a member of the public.

The execution of John Jones at Aylesbury Prison on 8th August 1870. The picture shows Prison Chaplain Thomas Bunbury reading the burial service, and William Calcraft adjusting the noose. The unfortunate John Jones awaits his fate above the trap door.

Original broadsheet in the custody of Thames Valley Police Museum.

It was none other than chief witness Charles Coombes. *Reynolds's Newspaper* mentioned his journey to the gaol:

> The witness Charles Coombes walked all the way from Uxbridge.[19]
> Mr Tindal gave special permission for him to see the execution at the last moment.[20]

It must have been a huge effort for Coombes to have travelled on foot all the way from Middlesex to Aylesbury, with no guarantee of being admitted. He had already been refused any 'reward' money following the trial. Mr Tindal must have taken pity on him when he arrived at the prison. Coombes was admitted and was there to see justice finally catch up with his one-time lodging 'friend', John Jones. It's a shame that history seems to have forgotten Mr Coombes after this point. We will never know how often he told people of the story of the Denham Murderer, but it was surely quite often.

The final seconds of John Jones's life were related by the *Oxford University Herald*:

> At three minutes to eight, the bell began to toll, and he was brought from his cell by two warders. Calcraft met him in the corridor, and the prisoner at once submitted to be pinioned. Calcraft found a little difficulty with one of the buckles. 'You will see better if I turn round to the light', said the prisoner and he at once turned round... The body seemed to fall heavily, death was almost instantaneous, and only one moment's convulsion marked his end.[21]

Reynolds's gave some final details about Jones's death;

> He was a strongly made, wiry fellow measuring 42' round the chest, aged 38. The body fell heavily with one convulsion. A black flag was raised at the prison. There were 500-600 people outside. When seen by the jury, the features of Owen exhibited no symptoms of a violent death.[22]

After being cut down from the scaffold, the officials went through the motions of an inquest into his death. The death certificate, which was issued by Henry Lewis, showed the informant to be the Coroner for Buckinghamshire, Mr Joseph Parrott. The cause of death was put simply as 'Executed by being hung for wilful murder'.

John Jones was photographed at Aylesbury Gaol in what appears

to be a prison issued suit. (The arrowed prison suit only came to English prisons at the beginning of the 1870s.) Although smiling in portraits is not something we associate with photographs of this period, the image is quite haunting. There is a coldness to his face and particularly his eyes. It is interesting to compare his likeness from the photograph and the drawing from the *Illustrated Police News*. It is probable that this image was taken at Aylesbury Gaol by local photographer Samuel Glendenning Payne[23] not long after Jones's arrival at the prison. The portrait was given to local police for identification purposes and then passed to Northamptonshire Constabulary.

The second picture of Jones is not one that could easily be placed on the family mantelpiece. Samuel Payne returned to the County Gaol to record the deceased's image on 8 August 1870, moments after he was executed. This image shows Jones as if sleeping peacefully.[24]

John Jones's unhappy life was finally over.

---

1   Centre for Buckinghamshire Studies, (www.buckscc.gov.uk/media/130617/bucksprisoners.pdf).

2   *Manchester Evening News*, 8 August 1870.

3   Thomas Edwin George Bunbury was the chaplain for Aylesbury Gaol. He was

born in Bath in 1837, the son of Commander George Benjamin Bunbury, Royal Navy. He attended Cambridge University. He married Anna McGhie Pugh, the daughter of a clergyman, on 1 June 1870 just a few weeks before John Jones's execution. The 1871 Census shows Thomas as a 34-year-old 'Chaplain of the County Prison'. He was also listed as naval chaplain to HMS Esk. Sadly, he died aged 53 after being admitted as a patient at Warneford Lunatic Asylum, Headington in Oxfordshire on 6 May 1891.

4   *Alnwick Mercury*, 13 August 1870.

5   *Berkshire Chronicle*, 13 August 1870.

6   A missal was a Catholic religious book for the celebration of Masses.

7   *Northern Standard*, 13 August 1870.

8   *Berkshire Chronicle*, 13 August 1870.

9   Ibid.

10 *Sydney Empire* (Australia), 4 October 1870.

11 *Salisbury & Winchester Journal*, 13 August 1870.

12 Rev Joshua Greaves (1821-1885) was the son of clergyman Richard Jarvis Greaves. He was educated at Trinity College, Cambridge. He married Mary Jane Walker on 15 January 1845 in Kington, Herefordshire. In 1851 they were living in Lee Hall Lane, Woodlands, Handsworth, Staffordshire, where he was the Curate of St Peters. Mary Jane sadly died later the same year. Joshua married Frances Sarah Dent in Streatham on 8 June 1852. In 1861 he was a 40-year-old vicar at Great Missenden, but Frances seems to have died soon after as in 1864 her father paid to have a stained-glass window put in St Peter and Paul Church in Great Missenden in memory of his late daughter. On 4 July 1865 he married for a third time, to Mary Wilson Bate. Joshua Greaves died on 25 June 1885 in Great Missenden. He left £1,523 in his estate to his son Leighton and his daughter Frances. The *Bucks Herald* of 4 July 1885 gave details of his funeral, stating that he had been in poor health for some time. He was described as one of the foremost men in the county in the cause of education. He was a treasurer at the Bucks Infirmary and was also a JP. Every shop in the village closed for the funeral. All the children attending the funeral carried flowers, with around a thousand mourners attending the burial.

13 *Illustrated Police News*, 13 August 1870.

14 Augustine Thomas Shelley was born in Chigwell Row c1826. He married Mary Ann Lyne in Edmonton on 24 May 1848. In 1851 he was an independent minister at Soham, Cambridgeshire, aged 25. By 1861 he had moved to Great Yarmouth and was living at 54 South Quay. He was listed in the Census as an independent minister and school teacher. In 1871, Augustine and Mary Ann were living at The Mount, Castle Street, Aylesbury. He was then aged 45. The *Bucks Herald* described how he suffered severe chest pains after catching a cold after conducting a funeral. Dr Eagles was later called and diagnosed bronchitis. A few days later, on the Sunday, his condition improved but the following day, Monday 4 December 1871, he suffered a violent attack and died two hours later. The *Herald* reported that he had been educated in Belfast and Cheshunt, and that he

had been a missionary in Ireland. He had ministered at Maidenhead for two years, Soham for seven, Great Yarmouth for seven and Ely for four years. He had gone to Aylesbury in May 1868. His obituary described him as an earnest and devoted pastor. He left £800 in his will.

15 *Illustrated Police News*, 13 August 1870.

16 *Berkshire Chronicle*, 13 August 1870.

17 *Sydney Empire* (Australia), 4 October 1870.

18 *Illustrated Police News*, 13 August 1870.

19 The distance from Uxbridge to Aylesbury is 25 miles and it would have taken at least 8 or 9 hours to have walked this distance on a good day.

20 *Reynolds's Newspaper*, 14 August 1870.

21 *Oxford University Herald*, 13 August 1870.

22 *Reynolds's Newspaper*, 14 August 1870.

23 Samuel Glendenning Payne (1835-1912) was a photographer in Aylesbury High Street with his sister's husband, Henry Jenkins, but by 1864 that partnership was dissolved and he set up his own business at 3 Serena Terrace, Aylesbury, where people could come to have their portraits taken. Both Samuel and his wife were involved in the business, which later moved to 43 High Street. Maria was recorded on the 1871, 1881, 1891 and 1901 census returns as being a photographic artist. Considering she was the mother of eight children it was remarkable that she could have been so actively involved in the business. The firm later expanded with new branches in both Thame and Tring. Samuel was a volunteer sergeant in the Territorial Army, a musician, an archaeologist and also a Freemason, being a Past Master at one point. He died on 7 February 1912 following 'a long and painful illness' through which he had been confined to bed for a year. He left an estate worth £2,200.

24 *Bucks Herald*, 20 August 1870.

CHAPTER 36

Superintendent Thomas Dunham

At the end of the investigation of the Denham Tragedy, Supt Dunham must have sighed with relief. The biggest challenge of his career was over. He had passed with flying colours. Jones had been brought to justice by the efforts of Dunham and his Buckinghamshire Constabulary colleagues. He had not needed the assistance of any high profile London detectives to solve the case. He had taken decisive action himself and acted with determination and bravery in the act of arresting an armed suspect who was desperate and on the run.

He had succeeded in getting Jones safely before the Assize Court in one piece, despite the best attentions of the mob. He had now obtained a conviction with the ultimate penalty being the outcome.

Added to this, the trial judge had given him a reward of £10 to show his appreciation for a job well done. Dunham had coped with the logistical nightmare of travelling from Slough to Reading, Denham and also Aylesbury, as well as ensuring that a host of witnesses attended the various court hearings.

Following on from the award from the trial judge, Dunham was to receive another award from the grateful public in the early part of 1871. The *Bucks Advertiser* gave details of the award:

> On Wednesday, at the Bucks Petty Sessions, held at Slough, a testimonial, subscribed to by a large number of the principle

The watch presented to Supt Dunham after the trial.

Thames Valley Police Museum

inhabitants of the neighbourhood, and consisting of a gold watch and Albert chain, with a purse containing 20 sovereigns, was presented to Mr Supt Dunham, by the chairman, Captain Rudyerd. The following inscription was engraved on the back of the watch; 'Presented to Supt T Dunham, by the inhabitants of Slough and the vicinity, in recognition of the zeal and ability displayed by him in the capture of the Denham Murderer, 24 May 1870' The testimonial was accompanied by a suitable address, signed by the 91 inhabitants.[1]

After the mass of work he had endured in this case, it's unlikely that any other case during his service excited him quite so much. This was the pinnacle of his career. It would set a marker down in history that he had been responsible for the daddy of all 'good arrests'. Police officers always like to talk about their best arrests, especially in retirement, and Dunham would always have commanded respect from any listener in later years when hearing about this infamous case. One of his best moments must have been when he arrived at Reading Police Station and told the station sergeant that he had arrested Jones on suspicion of seven murders.

Dunham continued to work in Slough for the rest of his service, but never achieved any further promotions. He never quite made it to the top job of Chief Constable. He served Bucks Constabulary from 1857 until 1890, reaching the post of Superintendent in January 1867. Considering how well thought of he was and his success at Denham, one might have expected him to have reached the top job but it never happened. Perhaps he liked Slough and did not want to live in Aylesbury?

In this period of English police history, the Chief Constable post more often than not went to men who had been in the military rather than career coppers who had worked their way up the ranks. Indeed, Dunham's own Chief Constable, John Charles Tyrwhitt-Drake, also known as 'Captain Drake', had entered the service after reaching the rank of Lieutenant in the 2nd Regiment of Foot.

Thomas Dunham featured in numerous articles in the *Bucks Herald* during his period of service. His cases were many and varied. Indeed, his adventures could fill a book on their own. He was involved in other, more 'routine' murders in his service, though without quite as much success as he enjoyed in the Denham case.

On 11 April 1881, Ann Reville was murdered in the family butcher's shop in Slough. Sixteen-year-old butcher's assistant Augustus Payne, who worked for the Revilles, was arrested by Dunham for the murder, but he was acquitted at the subsequent trial at Aylesbury Assize.

In 1886, local criminal Alfred Hitch murdered Charles Plumbridge in a field near Denham, when the pair were working together. Plumbridge is thought to have been hit on the head with a hoe. Hitch escaped but was found much later having attempted suicide. Dunham arrested him for the murder and he was duly found guilty and sentenced to death, though the jury asked for clemency. Hitch was reprieved by the Home Secretary but spent the rest of his life in prison, dying in 1919.

Another murder case that Dunham was involved in was the 1888 death of coal merchant Charles Dance in Chalvey near Slough. The 57-year-old had sustained a very serious head injury.

Evidence pointed towards one William James being responsible. He was arrested on suspicion of the murder, but he too escaped the hangman's noose when he was also acquitted at the Aylesbury Assize.

In 1881 Dunham was badly injured when a horse fell on him. The ever-informative *Bucks Herald* gives us the details:

> A serious accident occurred on Saturday when the County Volunteer Corps was passing from the station to Eton. Supt Dunham was in charge of the police. His horse was startled by the band and it reared up and fell on him, injuring him severely. He was conveyed to his residence at the police station. He is reported to be progressing favourably.[2]

Ill health began to affect Supt Dunham towards the end of his career. By 1889, a very serious sounding larynx problem required Dunham to undergo an operation. The *Slough, Eton & Windsor Observer* reported that Dunham had suffered this throat condition for twenty years, and that he was only able to speak by the use of great and painful effort. He had visited St Bartholomew's Hospital where he had been advised that a tracheotomy was the only solution. The paper described him as having 'indomitable pluck and energy in facing the difficulties of his condition' and that the operation was carried out at his house. It gave the following details of the medical difficulty:

> A cannula or tube was introduced into the windpipe. At first there was loss of blood with every expiration. From the pain of the operation and the loss of blood, the patient became greatly exhausted and for some time on Monday evening his condition was distinctly critical.[3]

A few days later, a second operation was required:

> Readers will regret to hear it was necessary to admit Supt Dunham to another operation for a disease of the larynx. It will be remembered that he was first operated on some days ago. On Sunday, the tube in the windpipe became displaced and was taken out. All efforts to replace it were ineffectual and on Tuesday another operation was performed with the use of the knife, that tube being put back in its former position. Surgeons were Mr Wilmer Phillips, house surgeon of Windsor Infirmary, and Mr Brickwell of Slough. Since that time

the respected Supt has been going on satisfactorily and when we enquired yesterday, we were informed that the improvement is decided and sustained.[4]

Inspector George Sutton took charge of the South Eastern Division during Dunham's illness.

On 13th January 1890, having been found medically unfit for further service, Superintendent Thomas Dunham finally handed in his resignation. He was 57 years old and he had served 'with diligence and fidelity' for 32 years and 305 days.

The *Reading Mercury* gave details of his retirement:

> Thomas Dunham, for 23 years a Supt, has resigned due to ill health. At Bucks Petty Sessions held at Slough last week, chairman, Mr E.C.S. Thompson and Mr Springnall Thompson referred with regret to Supt Dunham's resignation and spoke highly of his services while a Superintendent. He was granted a full pension, 2/3rds of his pay [£101.13s.4d. per annum]. Men of the South Eastern Division presented Mr Dunham with a handsome clock in token of their esteem for him. The presentation was made by Insp Sapwell and Insp Andrews.[5]

The inscription of the clock read: 'Presented by the officers and constables of the South Eastern Division to Supt Thomas Dunham as a mark of their respect on his retirement after 33 years faithful service in the Bucks Constabulary, 10 January 1890'.

Four months later, the residents of Slough clubbed together to show their appreciation of his services. A not inconsiderable sum was collected, as the *Bucks Herald* reported:

> This worthy & painstaking officer, who has just retired in consequence of broken health from his position as Superintendent of the South Eastern Division of the Bucks Constabulary was on Tuesday the recipient of a most gratifying presentation made by Mr G.S. Emanuel, chairman of the committee in the presence of some subscribers. It took the form of a handsome illuminated address, the work of Mr W Guest, accompanied and a purse containing over £180. On 20th May 1890 it was presented to Mr Dunham by the inhabitants of Slough as token of great respect in which he is held. [250 people had signed the address as subscribers.]

> Mr Dunham said: 'I acted as a police officer, I simply endeavoured to

The clock presented to Supt Dunham following his retirement.

Thames Valley Police Museum

do my duty according to the best of my ability, without fear or favour or affection, malice or ill will towards anyone whether they were rich or poor.'

He thanked the magistrates, the officers of Bucks Constabulary, the public and the Chief Constable, Capt Drake. Mr Drake gave him 10 guineas. He had received many kind letters including one from Mr Drake since his retirement. Mr Dunham stated that he would never forget the presents and thanked everyone on behalf of his wife and family.[6]

Following a nine-year retirement, ex Supt Dunham passed away on 21 March 1899 at his home, 59 William Street, Slough. The death certificate which had been signed by Dunham's surgeon Dr Brickwell[7] stated 'Exhaustion 10 days, chronic inflammation of the larynx and right lung, 9 years.'[8]

The funeral took place in Slough on Saturday, 1 April 1899. The cortege left the family home at 4.00 pm, proceeding along Windsor Road to the Parish Church. Both the Police and Fire Brigade accompanied the hearse. The coffin, which was covered in flowers, was borne on the shoulders of eight constables. The service was conducted by the rector, the Rev P.H. Elliot, and there was a large congregation. Serving and retired police officers came from far and wide to attend the service. The senior officer at the church was Supt Sutton, who had worked with Dunham on the Denham Murders and who was by now the Deputy Chief Constable.[9]

Soon after the death of Thomas Dunham was reported, the local magistracy paid their respects to the town's former Superintendent. *The Slough, Eton & Windsor Observer* reported their sentiments:

> Slough Petty Sessions – The Late Ex Supt Dunham
>
> Captain Higgins. I have been requested by my brother magistrates to say how sorry they were to hear of the death of Ex Supt Dunham. He was a very active and intelligent officer, and we know that he distinguished himself in many cases more particularly the capture of The Denham Murderer. Mr J Hartopp Nash, 'I agree with the chairman, we all regarded him as a most able and astute officer.'[10]

Thomas Dunham was buried in the churchyard of St Mary's Church, Church Street in Slough. The funeral was handled by undertakers E. Sargeant & Sons, conveniently situated right next to the church and who are still in business well over a century later. According to the burial records of the church, Thomas was buried in Row 5 Plot 1. Despite the best efforts of myself and the churchwarden, no headstone, if one ever existed, appears to have survived.

When Thomas died, leaving a widow and ten children, his probate entry gave details of his estate. It stated: 'Thomas Dunham, of 59 William Street, Slough, Bucks, died 21 March 1899. Probate, London, 19 April, to Carl Franz Wilhelm Theodore ROHDE, watchmaker, effects £474'.[11] Mr Rohde was married to the Dunham's daughter Alice Lucy. Thomas's widow Martha survived for a further fifteen years, passing away in Slough on 14 August 1914 aged 70. She was buried together with her husband.

Thomas and Martha Dunham have much to be proud of. He served his community faithfully and helped to make Buckinghamshire a safer place. Martha brought up a large family, some of whom went on to join the police who also wanted to make a difference. But more of them later.

It is perhaps possible for us to say that Thomas Dunham will go down in police criminal history as one of Buckinghamshire's finest.

---

1   *Bucks Advertiser*, 4 March 1871.

2   *Bucks Herald*, 16 July 1881.

3   *Slough, Eton & Windsor Observer*, 28 September 1899.

4   *Slough, Eton & Windsor Observer*, 5 October 1889.

5   *Reading Mercury*, 25 January 1890

6   *Bucks Herald*, 24 May 1890.

7   John Smith BRICKWELL, MRCS LSA. Joined the medical profession in about 1855. He started his career at the Warwickshire & Coventry Hospital. He then took a trip to Australia as a ship's surgeon. He subsequently joined Windsor Infirmary, and eventually purchased the practice of Dr Algey of Slough in 1867. He was the medical officer and public vaccinator for Stoke Poges, as well as to the Loyal Herschel Lodge of Oddfellows. He retired due to ill health in May 1909. It was said that he never refused to attend a call at whatever hour of the day or night it came. He died aged 73 years at 'Pinwell', the residence of his partner, Dr T.H.E. Meggs, his son in law in September 1909. (*Windsor & Eton Express*, 30 October 1909.)

    Dr Brickwell was born in Sawbridgeworth, Herts on 28 October 1835, the son of John Brickwell, surgeon. He was baptised in Sawbridgeworth on 30 December 1835. He married Annie Sargeant at St Georges, Bloomsbury in London 28 April 1867 (page 86 marriage register); the couple had four daughters and four sons. He left £1,922 in his will (Probate 3 December 1909, Oxford, page 239).

8   Death Certificate.

9   *Bucks Herald*, 1 April 1899.

10 *Slough, Eton & Windsor Observer*, 1 April 1899.

11 Probate Record.

CHAPTER 37

Assorted Intelligence

This chapter brings together a number of unrelated, but interesting items connected to the Denham murders.

Following the execution of John Jones, as he was now England's most notorious murderer it was no surprise that Madame Tussaud's decided that a waxworks effigy was needed of him.[1]

The waxwork of Jones came to a sticky end when a serious fire at Tussaud's in London in March 1925 destroyed it, along with all the other models. Twenty-five fire engines attended the scene, with the fire almost destroying the whole building. There were only two 'survivors'; 'PC Robertson' and a green parrot. PC Robertson was a wax policeman at the front door of the building. The parrot was apparently the only living thing in the building when the fire started at 10.15 pm. The Salvage Corps struggled out of the building with a cage containing a parrot who looked dead. After some fresh air, the bird shook off its stupor, hopped onto its perch and began to behave like a healthy bird. It then startled everyone by remarking, 'This is a rotten business'. It certainly was.[2]

*

The Denham Murders were a shock for the whole country. Who up to that point could imagine seven inhabitants of a single house all being killed by an intruder? The news was enough to make some people tip over the edge. *The Era* newspaper reported a shocking incident which led to another victim of the murders:

> DISTRESSING DEATH – on Friday morning Mr Carttar held an inquiry at the Warwick Arms, Warwick Road, respecting the death of Mrs Mary Ann Reynoldson, aged about 57 years, who committed suicide through depression of mind caused by being informed of the murders at Uxbridge. On Tuesday morning she was standing in the street door of her house when she was suddenly informed by a neighbour of the Uxbridge Murders. She became greatly excited. She shut the door, went upstairs, and took some prussic acid. The Jury returned a verdict that the deceased committed suicide by taking poison while of unsound mind.[3]

*

Following his execution, great interest was paid into mind of the perpetrator, John Jones. What would have made a man commit such a crime? In the Victorian period, phrenologists believed that the human mind had a set of various mental faculties, each one represented in a different area of the brain.

Phrenology was a process that involves observing and/or feeling the skull to determine an individual's psychological attributes. Franz Joseph Gall believed that the brain was made up of twenty-seven individual organs that determined personality; the first nineteen of these 'organs' he believed to exist in other animal species. Phrenologists would run their fingertips and palms over the skulls of their patients to feel for enlargements or indentations. The phrenologist would often take measurements with a tape measure of the overall head size.

After Jones' execution, a cast of his skull was examined by Professor Cornelius Donovan,[4] who had founded the London School of Phrenology in the Strand, London, in 1840.

Donovan's findings after his examination were printed in the newspapers, though this does not make for easy reading. His findings seem to intimate a dangerous man, as reported in the *Bucks Herald*:

> In the face there is nothing repulsive. The physiognomy of the head is vile indeed. The skull bulges out at the sides – in the region of

combativeness, destructiveness – with enormous disproportion. The organ of self esteem in which originates self love, is fully developed, but the arch of conscientiousness, and caution is flat and low. The head was above average size, around 23 and a half inches.

Phrenologically viewed, this is the head of a man in whom the animal organs so far exceed in size the organs of the moral and the reasoning faculties that nothing but the hardest labour and prevention from immoral seductions could have kept in anything like safety. The good looks of the face were in strange contrast with the dangerous features of the mental organ.[5]

*

Seven months after the funeral of the Marshall family, a proper headstone was finally erected in the churchyard at Denham Parish Church. The local residents had clubbed together in order to purchase a proper memorial. The *Bucks Herald*, as ever, reported the circumstances:

Denham, the Marshall Family. The inhabitants of the parish of Denham have shown their great sympathy for the cruel and barbarous murder of the above family, by erecting to their memory a neat and exceedingly chaste monument in the churchyard. It consists of a large slab of Bath stone, and is inscribed as follows;-

'Beneath this stone lie the remains of Emmanuel Marshall, and Charlotte his wife; also Mary Ann his sister; Mary, Thirza, and Gertrude his children; who together with his mother Mary Marshall, were all barbarously murdered on Sunday morning, 22 May 1870, by John Owens, a travelling blacksmith, who was executed at the county Gaol at Aylesbury, 8 August 1870. Mary aged 8 years; Thirza aged 6, Emmanuel, aged 35; Charlotte aged 34; Mary Ann aged 32 years; Gertrude aged 4 years'.[6]

*

It is good to note that the other officer involved in the arrest of John Jones was not forgotten, with all the glory going to senior officer Supt Dunham. William Toulman was also at the sharp end of policing, taking the armed and dangerous Jones into custody on 24 May 1870. The *Bedfordshire Mercury* recorded the award that was made to him:

> Testimonial to a Detective Officer; On Tuesday, Detective Toulman, of the Reading Borough Police Force, was presented with a valuable testimonial, subscribed for by the residents in that town and neighbourhood, in recognition of the important services he rendered in connection with Owen, the Denham Murderer, in one of the lodging houses in Reading.

> The testimonial consisted of a handsome watch, with gold chain, the inner case of the former bearing the following inscription:- 'Presented to Detective Toulman, by the inhabitants of Reading, as a testimonial of his vigilance and courage in assisting in the capture of John Owen, the Uxbridge Murderer, on 24 May 1870.'[7]

William and Margaret Toulman were living at 39 Chatham Street, Reading at the time of the 1871 census.[8] He was serving as a police officer in Reading in 1881,[9] but by 1891 had retired and was living in Alvenstoke, Hampshire.[10] He must have done well for himself, as by the 1901 census he had returned to his birthplace and was listed as a retired police inspector.[11]

Things did not end well for William. His burial record in Bothenhampton in Dorset recorded his death as occurring on 1 October 1903, at the age of 60.[12] It gave no clue as to the cause. Two newspaper articles (*Reading Mercury*, 3 October 1903 and *Cheltenham Chronicle*, 3 October 1903) gave details from the coroner's inquest in relation to his apparent suicide.

It appears that William had been assaulted in a scuffle with some 'gypsies' some year before his death which had left him suffering from occasional bouts of depression. He was later found hanged near his home in Bothenhampton in Dorset. At the hearing his brother asked the Coroner if he could keep the noose which had been used. The Coroner acceded to the request, describing it as a 'melancholy relic'. The brother said he would keep the rope for the rest of his days.[13]

*

Two callers at Denham Police Station over 100 years after the murders made the case for a ghost of the Marshalls still being at work in Cheapside Lane. An article appeared in the *Police Review* magazine in 1986 which makes for 'interesting' reading. The article was written by Inspector John Pearson, who had worked in the Denham area for many years. Make of it what you will:

> It was 2am, the police station door flew open and a man & woman rushed in with faces white as snow. These two frightened people were very anxious to relate their story to someone. The wife told me that their house stood on or around the site of the old smithy where seven people had been murdered. She said the spirits had been sorely disturbed. She and her husband could not stay in the house any longer.

> On several occasions the wife had heard a body, as if in severe torment, rushing from one corner of the room to another in the bedroom above her. When she went up the stairs to investigate, a cold damp wind always blew strongly in her face. Black fungus grew overnight in the high alcoves of the staircase.

> On this very evening she had gone up to find her husband was sleeping soundly in bed but his body was cold as death. Sweat had soaked his pyjamas and sheets to such an extent that it could be wrung out afterwards.

> Things often moved around in the house and ornaments shifted as if moved by some unseen hand. The house, 'The Murder House' as it was known, remained standing until a few years ago when it was demolished to make way for flats.[14]

*

At the time of the murders it was suggested that the house where the crimes took place was going to be demolished. Houses belonging to the likes of Fred and Rose West and Soham murderer Ian Huntley were quickly knocked down. The Marshalls' building stood for around 87 years after the murder. It was later renamed Orchard Farm, which probably refers to the fact that the plot contained an orchard originally planted by William Marshall. In 1970 *The Post* local newspaper carried an article marking the centenary of the murders. The piece, including a photograph of the property looking forlorn and overgrown, with a Frost & Co. 'For Sale' sign, described the building as 'now demolished.'[15]

It's hard to imagine anyone having a peaceful night's sleep in that building, but the Bronsdon family lived there for many years.

During my research for this book I was lucky enough to meet a descendant of Daniel Bronsdon, who was churchwarden at the village church and captain of the bell ringers, and who lived in the house in Cheapside Lane for forty-six years. Ann Collins, who still lives in Denham, told me that her parents and grandparents lived in the house.

The family apparently liked the property and never had any untoward experiences there. Ann played in the house for several years as she was growing up, and had many happy memories there.

After the house was pulled down in the late 1950s it was replaced by some modern terraced houses in a small cul de sac which were aptly named Bronsdon Way. Cheapside Lane today contains a number of unremarkable modern properties with nothing of the house or the orchard left to show it ever existed.

*

The Bucks Constabulary was a relatively new police force when the murders took place. The Metropolitan Police was formed in 1829, but other provincial forces were much slower to arrive. In 1856, the Government passed an Act making it compulsory to establish a paid police force in the county, and on 6 February 1857 the Buckinghamshire Constabulary was established.

The county was split into 5 Divisions, with a Superintendent in charge of each: Aylesbury (which was to be the Headquarters of the Force), Fenny Stratford, Steeple Claydon, High Wycombe and Slough. The force strength at its inception was 100 men. A constable's shifts consisted of six hours during the night and three hours during the day.

After 111 years of service, the Bucks Constabulary ceased to exist on 1 April 1968 when it was amalgamated with other local constabularies at Oxford, Oxford City, Berkshire and Reading to become Thames Valley Police.[16]

*

Finally, when I first started researching this book, I checked the website ancestry.com as I was trying to find out more about Supt Dunham. I discovered a lady in the United States who was distantly related to him. I decided on a whim to email her, to see if she was aware of her famous ancestor. Within twenty minutes of my message she emailed back saying how interested she was in my research, but that she was rather tied up as her own son had been recently murdered. How ironic and sad.

1 *Bucks Herald*, 20 August 1870.

2 *Western Times*, 20 March 1925.

3 *The Era*, 29 May 1870.

4 Professor Cornelius Donovan was born in Cork in 1795. He married Henrietta Maria Sarah Walsh at Paddington in 1835. In 1871, shortly after the Denham Murders, he was living at 44 Manor Road, Lewisham, with his wife and children, aged 75 years. His title recorded in the Census of that year was 'Professor of Phrenology'. He published a book called A Handbook of Phrenology in 1870. He died on 30 December 1872 at 44 Manor Road. Probate records showed that Donovan only left £20 in his estate.

5 *Bucks Herald*, 20 August 1870.

6 *Bucks Herald*, 31 December 1870.

7 *Bedfordshire Mercury*, 10 September 1870.

8 1871 Census.

9 1881 Census. Toulman was listed as a 'detective officer of police' aged 37 years. His address was 44 Sherman Road, Reading. The tiny two bedroom terraced house still stands.

10 1891 Census, on which he is recorded as 2 Little Anglesey, Alvenstoke, as a 45-year-old retired police officer.

11 1901 Census.

12 Burial parish records for Bothenhampton, Dorset, page 94, entry number 748: William Toulman, abode Baunton, age 60, died 1 October 1903, curate Malcolm Foster.

13 *Reading Mercury*, 3 October 1903; *Cheltenham Chronicle*, 3 October 1903.

14 *Police Review*, 14 March 1986.

15 *Bucks Herald*, 20 August 1970.

16 Mike Shaw, retired police officer, Buckinghamshire Constabulary website (www.mkheritage.co.uk/bch/docs/bconstab.html).

Review of the Evidence

When I was writing the last few pages of this book, I was feeling quite pleased with myself for having completed a large research project of three years. I was happy with the narrative and the illustrations, and I hoped it made an interesting read. I had considered the Denham Murders a fascinating story with a successful prosecution to end the story.

Imagine my surprise when I discovered that just prior to my approaching a publisher, someone released a book about alleged miscarriages of justice in Buckinghamshire in the latter part of the 19th century. Always being interested in anything crime-related, this book was of interest but it became a lot more interesting when I discovered that the author had written a section of the book on the Denham Murders. The book gave details of a number of murders in Buckinghamshire, all of which were investigated by Supt Thomas Dunham.[1]

It soon became clear that this was no ordinary scholarly account written in an objective and unbiased way. It turned out that the author, Martin Taylor, was related to a lady who was murdered in Slough in 1881. She turned out to be his great, great grandmother, Ann Reville. His research of that crime led to him 'investigating' other Thomas Dunham murders. Mr Taylor was a man on a mission. He has not been afraid of upsetting people and organisations along

221

the way.

Mr Taylor demanded, unsuccessfully, that the Chief Constable of Thames Valley Police funded a memorial to John Jones as he was buried in an unmarked grave in Aylesbury Gaol. He has attempted, again unsuccessfully, to force the Attorney General to re-examine the inquests into the Marshall family murders. He also wants the death certificates 'corrected' to remove the section of the document which gave the cause of death as being murdered by John Jones. His book criticises Ancestry, the Government, *Daily Mail* readers, democracy in the UK, the General Register Office, the Attorney General and Thames Valley Police Freedom of Information department.

It's a shame that Mr Taylor didn't simply stick to telling a story about the murders. His accounts are tiresomely sarcastic, repetitive, and at times hard to understand. This is a shame, as he has clearly done a huge amount of research. He has an axe to grind and uses the pages of his book to deride, in the worst possible terms, Supt Dunham, Chief Constable John Tyrwhitt Drake, Buckinghamshire Constabulary, the Coroner Mr Charsley, Thames Valley Police and the Thames Valley Police Crime Commissioner.

The venom that emanates from the pages of this shocking book is quite astounding. It is quite the most sarcastic piece I have ever read. It's hard to take seriously someone who writes like a spoiled child. He was also scathing about two former policemen who had written small articles about Denham. He lambasted both Len Woodley, who wrote *Murder in Buckinghamshire*, as well as A. Hailstone, who wrote the book *Buckinghamshire Constabulary Centenary 1857-1957*.

The only good thing about the publication of Mr Taylor's book is that it prompted me do some more research, especially into John Owen's life and criminal record, which has been shown to be considerable. Mr Taylor claimed he was not a career criminal. It also encouraged me to re-examine the evidence that I had gathered in order to reassess the outcome of the case. Had I come to the wrong conclusion?

Mr Taylor is convinced that everyone who Thomas Dunham dealt with had been 'fitted up', and that Dunham was incapable of successfully investigating any crime. In particular, he claims that the Marshall family were NOT murdered by John Jones/Owen.

The early days of the Bucks Constabulary would not have had the scientific aids that we commonly see now in modern day policing. These were still years away. Dedicated detectives were operating at Scotland Yard, but forensic science did not exist in 1870 as we know it today. Fingerprinting only arrived towards the end of the 19th century, while DNA testing was a late 20th century development.

Policing in Dunham's day would have been far from perfect and mistakes were made then, as they are now, as police officers are human and therefore fallible. What Mr Taylor argues, however, is that Mr Dunham, the coroners and others deliberately perverted the course of justice and that, having decided who the killer may be, built a case around it.

I have not investigated the other murders which Mr Taylor has written about so I can make no comment about these cases. But I do feel qualified to speak about the Denham Murders, having spent three years researching the case in great detail. Unlike Mr Taylor, I don't have a reason for writing the book one way or the other. I entered my research with an open mind and have made my conclusions based only on those findings. Although I am a retired police officer, I have recorded all the facts that I have discovered without bias. I have to say that I did not find any evidence that led me to believe that John Jones was not the culprit.

I'm sure that Thomas Dunham was no Victorian wonder cop. I'm also sure that if we looked hard enough, we would find out about cases that he lost and investigations that went wrong. That is, however, par for the course for any police officer. No officer who completes his full years of service wins every case. Policing is also a complicated and difficult job, where you learn things every day. It's hard to believe that Thomas Dunham could have reached the rank of Superintendent and completed his full service if he was either a serially unsuccessful or corrupt policeman.

As far as you and I are concerned, the only case that we are interested in at this point is the Denham Murders. Did Dunham make mistakes? Almost certainly. Did he collude with numerous independent witnesses in order to make them give false evidence against the first suspect that came along? I don't think so. Mr Taylor makes great play on Charles Coombes, and how he told Dunham that Jones was the murderer. He belittles this witness and the importance of his intervention into proceedings.

Mr Taylor tries to suggest that Dunham colluded with several witnesses, not to mention the local coroner. How likely was this? He makes a lot of a supposed conflict of evidence about the clothing found at the scene. This is a red herring from Mr Taylor, as Jones claimed that the victim's clothing had been given to him by the 'real' murderers. What Taylor forgets is that the evidence from Mr Coombes did lead to Jones's apprehension. On being arrested, Jones said he did not commit the crime but he knew who did. This was the sort of vague story that criminals often come up with when they know the evidence is against them and they have been caught 'bang to rights'.

It's a common thing for criminals to attempt on being confronted with strong evidence of their guilt when being interviewed by the police. The 'trick' is to give an explanation that the police will be unable to easily test.

The conversation would go something like this:

Police: 'Where did you get the (suspected stolen) property from?'

Suspect: 'A man in a pub sold it to me for £50.'

Police: 'Who was the man?'

Suspect: 'I don't remember his name, I think he lives somewhere in London. He is 5'9' tall and is medium build. He gave me a receipt for the goods.'

Police: 'Where is the receipt now?'

Suspect: 'I put it in my jacket pocket, but when I got home it was missing. I think it must have fallen out when I took my jacket off on the bus.'

The point I am trying to make here is that Mr Taylor is looking at Jones's explanation of his being found in possession of the clothing and property naïvely. He has accepted Jones' explanation at face value, without stopping to think that he may have been lying in order to save his own skin. His explanation was a simple one to come up with. It was convenient for him, as he knew that the police would never be able to find these men, if indeed they actually existed.

He told the police that two men had committed the crime, and who then gave him items from the victim's property. Being a regular in various courts in the south of England, Jones would have known how the system worked. Would he have chanced wearing a murder victim's clothing, as this evidence would surely have consigned him to the gallows?

Was it more likely, instead, that having himself committed the murder, his own clothing was covered in blood and he simply needed the victim's clothes in order to make good his escape but without the incriminating bloodstains?

In any event, what were the chances that Jones would have been passing the Marshall home in the early hours of the morning at precisely the moment when the two murderers were leaving the building? Also, why would he have taken possession of the front door key of the house? What possible value would it have been to him?

Let us imagine for a moment that you were the two murderers. You have just killed seven people in a frenzy of violence. As you leave the victims' house you see an unknown man passing by. You would know that every policeman in the country would soon be looking for you. The passerby could be someone that could describe you to the police. Would you give him money and property and make him promise to keep quiet, or would you have killed him as well, as dead men tell no tales? Why would they have taken a chance on him keeping quiet? Having killed seven people, another murder was not going to add to their sentence.

One thing that Mr Taylor does not seem to have grasped is the importance of circumstantial evidence. Many murders take place when only the victim and the assailant are together, unseen by any witnesses. No one saw the Marshall murders take place, so the only evidence that was ever going to convict Jones or anyone else was circumstantial evidence.

There comes a tipping point in many cases when the weight of the circumstantial evidence becomes overwhelming, and where there are just too many pieces of evidence that point to the guilt of a suspect. With the Denham Murders case, there was far too much circumstantial evidence that pointed at John Jones being the murderer.

Mr Taylor has tried to give John Jones the status of an innocent martyr to police corruption. He described him as 'an innocent man'. Jones was no innocent as we have proved by his long criminal record. He was by his own admission 'involved' in the murder. He said two unknown men committed the crime and simply gave him some items from the crime scene to keep quiet. He was therefore at the very least guilty of receiving stolen goods.

He had also failed to inform the police about the crime. The modern offence of Assisting an Offender (Contrary to Sec 4 (1) Criminal Law Act 1967) may also have been committed by Jones in this regard.

Even if he had not been convicted of the murder of the Marshalls, Jones would probably have also been convicted of the modern offence of using a firearm with intent to resist arrest. (Contrary to Sec 17 Firearms Act 1968).

We might conclude from all this evidence, however, that the two men were a smokescreen and that he was the murderer. There are several possibilities. Perhaps three men committed the murders - Jones and two unknown others.

Mr Taylor has recently demanded that Thames Valley Police erect a memorial to John Jones. He has used a large helping of speculation in his book to try and discredit both the police and the evidence. Miscarriages of justice will always happen, but not in this case. I don't think a memorial to John Owen/Jones is going to happen any time soon.

All the evidence screams out at Jones being the guilty party. Jones had a motive. He had the opportunity, and all the evidence points at him. He was a man who lived his life breaking the law and using violence. As a young man he had sustained a very serious head injury.

Jones was, in my view, rightly hanged based on the evidence.

In conclusion, I don't want to tell you Jones was guilty of the crime unless I can prove it to you. I would therefore like to sum up to you, the jury, with the main facts of the case, and then let you decide.

Mr Taylor says he does not know who killed the Marshalls. After reading the evidence below, I hope that you *will* know.

Main points of circumstantial evidence against John Jones

1. Jones knew Emmanuel Marshall and had done work for him.
2. He would have known the location, the house and forge.
3. He would have known the family.
4. He had a grudge against Marshall, who refused to pay him for some bad work he had performed.
5. Jones was a career criminal. His usual crime was theft.
6. He had used violence previously, assaulting a policeman and shooting cats with a pistol.
7. He had received a life-changing head injury aged 15 which may have changed his personality.
8. He had possibly served in the army and was reported to have been flogged against a crossbar. He may have had experience killing people in the army in wars overseas.
9. Daniel Love of Reading Gaol identified the clothing left at the scene of the murder as belonging to Jones.
10. Jones told him on being released that he knew a man who had some money and he wanted it and would kill the man. He also asked the way to Uxbridge.
11. Jones was seen at 3.00 am near the Marshalls' house in Denham by PC Trevener wearing old clothing.
12. The murder weapons were all blacksmiths' tools; Jones would have been very adept at using them.
13. Marshall's boots were removed from his feet; Jones was reported to be wearing boots that were too tight. Why would anyone, who had just murdered seven people, bother to steal an old pair of boots, unless your own pair were saturated in blood?

14. Warder Thomas Paulton identified the hat and clothing found at the murder scene as those worn by Jones on his release from prison.

15. If strangers had murdered Emmanuel Marshall they could have escaped without killing the rest of the family, as they would not have been unable to identify them. If the family had seen Jones he would have had to kill them as well, as they knew who he was.

16. The smashing of the photograph of Emmanuel Marshall in the bedroom indicates someone with a grudge against him.

17. When Jones arrived in Uxbridge on Saturday he had no bag and only old clothing, and no money. The following day he had new clothes, money and a bag and property – obviously come by illegally.

18. Jones stated he was getting items from his brother, but he had no brother in the area. He mentioned a brother before and after the murders. This shows his intention of going to Marshall's, not the 'brother'. His 'brother' never appeared in court as a witness for the defence.

19. He destroyed a straw hat he had come by from the victim – why?

20. On the Sunday he was being extravagant with money.

21. When Jones heard about the murders in the pub he hung his head and trembled violently. He left hurriedly saying he had to go away in the morning. This suggests guilty knowledge.

22. Jones had a pistol in the brothel which he held at the woman's forehead, and threatened to use on those there for no apparent reason. He threatened to 'do for them all'.

23. Jones left Uxbridge in a hurry and travelled miles away to Reading. He told people that he had to get away in the morning to West Drayton, Southall or Brentford. He did not say why he had to leave. Was it to avoid capture? He had no home to go to, so why was he in such a hurry to go there?

24. On his arrest he stated that he knew who the murderers were.

25. He pulled out a pistol on being approached by the police – a run-of-the-mill thief would not have pulled out a gun in such circumstances. This was a man fearing the hangman's noose.

26. The pistol was one of an identical pair stolen from the Marshall's house.

27. He was found wearing the victim's boots and clothing.

28. He was in possession of a key to the Marshalls' house – did he use it to lock up the house on departure?

29. He tossed the key into a cupboard in Reading to try and dispose of the evidence. It was discovered and found to fit the Marshalls' door.

30. Mr Boyce, the Deputy Prison Governor, recognised Jones, despite him giving a false identity.

31. Jones acted erratically in custody, with furious outbursts. He looked to try and escape while on the train.

32. Jones sold Marshall's coat in Reading, wanting to get rid of the evidence.

33. When his case was heard at Slough he was asked if there was anything he wanted to say about the murder charge. He responded: 'Not a word sir.'

34. Old cord trousers left at the scene were almost unmistakable, with black patches on white. Other clothing was identified as belonging to Jones.

35. He stated that he was passing the murdered people's cottage on the Sunday morning when he saw two men standing there, who called him and gave him money and clothes. What is the likelihood of this?

36. If these men were real rather than imaginary, why would they have given the items to Jones? How would it benefit them?

37. Clothing was stolen in the burglary subsequent to the murder. The murderer might want to steal items of value, but why steal clothing?

38. Jones gave a false name on his arrest.

39. Where was Jones going at 3.00 am on the Sunday?

40. When arrested he said: 'I have not murdered man, woman nor child', showing he had knowledge of the murders. The papers had not yet reached Reading with the news, so he must have known it before leaving for Reading.

41. During his arrest Dunham said: 'Why you scoundrel, you have the murdered man's boots and trousers too!' Jones replied: 'I know that.' How did he know this?

42. Jones demanded a drink in a pub in Denham at 8.00 am. He had been seen at 3.00 am by police. What had he been doing between 3.00-8.00 am. Why was he so desperate for a drop of beer?

43. Jones pawned a watch and chain in Uxbridge. He told James Weston that his name was George Wilson of Reading. He said the property belonged to him. He pleaded for some money on the items, saying he had to get back to see his father in Reading.

44. Henry Salter picked up Jones in his cart. He told him he was going to get money from his brother near Uxbridge, and that he was going after dark. He refused to say where his brother lived when asked. Was this because mentioning the blacksmith Marshall would have given the game away?

45. Elizabeth Simpson saw Jones coming out of the Marshalls' gate at about 7.00 am. She engaged him in conversation, believing him to be Emmanuel Marshall. He told her the family had gone on an excursion early that morning at 5.30 am. He asked Mrs Simpson if Marshall kept any man. This was an interesting question - was it jealousy of anyone else who might be employed by Marshall?

46. John Smith was offered a watch by Jones at 8.00 am, despite him having had no money the previous night.

Not all of the evidence / information above was presented at the trial of John Jones. Though most of it was, some of the information was reported in the newspapers but never tested in court.

I have included this information in order to help us make an informed decision about the guilt of John Jones.

———————————————

1   Martin Taylor, *Buckinghamshire in Crisis – A County Rotten to the Core* (Grosvenor House Publishing, 2016).

List of Main Characters

Abdy, John Thomas
Defence Counsel at the trial at Aylesbury.

Alderman, Charles
Broke into the Marshalls' house in order to find the bodies.

Alderman, Sarah
Landlady of the Dog and Duck Pub, Denham – served Jones a drink of beer.

Alexander, Hannah (Russell)
Wife of John Owen.

Amor, George
Husband-to-be of victim Mary Ann Marshall.

Armstrong, Mr
Chief Warder at Aylesbury Gaol who was present at the execution of John Jones.

Balham (or Bollam), Charlotte
Landlady of Bell Yard, Uxbridge.

Bampton, Lizzie
11-year-old child, took dress to the Marshall house on the day the bodies were discovered.

Bowden, Sgt Elijah
Sergeant of Bucks Constabulary who assisted in the discovery of the murders.

Boyce, Robert Walter
Deputy Governor of Reading Gaol who identified Jones.

Brickwell, Dr John Smith
Thomas Dunham's Surgeon.

Bunbury, Thomas Edwin George
Chaplain to Aylesbury Gaol.

Burton, Susan
Prostitute, possibly with Jones on Sunday.

Calcraft, William
Hangman.

Ceely, Mr Robert
Surgeon of Aylesbury, present at Jones's execution.

Channell, Sir William Fry
Trial judge.

Charsley, Frederick
South Bucks Coroner, conducted the inquest at the Swan Inn.

Churchley, PC Henry
Shipston-on-Stour police officer who found stolen pistol on Jones.

Coleman, Edward John
Magistrate at the examination of Jones.

Coombes, Charles
Bricklayer. Important witness, first to report to Supt Dunham about Jones as a suspect.

Cooper, Sgt 13X
Met Police Sergeant, Uxbridge Police.

Cooper, William
Defence counsel at the trial

Davis, Jane

21-year-old needlewoman and possible prostitute who spent the night with Jones.

Denson, Job

Superintendent, Bucks Constabulary.

Donovan, Professor Cornelius

Phrenologist who examined cast of John Jones's skull following his execution.

Drake, Captain John C. Tyrwhitt

Chief Constable of Bucks Constabulary.

Dunham, Frederick John

Son of Supt Thomas Dunham. PC 158 Bucks Constabulary, later RSPCA inspector.

Dunham, James Branwood, Chief Supt

Grandson of Supt Thomas Dunham. Warrant number 122526. Chief Supt Met Police X Division.

Dunham, Martha (née Wiggins)

Wife of Supt Thomas Dunham.

Dunham, Thomas

Superintendent of Bucks Constabulary, arrested and convicted John Jones.

Dunham, William

Brother of Supt Thomas Dunham.

Du Pre, Caldon George

Foreman of Grand Jury at the trial, local MP.

Farrer, Captain W.F.

Magistrate at Slough who examined Jones.

Fassnidge, Mr

An ironmonger in Uxbridge who Jones would often ask for work.

Ferris, John Spencer MRCS of Uxbridge

Performed Post Mortem. The main medical witness.

Forbes, Sgt Charles

Reading Police - Guarded Jones at Reading.

Fox, Dr Cornelius

Of Scarborough, performed Post mortem.

Greaves, Joshua

Vicar at Great Missenden. Visiting Justice of the Peace who went to meet John Jones at Aylesbury Gaol.

Harper, William

Superintendent Station Master, Slough Railway Station.

Harvey, Sir Robert Bateson

Chairman of Magistrates at Slough.

Henderson, Col Edmund

Metropolitan Police Commissioner. Offered to send a detective inspector to assist Bucks Constabulary.

Hickman, Joseph

Furniture dealer of Rockingham Road, Uxbridge, who assisted in arresting Jones for theft of stockings in 1870.

Hitch, Alfred

Murdered Charles Plumbridge in Denham in 1886 and was arrested by Supt Dunham.

Holloway, Insp William H

Inspector 'X' Division, Met Police.

James, William

Arrested by Supt Dunham on suspicion of the murder of Charles Dance in 1888. He was acquitted at Aylesbury Assize.

Jervis, Supt James

Supt Bucks Constabulary, produced the lock of the door of the house and was present at Jones's execution.

Johnson, PC Charles

Guarded Jones at Reading Police Station.

Jones, John
Murderer. Alias John Owen, John Reynolds, John Jenkins. Also known as 'Jack'.

Josey, Sgt William
Reading police officer who assisted at Reading Railway Station.

Joyce, Rev Charles
Conducted the funerals, foreman of the Inquest jury. Curate at Denham Church.

Leaver, PC George
Reading police officer, guarded Jones at Reading Police Station.

Love, Daniel
Warder at Berkshire County Gaol, Reading.

Lyons, Margaret
Owner of clothes shop in Reading who bought items from Jones.

MacNamara, Dr George Housman
Doctor who performed post mortems.

Marshall, Charlotte
Wife of Emmanuel – Victim. Aged 34 years.

Marshall, Emmanuel
Victim – Blacksmith. Head of the Family. Aged 35 years.

Marshall, Francis William
Son of Emmanuel Marshall. Escaped the murders but died of TB age 18.

Marshall, Gertrude (Maud)
Victim - aged 4 years. Found in the arms of her grandmother.

Marshall, Mary (Senior) née Herbert
Victim - aged 77 years. Mother of Emmanuel.

Marshall, Mary Ann
Victim - aged 32 years. About to be married to George Amor.

Marshall, Mary Charlotte Sophia
Victim - aged 8 years.

Marshall, Philip

Brother of Emmanuel who went to Australia.

Marshall, Thirza Agnes

Victim - aged 6 years.

Marshall, William Francis

Brother of Emmanuel who went to Australia and died there in 1865, five years prior to the murders.

Mason, Thomas

Blacksmith of Byfield, Northants who accidentally struck his apprentice, John Jones, on the head, nearly killing him.

Metcalfe, James William

Prosecution barrister at trial

Nightingale, PC

Wolverhampton Borough Police officer who had a violent struggle with Jones whilst drunk.

O'Malley, Peter Frederick

Prosecution barrister at trial.

Owen, Elizabeth

Sister of Jones.

Owen, George

Brother of Jones.

Owen, John

Father of John Jones, a tailor.

Palmer, William

Detective Inspector – Scotland Yard detective who visited Uxbridge and Slough.

Paulton, Thomas

Prison warden at Coldbath Fields Prison, identified the clothes used by Jones on release the day before the murders.

Payne, Augustus

Was arrested by Supt Dunham on suspicion of the murder of Ann Reville in 1881. He was acquitted at Aylesbury Assize.

Peach, John

Great Western Railway Station Master who assisted at Reading Railway Station.

Pennifold, PC Michael

Met Police constable, Uxbridge. Adopted father of orphaned Francis Marshall.

Phillips, Sgt

Police officer who arrested Jones for selling tobacco on a Sunday.

Platt, Samuel Eli

Clerk of Aylesbury Assize Court.

Pratt, Dr

Doctor of Uxbridge, performed post mortems.

Purchase, Supt James

Reading police officer who assisted at Reading Railway Station.

Reynoldson, Mary Ann

Committed suicide in London on hearing news of the Denham Murders.

Robinson, John

Man arrested on suspicion of being involved in the murder but was released without charge.

Salter, Henry

Carman, gave Jones a lift to Uxbridge in his cart.

Selwood, Elizabeth

Spent an evening with Jones, possibly a prostitute.

Shelley, Augustine Thomas

Independent Minister of Aylesbury, visited the prison to unsuccessfully obtain a confession from Jones.

Simms, Sarah

Present at time of breaking the Marshalls' door down.

Simpson, Elizabeth

Saw Jones come out of the Marshalls' house on the morning of the murders.

Smith, John

Coal dealer living at Denham Turnpike, was offered a watch by Jones.

Sparke, Job

Brother of Charlotte Marshall (nee Sparke).

Sparke, Loyal

Father of victim Charlotte Marshall (nee Sparke).

Sparke, Mary Ann

Sister of victim Charlotte Marshall (nee Sparke).

Spooner, Thirza (née Marshall)

Sister of Emmanuel Marshall. Aunt and guardian to Francis W. Marshall.

Sutton, Insp George

Bucks Constabulary, assisted with the initial investigation.

Thompson, Supt

Warwickshire Constabulary. Sent report on Jones's history to Supt Dunham.

Tindal, Acton

Clerk of the Peace and Under Sheriff for Buckinghamshire. Present at the execution of Jones.

Toulman, Detective Constable William

Reading Police, assisted in arresting Jones with Supt Dunham.

Townsend, Inspector John

Door key found at Oxford Arms given to him which fitted the door to the Marshalls' house.

Trevener, PC Charles William

Denham village policeman PC 27, Bucks Constabulary.

Walker, Detective Sergeant Robert

Met Police detective, Scotland Yard.

West, David

Neighbour of the Marshall family.

Weston, James

Pawnbroker in Uxbridge.

Williamson, Superintendent Adolphus Frederick

Met Police, Scotland Yard. Senior detective. Superior of Insp Palmer, who offered assistance to Bucks Constabulary.

Willis, Harriett

Found key in cupboard at Oxford Arms.

Wooderton, James

Was with Jones at Lyons shop in Reading selling coat, also saw Jones dispose of a key in a cupboard at Oxford Arms.

Calendar of Events

21 May 1870
Marshalls last seen alive. Jones released from Coldbath Prison 9.00 am.

22 May
Marshall family murdered in early hours.

23 May
Bodies of Marshall family found at the house.

24 May
Intended wedding day of Mary Ann Marshall.
Jones arrested.
Inquest opens: First day.

25 May
Jones appears at Slough Magistrates' Court.

27 May
Inquest resumes: Second day.
Funerals of the victims.

31 May
Second Magistrates' court hearing at Aylesbury Prison.

22 July
Trial at Aylesbury Assize. Jones found guilty.

8 August
Jones executed at Aylesbury Prison at 8.00 am.

Rules To Be Observed By All Police Constables

(Drawn up in the reign of Queen Victoria)

1. Constables are placed in authority to protect and not to oppress the public.

2. To which effectually they must earnestly and systematically exert themselves to prevent crime.

3. When a crime has been committed, no trace should be lost, nor exertion spared to discover and bring to Justice the offenders.

4. Obtain a knowledge of all reputed thieves, idle and disorderly persons.

5. Watch narrowly all people having no visible means of subsistence.

6. Prevent vagrancy.

7. Be impartial in the discharge of duties.

8. Discard from the mind all political and sectarian prejudices.

9. Be cool and intrepid in the discharge of duties in emergencies, and avoidable conflicts.

10. Avoid altercations, and display perfect command of temper

under assault, and gross provocation, to which all Constables must occasionally be liable.

11. Never strike but in self-defence, nor treat a prisoner with more vigour than may be necessary to prevent escape.

12. Practice the most complete sobriety; one instance of drunkenness will render a Constable liable to dismissal.

13. Treat with the utmost civility all classes of Her Majesty's subjects and cheerfully render assistance to all who may have need of it.

14. Exhibit deference and respect to the Magistracy.

15. Promptly and cheerfully obey all superior officers.

16. Render an honest, faithful and speedy account of all monies and property whether entrusted with them for others, or taken possession of in the execution of duty.

17. With reference to the foregoing, bear especially in mind that honesty is the best policy.

18. Be perfectly neat in person and attire.

19. Never sit down in any public house or beer shop.

20. Avoid tippling.

21. It is in the interest of every man to devote some portion of his spare time to the practice of reading and writing, and the general improvement of the mind.

22. Ignorance is an insuperable bar to promotion.

Victorian Slang Words used by the Lower Class and the Criminal Underworld

Slang word / Meaning / Relevance to Denham case

Barking Irons
Guns or Pistols
Jones stole a barking iron from the Marshalls' house

Beak
Magistrate
Jones was often 'Up before the Beak'

Blag
Steal or snatch

Blower,
Nose; Informer
Charles Coombes was an informer

Bludger
A violent criminal
Jones was certainly a bludger

Blue Bottle, Crusher, Rozzer
A policeman

Boat, get the
To be sentenced to transportation (Australia)

Broad Arrow or Devil's claws
The arrow-like markings on a prison convict's uniform
These were introduced just after Jones was executed

Crapped
Hung, hanged
Jones was 'crapped' in Aylesbury

Derbies, Ruffles
Handcuffs
Jones was often handcuffed

Dipper
Pickpocket

Dollymop, Ladybird, Judy
A prostitute, often an amateur or a part-time street girl
Jones consorted with prostitutes in Uxbridge

Drag
A three month gaol sentence
Jones received three months for theft

Drum
A building, house or lodging; the location of a gaol
Jones had been in several different 'drums'

Family, the
The criminal Underworld

Flash house
A public house patronised by criminals

Jack
Detective

Jerryshop
Pawnbrokers
Jones tried to sell stolen property at a pawnbrokers

Lag
A convict
Jones was certainly one of these

Lump Hotel
Work House

Mot
Woman, especially, the proprietor of a lodging or public house
Mrs Balham in Uxbridge was one of these

Moocher
A rural vagrant
Jones was one of these

Mug-hunter
A street robber or footpad. Hence the modern 'Mugger'

Mumper
Beggar or scrounger

Muck Snipe
A person who is 'down and out'
Jones was often this

Salt Box
The Condemned Cell
Jones was in one of these

Scroby
Flogging in gaol
Executioner William Calcraft started his career flogging

Snowing
Stealing linen, clothes, that have been hung out to dry.
Jones did this in Uxbridge

Topping
A hanging
Jones was topped at Aylesbury

APPENDIX E

Careers of the
Police Officers Involved
in the Case

John Charles Tyrwhitt-Drake,
Chief Constable of Bucks Constabulary

John was often known during his police service at 'Captain Drake'. He was born in Amersham, Buckinghamshire in 1835 into the wealthy Drake family. He later attended Rugby School, in whose records he is listed as follows:

> Drake, John Charles Tyrwhitt, son of the Rev John Tyrwhitt Drake, Amersham Rectory, aged 14, 14th April, Mayor.[1]

He was later to become a captain in the Queen's Regiment before being appointed Chief Constable of Bucks Constabulary on 1 November 1867, taking over from Captain Willoughby Harcourt Carter. The Police Committee decided to appoint Drake after hearing details on the eighteen candidates and then voting for them. Drake had influential allies in Lord Chesham and C.G. Du Pre MP. It was interesting to note that most of the candidates appeared from their titles to be military officers.

The *Bucks Herald* reported a testimonial from Lord Chesham and Mr Du Pre for Drake:

[Drake] was living in the county and was a young and active man. He thought that the committee would not find a better man. Du Pre stated that Drake had earned the esteem of his comrades as well as his commanding officers and that he would devote his best energies to his office. After the voting, Drake was found to be well ahead of any of his rivals and was duly elected as chief constable.[2]

Drake retired in 1896. He was 62 years of age. His report of 31 July read as follows:

The Chief Constable, in taking leave of the Officers and Constables of the Bucks Constabulary begs to thank them heartily for the cheerful and ready manner in which they have always rendered him assistance in the execution of his duty and after nearly 29 years service. He can but leave the force with much regret and will always take an interest in their future welfare.

John Tyrwhitt-Drake retired on a pension of £266 13s 14d.[3]

The *Bucks Herald* gave details of the retirement of Mr Drake, where he was given a present of a silver tea and coffee service marked with the Drake family crest as well as a silver mounted oak tray.[4]

He had married Emily Harriet Anna D'Urban in 1861 in King Williams Town, Eastern Cape, South Africa. Emily died in 1869 and John then married Lydia May Hamilton in Devon in 1873.

Towards the end of his life he retired to a grand house at Dulas Court in rural Herefordshire where he had eight servants to look after him and his daughter Gertrude. When he died in 1915 his estate was worth £28,953.[5]

The 1911 census showed him to be a J.P. living on his own means. Interestingly, in the 1901 census he described himself as a 'retired officer of army' rather than a retired police chief constable.

I feel sure that Drake would have gained a good amount of reflected glory from the activities of Supt Dunham during the investigation of the Denham Murders. The clear up rate for murders would have certainly looked healthy that year.

PC Charles Trevener

PC Charles Trevener, collar 27, had a 'colourful' police career with ups and downs. This is a resume of his service:

Appointed 3rd Class Constable, 20 May 1867

Posted to Eton (South Eastern Division), 11 June 1867

Promoted to 2nd Class Constable, 13 January 1868

Promoted to 1st Class Constable, 21 October 1868

Posted to Denham (South Eastern Division), 11 May 1869

Appointed Acting Sergeant, 22 August 1870

Posted to Burnham (South Eastern Division), 22 January 1872

Posted to Colnbrook (South Eastern Division), 21 May 1874

Promoted to 3rd Class Sergeant, 26th March 1877

Posted to High Wycombe (South Western Division), 24 March 1880

Posted to Lee Common (Central Division), 20 May 1880

Reduced to Merit Class Constable for being drunk and absent
from his station at High Wycombe, 9 August 1880

Promoted to 3rd Class Sergeant, 19 May 1884

Posted to Princes Risborough (Central Division), 20 May 1884

Promoted to 2 Class Sergeant, 9 April 1888

Posted to Ivinghoe (Central Division), 11 March 1890

Promoted to 1st Class Sergeant, 2 May 1892

Posted to Stony Stratford (Northern Division), 4 August 1892

Discharged, 17 October 1893[6]

Charles Trevener was born in Purfleet, Essex c.1842. He was sworn in with the Buckinghamshire Constabulary on 1 June 1867. He was 26-years-old and single. His trade was given as a labourer, although he served for some time in the City of London Police, being stationed at Bishopsgate. Prior to that he had served in the Kent Constabulary for nearly three years. He was described as 5 feet 10½ inches tall, proportionate build with hazel eyes and brown hair.

Although PC Trevener was promoted several times, he was demoted once, in 1880. On another occasion, in 1874, he was reprimanded for remaining at and drinking beer in a public house at Taplow. Offences in relation to drinking on duty were common among police officers in the Victorian period.

He was a first class sergeant by the time of his retirement after 26 years and 4 months service. It is interesting to note that his first significant promotion from constable to sergeant came on 22 August 1870, just two weeks after the execution of John Jones. It may have been in the minds of the Bucks Constabulary hierarchy to in some way reward him for his part in the Denham Murders. Charles Trevener retired in 1893 with a pension of £53 14s 8d. Following his retirement he became the landlord of the Plough Inn on the Bath Road, Colnbrook.[7]

He married to Ann Good at Upton-cum-Chalvey, Slough, on 22 February 1868 and the couple had seven children, one of whom was Charles William Trevener who was born at Slough in 1869. Charles Jr was a baby living in Denham at the time of the murders. He later joined the Bucks Constabulary as PC 35, on 28 December 1886. He was promoted to Sergeant in 1891, Inspector in 1902 and to the rank of Superintendent on 1 January 1909. He retired on 12 May 1920 being in receipt of pension of £306 13s 4d. He was awarded the George V Coronation Medal in 1911.

Another son of Charles Sr was Walter John Trevener, who joined the Bucks Constabulary in 1894 as PC 50 but was called upon to resign in 1897 when he was 'found to be unsuitable for the Force'. Further bad news awaited his family. He joined the Royal Navy as a petty officer stoker on board HMS *Cressy* and was killed when the ship was sunk by a U-Boat on 22 September 1914. Of a crew of 760 officers and men, Walter was one of 559 men lost during the sinking. His body was never recovered and his name appears on the Chatham Naval Memorial.[8]

George Sutton

Buckinghamshire Constabulary records contain a lot of information on Sutton's service. He was born in Beaconsfield around 1837. He was 5' 7" tall and was a chairmaker by trade. He had also served in the 7th Royal Fusiliers for five years and six months, leaving on 6 January 1860.

After leaving the army he joined the Bucks Constabulary as a 3rd Class Constable on 8 March 1860. His shoulder number was 94. At the time of the Denham murders he was a 2nd Class Inspector based at Iver but he rose through the ranks to become Deputy Chief Constable on 6 January 1896.

By 25 October 1862 he was being marked out for higher things. A report at the Chief Constable's office commented:

> In consequence of the very marked zeal, energy and intelligence exhibited by P.C. 94 George Sutton in numerous cases during the last 12 months and in which his perseverance and tact were alone the cause of detection, he is promoted to the rank of 1st Class Constable and the Chief Constable feels it is his duty to uphold this promising Officer as an example to others.

By 24 September 1889, a significant promotion was announced by Chief Constable W.H. Carter. The report stated: 'Inspector George Sutton will proceed to Slough on Wednesday the 25th inst. for the purpose of taking charge of the South Eastern Division during the illness of Superintendent Dunham'.

After being promoted to Superintendent on 13 January 1890, his final promotion to Deputy Chief Constable was announced on 6 January 1896.

Census records showed George Sutton living with parents John and Rebecca Sutton in Shepherds Lane, Beaconsfield in 1851, working as a baker's boy. Subsequent census returns show him living at various Buckinghamshire police stations including Waverdon (1861), Iver (1871), Wing Road, Linslade (1881) and Upton-cum-Chalvey, Slough (1891).

The 1901 census recorded him living with his wife Sarah, both aged 64, at Slough Police Station. His occupation was given as Deputy Chief Constable.

Sadly, Sutton died in service. The report on his death dated 26 December 1902 from Chief Constable Otway Mayne gave the following sad tidings:

> It is with extreme regret that the Chief Constable has to announce to the Force the death of Superintendent George Sutton. Deputy Chief Constable, at Slough on Christmas Day. Supt. Sutton has served the County long and faithfully for a period of nearly forty three years in the Bucks Constabulary, and the Chief Constable feels that his

death will be deplored by all who knew him and have served under him. Superintendents and Inspectors will wear a mourning band on the left arm for one month from this date. Gratuity paid to widow £682.10.0.

George Sutton's death was reported in the *South Bucks Standard* of 2 January 1903. It described him as 'worthy, courteous, sympathetic and just.' He had had a long career and was much respected by all who knew him, having served Bucks Constabulary faithfully for 42 years. Sadly, his health started to fail and he offered his resignation only two weeks before passing away aged 66 on Christmas Day 1902 before he could enjoy his pension. One of the floral tributes at his well-attended funeral was from the widow of the late Supt Thomas Dunham. Before his death, Sutton was quoted as saying that his career had seen him having to deal with all kinds of criminals from 'a murder down to ferret stealing'.

Superintendent James Jervis

James Jervis was born in West Derby, Lancashire in 1845. He came from a police family, being the son of William Jervis who was a Superintendent of Police in St Helens, Lancashire.

His brother Richard became a police inspector in Southport, Lancashire. Richard Jervis was a very famous policeman of the period. He is mentioned in the book *The Great British Bobby* by Clive Emsley, and in fact in 1908 Richard had published his own memoirs, entitled *Lancashire's Crime & Criminals* following his retirement from Ormskirk Police Station in 1907.[9]

James Jervis first worked in a solicitor's office in Lancashire before moving to London to take up a post in the general manager's office on the Great Western Railway.[10] He then worked for Hanson & Son, Colonial Merchants in London before joining the Bucks Constabulary. He quickly became a Superintendent (on 1 June 1868), and became the Chief Constable of Portsmouth Police in 1875.

The *Bucks Herald* stated in their 13 November 1875 edition that:

Supt Jervis occupied the post of head clerk to the Chief Constable, (of Bucks Constabulary), at Aylesbury for the last 9 and a half years. He has been elected to the post of Chief Constable of Portsmouth on a salary of £300 per annum.

The same newspaper reported Jervis' next promotion in their 4 December 1880 edition:

> At the age of 23, he was promoted to the rank of Superintendent at Bucks Constabulary. He was the youngest man in any similar position in the country. At Blackburn his salary will be £400 per annum. During his career he has been involved in some of the most important criminal proceedings which have ever taken place in this country.

In 1880 he returned to Lancashire to become the Chief Constable of Blackburn Police. His reputation was good as he started his new posting, but tragedy was to strike when his wife Alice died suddenly of 'brain fever' in December 1881.[11]

Jervis was left a widower with three young children at the age of 35. This was the turning point in his career, as only six months later he resigned from that post under mysterious circumstances. The *Blackburn Standard* reported the matter on 3 June 1882, with what appeared to be hurt indignation:

> Mr Jervis has been the Chief Constable of Blackburn for 18 months. He was on a salary of £400 P.A. as well as having a house within a mile of the Town hall. On his appointment he said he was 35 years old and had 14 years police experience. He arrived in Blackburn on Monday 20 December 1880 to take up his duty. Most of his relatives have been in high positions in the police. He was appointed Chief Constable for Portsmouth in 1875. There were 50 candidates for the office. He held that post for 5 years. He has now added flight to his offences against good conduct. Most people were under the illusion he was a modest Chief Constable, sober, industrious and sagacious. Out of town, he seems to have made himself notorious for unbecoming behaviour on one or two occasions, and had been warned by the Watch Committee but their cautions went unheeded. He was summarily called upon to resign, and his resignation was accepted. Mr Jervis has sadly betrayed them. The late Chief Constable left Blackburn on Tuesday and said he would return, it is doubtful if reliance can be placed on this statement. He left in a cab from the Fox & Grapes Inn, Preston New Road to Pleasington Station and thence to Preston, his further destination being unknown.

Another article in the same edition of the paper commented:

> He seems to have hopelessly broken down. Some time ago he suffered severe domestic affliction with the loss of his wife. Since then it does not seem that he has been able to steady himself, with at length he neglected his duties so greatly that the authorities called upon him to demand his resignation.

It's unfortunate that Mr Jervis's career descended so relatively quickly. *The Blackburn Standard* of 7 January 1882 had earlier stated that the Watch Committee had passed a resolution of sympathy upon the decease of Mrs Jervis. The same article quoted the crime figures for local robberies in November 1881, with 25 committed and 21 detected. The figures for November 1880 were 33 committed, 23 detected. These were indeed impressive clear up rates.

Frustratingly, no further trace has been found of James Jervis following his departure from Blackburn with his reputation tarnished. He appears to have disappeared completely.

Officers who assisted at Reading Railway Station

A number of senior police officers and the Reading Slough Station Master were all involved in the exciting incidents at the station. They are described here.

John Peach is an interesting character. He was the Railway Superintendent at Reading Great Western Railway Station at the time of the murders. Born at Atcham near Shrewsbury, he dedicated most of his working life to the GWR. He joined the company aged 28 in Maidenhead in 1854, earning £70 per annum. He worked his way up to the rank of District Superintendent before retiring in Cornwall. He was earning £350 a year by the time he retired in 1894. He had also worked at Hungerford, Paddington, Didcot, Reading and Penzance.[12]

According to the 1871 census, he and his wife were living at the GWR station at Reading. He was shown as being the married head of the household, aged 43 years and employed as Great Western Station Master.[13]

When he moved from Reading to Cornwall in September 1880 he was presented with a handsome gold English lever watch and £55 from the staff at Reading.[14]

Following his death on 26 April 1900, his funeral was attended by a large number of people including GWR staff from as far away as Paddington.[15] He left his wife Louisa £1,137 in his will.[16]

Supt James Purchase was born in Christchurch, Hampshire in 1826. In 1851 he was shown on the census as a garden labourer living in Christchurch.[17] By 1861 he was living at the County Police Station in Reading aged 35. He was listed in the census as head of the household, and was a Sergeant in the County Police.[18]

By the 1871 census, just after the Denham murders, he was at the police station at 1 London Street, Reading, but was now described as a Chief Superintendent of police.[19] In 1881 he was now aged 56 and was still living at the same police station in London Street. After his retirement he moved to 'Fernleigh' on Waldegrave Road, Teddington. The 1891 census showed him as a 67 year old, superannuated police officer.

The short obituary in the *Reading Mercury* of 2 April 1892 described Purchase as being greatly respected in Reading, and that he had been the chief officer in the town since 1865, when he was elected. His rank had only been that of sergeant when his promotion took place. The report added that had joined Berks Constabulary in 1857 after 5-6 years in Hampshire Constabulary. It was also noted that he was an excellent cricketer.

Probate records show that he died on 27 March 1892, leaving £370 to his wife Catherine and his son, the Rev Edward James Purchase.[20]

Sgt William Josey was born in 1840 in Goring, Oxfordshire. He joined the Reading Borough Police. The 1871 census records him as a 31-year-old married head of the household. He was married to Alice Patey, the couple living at 2 Oatland Cottages, Reading. His occupation was police sergeant. The *Berkshire Chronicle* reported his retirement in their edition of 6 June 1874.

Supt Job Denson had a long and eventful career. He was born in Chester around 1823. During his time in the police, he had seen service in Ireland, Chester and Wales. He spent 30 years in the Bucks Constabulary with 15 years' service elsewhere before that according to a local newspaper report.[21] The 1851 census showed him living in Swan Lane, Denbigh, Wales. He was listed as Head of the household, married, aged 29 years, a police inspector born in Chester. He was married to Ann Evans who he had wed at Manchester Cathedral on 1 March 1847.[22]

By the 1861 census he had moved to Buckinghamshire and was living at Watson Lane, Aylesbury. He was a Superintendent of County Constabulary aged 38 years. In 1871 he was living at Exchange Street, Aylesbury, age 48 and still a Police Superintendent.[23] The police station contained a Superintendents' House in Exchange Street, so he would have almost have been 'living over the shop.' In the 1881 census he was aged 58 and was at 1 Exchange Street as a Superintendent of Police.[24]

He retired in 1888 and was given a purse of £70 as a retirement present at a meeting at The George Hotel. The *Bucks Herald* of 17 November 1888 described him as Superintendent and Deputy Chief Constable, who had served the county faithfully for 30 years and stated that he had 45 years service in total, his first station being at Stewkley, Bucks.

He died on 13 April 1899 at his home Gordon Cottage, Castle Road in Newport, Isle of Wight. He left £288 to his widow Ann Denson.[25]

It is interesting to note that Supt Denson's brother **William Biggs Denson** was also a member of Bucks Constabulary. Born in 1834, he had joined the Force on 4 December 1866 after transferring from Flintshire Constabulary, where he had served for five years. After being promoted to the rank of Acting Sergeant in 1867 he fell foul of the discipline code the following year. A report at the Chief Constable's Office, Aylesbury dated 4th August 1868 reads as follows:

> Acting Sergeant, William Denson is fined 2/6 for being drunk at Princes Risborough on the 20th July when on leave of absence.

The entry was signed by none other than his brother, Job Denson, Superintendent and Deputy Chief Constable. He then resigned by permission of the Chief Constable.[26]

---

1   Rugby School records.

2   *Bucks Herald*, 19 October 1867.

3   Bucks Constabulary records (Michael Shaw).

4   *Bucks Herald*, 18 July 1896.

5   Probate Record.

6   Buckinghamshire Constabulary records, Thames Valley Police Museum.

7   1911 Census, which showed that he had been married to wife Ann for 43 years and had had ten children, six of whom were alive and four who had died.

8   Thames Valley Police Museum archives re PC Trevener.

9   A Loving Cup listed for sale at auction in 2013 at Gerard's Auction Room, St Annes, Lancashire was inscribed 'A Present From A Friend To Richard Jervis Inspector Of Police, Southport, October 28th 1859'.

10 *Bucks Herald*, 4 December 1870.

11 *Blackburn Standard*, 10 December 1881.

12 GWR Employment Registers.

13 1871 Census.

14 *Reading Mercury*, 16 October 1880.

15 *The Cornishman*, 3 May 1900.

16 Probate Record, Bodmin.

17 1851 Census.

18 1861 Census.

19 1871 Census.

20 Probate record.

21 *Bucks Herald*, 17 November 1888.

22 Parish record marriages, Manchester Cathedral.

23 1871 Census.

24 1881 Census.

25 Probate record.

26 Bucks Constabulary records.

Police Descendants
of Thomas Dunham

Police officers often talk these days about the 'police family'. As we have seen in other parts of this book, the profession of police officer often ran from one family member to another. Brothers would often join up, as is the case with Thomas Dunham's brothers. It is also true that sons follow fathers into the same line of work. And so it was with the Dunhams.

One of Thomas Dunham's sons followed in his father's footsteps when he joined Bucks Constabulary on 4 May 1903. Sadly, Thomas did not live to see his son, Frederick John Dunham (born 3 July 1882) join up, which would have been a proud moment. PC 158 Dunham was posted to Northern Division at Fenny Stratford. Unfortunately, Frederick did not complete his service as he left the force on 11 January 1909.[1] Public service still beckoned, however, as he joined the RSPCA the same year.

In 1909 Frederick married Josephine Elizabeth Bramwood at St James Church, Muswell Hill. They had a daughter, Enid Marian, and a son, James Bramwood Dunham. The marriage register described Frederick as an 'Inspector in the RSPCA'.[2]

After two months with the RSPCA at Filey, Frederick was posted to Hertford in 1909, and then to Exeter in 1912. He later served in

WWI as a lieutenant in the Royal Devon Hussars. Following the war he re-joined the RSPCA in 1919 serving at Barnstaple. Frederick resigned from the RSPCA on 24 April 1921 owing to ill health.[3]

Thomas Dunham's grandson, James Bramwood Dunham, was the third generation to join the police. He was born in Hertford on 17 May 1912, well after his grandfather's death. He was rather more successful that his father Frederick, reaching the rank of Chief Superintendent in the Metropolitan Police. He had joined the Met on 31 October 1932 and retired on 31 March 1966. His warrant number was 122526, and his first posting was to S Division as PC 487S.

James married Violet Evelyn Churchill in 1935 in Edgware. Prior to his retirement he was Chief Officer of X Division (West London). He rode his horse at the funeral of Winston Churchill in 1965. He died in 2007 in Portslade at the age of 89.

───────────────

1   Buckinghamshire Constabulary Records (Mick Shaw).

2   St James Church, Muswell Hill Parish Register.

3   RSPCA personnel records.

A Brief History of the
Detective Branch at Scotland Yard

The history of the detective branch at Scotland Yard and Supt Williamson makes interesting reading:

Known to friends and colleagues as 'Dolly', Adolphus Williamson was a Scot whose father had been Superintendent of T Division (Hammersmith). His first job was as a temporary clerk in the War Department before he decided to follow his father into the Metropolitan Police in 1850. Initially working as an assistant clerk in P Division (Camberwell), he gained promotion and joined the detective department as a Sergeant in 1852. He later went on to become the Head of Scotland Yard's Detective Department, achieving the ranks of Chief Inspector, Superintendent and District Superintendent, Chief Constable en route.

During his long 36-year career at Scotland Yard, Williamson was involved in many of the high profile criminal investigations of his day. This included his early work with Inspector Whicher on the initially 'unsolved' case of the Road Hill House murder. Once Constance Kent confessed to the crime several years after the initial investigation had failed to reach a satisfactory conclusion, it was Williamson as Head of Department who concluded the case.

He was at the forefront of the Detectives' involvement in

investigations of Irish Terrorism on the British mainland, during the Fenian Conspiracy (1865-1868) and in the 1880s when a bomb explosion in London in March 1883 marked the start of another Fenian campaign. A 'Special Irish Branch' (the forerunner of Special Branch) was established under his leadership a month later.

Well-liked and respected by his colleagues, Williamson's reputation was nonetheless fortunate to survive, apparently unscathed, when, in 1877, his Department's three Chief Inspectors (George Clarke, Nathaniel Druscovich and William Palmer), were arrested and tried for corruption in the now notorious, 'Trial of the Detectives.'[1]

Williamson is said to have had a great capacity for hard work, combining it with a dry sense of humour. He died on 9th December 1889, still in post, though for some months prior to his death his health had failed.

The Home Secretary expressed his '...deep regret with which he hears of Mr Williamson's death, and of his sense of the great loss which the Police and Public have sustained in being deprived of an Officer distinguished for his skill, prudence and experience and whose life has been unsparingly devoted to the Public Service.' The Prince of Wales (later King Edward VII) expressed similar sentiments. Williamson's well-attended funeral service was held at St John Evangelist church in London's Smith Square.

On 12th May 1869, Chief Inspector Adolphus ('Dolly') Williamson was promoted to Superintendent and head of an expanded Detective Department at Scotland Yard. At the same time, the man who was to become Williamson's deputy, Inspector George Clarke, was promoted to Chief Inspector during the most radical changes to the detective force in London since 1842.

When the London Metropolitan Police Force was established in 1829, its principal role was crime prevention. Crime detection was given a lower priority, and the delay in establishing a plain clothes detective force was also attributable to concerns that this would lead to a civilian-spy system similar to those found in some European countries.

There were additional fears that men in plain clothes would also be more susceptible to corruption. Nonetheless, by 1842 the overriding need for a detective force in London had become apparent and a small Detective Department containing 8 men was established.

Long-serving Police Commissioner Sir Richard Mayne, died in December 1868 and was replaced by a new broom, Colonel Edmund Henderson.

Henderson had few reservations about increasing the number of detectives in London and, on the same day that Williamson and Clarke were promoted, Henderson announced that the Scotland Yard Detective Department would be increased to 27 staff including a Superintendent (Williamson), 3 Chief Inspectors, 3 Inspectors and 20 Sergeants. In addition, a few days later, approval was given for a total of 180 new detectives (Sergeants and Constables) to be appointed across the Metropolitan Police's Divisions.

As a consequence, the number of detectives in the force had, on paper, increased from 15 to 207. The team of 27 at Scotland Yard reported direct to the Police Commissioner, and the remaining 180 to their relevant Divisional Superintendents. This divergence in line-management was to remain a bone of contention until the later establishment of the CID (Criminal Investigation Department) in 1878.

---

1   Blog by Chris Payne, author of *The Chieftain, Victorian True Crime Through the Eyes of a Scotland Yard Detective*. See www.chrispaynebooks.com/blog/the-senior-detectives-at-scotland-yard-1869-inspector-william-palmer.

List of Illustrations

Select Bilbiography

William Calcraft, Executioner Extra-Ordinaire
Geoffrey Abbott

Buckinghamshire Constabulary Centenary 1857–1957
A. Hailstone

Buckinghamshire Murder and Crime
Scott Houghton

Foul Deeds and Suspicious Deaths Around Uxbridge
Jonathan Oates

The Chieftain: Victorian True Crime Through the Eyes of a Scotland Yard Detective
Chris Payne

Buckinghamshire in Crisis – A County Rotten to the Core
Martin Taylor

Murder in Buckinghamshire
Len Woodley

Index